Trends and Challenges in Digital Business Innovation

Vincenzo Morabito

Trends and Challenges in Digital Business Innovation

 Springer

Vincenzo Morabito
Department of Management and Technology
Bocconi University
Milan
Italy

ISBN 978-3-319-04306-7   ISBN 978-3-319-04307-4   (eBook)
DOI 10.1007/978-3-319-04307-4
Springer Cham Heidelberg New York Dordrecht London

Library of Congress Control Number: 2013958136

Printed on acid-free paper

Springer is part of Springer Science+Business Media (www.springer.com)

Foreword

This book aims to improve the understanding of trends and challenges in digital business innovation at the European as well as at the global level. It helps create a connection between business readers and academic research. The book summarizes what is hot—each year—in digital business, but with a focus on showing something new to professionals from an academic perspective. In this book, Vincenzo has put together several topics, clustering them in three Parts that could be seen as the steps of a roadmap. The book focuses first on the main digital systems' trends (Part I), trying to examine technological issues such as Big Data, Cloud Computing, Mobile services, etc., from a managerial perspective, aiming to reach a wide spectrum of executives, including those without an IT background. These last two Chapters shift the perspective of Part I, introducing the reader to Part II, which analyses and discusses the managerial challenges of technological trends focusing on governance models, the transformation of work and collaboration as a consequence of the digitization of the work environment, and finally dealing with what may be considered the real challenge to digital business: how to manage, control, and exploit a company's identity and brand in a competitive digital environment. Part II frames the managerial challenges so that they can complement the IT manager's perspective, while providing a useful summary of the state of the art for other non-IT executives. Part III discusses how companies have carried out "innovation in practice", providing easy to read and structured forms on what were some of the more interesting experiences at a global level in 2013. It is a challenge for any scholar to identify the most popular digital business topics in any given year. Given this, summarizing the vast literature in information systems, digital marketing, and computer science and identifying the most cutting edge phenomena is an arduous task. I congratulate Vincenzo for this book and look forward to seeing it in print soon.

Anindya Ghose

Preface

This book aims to discuss and present the main trends and challenges in Digital Business Innovation to a composite audience of practitioners and scholars. Accordingly, each considered topic will be analyzed in its technical and managerial aspects, also through the use of case studies and examples, the book having two main objectives:

- to review and discuss recent digital trends emerging from both managerial and scientific literature. Furthermore, the book aims to summarize, compare, and comment challenges and approaches to business digital transformation of organization, being a simple yet ready to consult scientific toolbox for both managers and scholars;
- to be the first of a yearly outlook focused on digital trends emerging from both the managerial and scientific literature, supporting organizations to identify and take advantage of digital business innovation and transformation, as well as its related opportunities.

As for the review objective, it is yet challenging to find a unified survey of current scientific work concerning relevant topics to digital business innovation, such as, for example, the different perspectives of Information Systems research (from management to computer science and engineering, among others). Furthermore, it is yet difficult to find such kind of unified survey acting as an instrument for providing practitioners a perspective on academic research, suitable to be used by them in their day-to-day activities or simply as an update on what academia may offer with regard to the industry proposals. Notwithstanding some journals such as, e.g., MIT Sloan Management Review, IEEE Computer, or the Communications of the ACM (CACM) have such a mission of connecting research and industry practices, at the best of the author knowledge they do not provide a yearly integrated summary or critical review, encompassing their respective areas (management, engineering, and computer science). However, these publications are going to be a part of the large set of information and body of knowledge together with other journals such as, e.g., Management of Information Systems Quarterly (MISQ), Communications of the Association for Information Systems, Management of Information Systems Quarterly Executive (MISQE), Information Systems Research, European Journal of Information

Systems, Journal of Information Technology, Information Systems Journal, and conferences such as International Conferences of Information Systems (ICIS), European Conferences of Information Systems (ECIS), America's Conferences of Information Systems (AMCIS) (just to mention some of the Management of Information Systems research sources), that this book aims to consider for identifying the challenges, ideas, and trends, that may represent "food for thoughts" to practitioners.

Notwithstanding the book adopts an academic approach as for sources collection and analysis, it is also concrete, describing problems from the viewpoints of managers, further adopting a clear and easy-to-understand language, in order to capture the interests of top managers as well as graduates students.

Taking these issues into account, this book is distinctive for its intention to synthesize, compare, and comment major challenges and approaches to business digital transformation of organization, being a simple yet ready to consult scientific toolbox for both managers and scholars. Finally, as said above, the book aims to be the first of a yearly outlook focused on digital trends emerging from both the managerial and scientific literature. In what follows an outline of the book is provided.

Outline of the Book

The book argument is developed along three main axes. In particular, Part I first considers *Digital Systems Trends* issues related to the growing relevance, on the one hand, of *Big Data, Cloud Computing,* and *Mobile Services* for business; on the other hand, it discusses the drivers and challenges of *Social Listening* and *IT Consumerization*, topics of strategic interest for IT and Marketing executives, in order to enable an effective understanding of today's organizations as well as users behavior and needs. Thus, in this part of the book the main technological trends, actually debated in both academia and industry, will be discussed and analyzed in their managerial challenges and opportunities. The trends have been selected also on the basis of focus groups and interviews to 80 European IT executives from different industries (finance, manufacturing, utilities, service, among others). Focusing on systems evolution trends from a technology push perspective, the analysis will move from information and service infrastructure topics such as *Big Data* and *Cloud Computing*, through *Mobile Services* as platforms for socializing and "touch points" for customer experience, to emerging paradigms that actually are transforming marketing, governance, and the boundaries of organizations as well as our own private life (i.e., *Social listening* and *IT Consumerization*).

Subsequently, the Part II of this book considers *Digital Management Trends*, focusing on work practices, identity/brand digital transformation, and governance. In this Part, the analysis will focus on the main managerial trends, actually answering and reacting to the systems' trends surveyed in Part I. Also in this case the selected topics result both from academia and industry state-of-the-art analyses and from focus groups and interviews to 80 European IT Executives from different industries (finance, manufacturing, utilities, and service, among others), likewise. Focusing on management evolution trends, the argumentation adopts a management pull perspective to consider how *work and collaboration* may be reconfigured or adapted to the new digital opportunities and constraints emerging from social networks paradigms, such as, e.g., crowdsourcing and people services. Moreover, this part of the volume will explore the identity challenges for businesses both as security and privacy issues; digital identity will be discussed also as with regard to brand management in the actual digital ecosystems, and the consequent constant revision of value propositions and business models for rebranding a company digital business, due to strict time to market. Furthermore, the last Chapter of this part of the volume will discuss the governance defies raised by the previous-mentioned changes and reconfiguration of organizational resources and structure.

Finally, Part III will discuss first (Chap. 9) the underlying issues and the most relevant concepts for understanding Business Model Innovation, providing general insights on the state-of-the-art and basic constructs of this research stream, suitable to support an understanding of its evolution in current digital business innovation experiences and practices. Then, Chap. 10 will present and review case studies of digital innovation trends at global level. Thus, the Chapter aims to discuss examples of digital innovation in practice, providing fact sheets suitable to build a "map" of the 10 most interesting digital innovations actually available worldwide. Besides an introduction to the factors considered in the choice of each innovation, a specific description of it will be developed. The considered 10 innovations will be discussed in their relationship to the topics of the previous Parts/Chapters, both providing insights on their potential evolution trends and unmatched characteristics, likewise. Finally, the conclusion will provide a summary of all arguments of the volume together with general managerial recommendations.

Vincenzo Morabito

Acknowledgments

This book is the result of a comprehensive research, where several people are worth to be acknowledged for their support, useful comments and cooperation. A special mention to Prof. Vincenzo Perrone at Bocconi University, Prof. Vallabh Sambamurthy, Eli Broad Professor at Michigan State University, and Prof. Franco Fontana at LUISS University as main inspiration and mentors.

Moreover, I acknowledge Prof. Giuseppe Soda, Head of the Department of Management and Technology at Bocconi University, and all the other colleagues at the Department, in particular Prof. Arnaldo Camuffo, Prof. Anna Grandori, Prof. Severino Salvemini, and Prof. Giuseppe Airoldi, all formerly at the Institute of Organization and Information Systems at Bocconi University, who have created a rich and rigorous research environment where I am proud to work.

I acknowledge also some colleagues from other universities with whom I've had the pleasure to work, whose conversations, comments, and presentations provided precious insights for this book: among others, Prof. Anindya Ghose at New York University's Leonard N. Stern School of Business, Prof. Vijay Gurbaxani at University of California Irvine, Prof. Saby Mitra at Georgia Institute of Technology, Prof. Ravi Bapna at University of Minnesota Carlson School of Management, George Westerman at MIT Center for Digital Business, Prof. Ritu Agarwal at Robert H. Smith School of Business, Prof. Lynda Applegate at Harvard Business School, Prof. Marco de Marco at Unversità Cattolica del Sacro Cuore di Milano, Tobias Kretschmer, Head of Institute for Strategy, Technology and Organization of Ludwig Maximilians University, Prof. Marinos Themistocleous at the Department of Digital Systems at University of Piraeus, Prof. Chiara Francalanci at Politecnico di Milano, Wolfgang König at Goethe University, Adriano Solidoro at University of Milano-Bicocca, Luca Giustiniano at LUISS University, Prof. Zahir Irani at Brunel Business School, Prof. Sinan Aral at NYU Stern School of Business, and Ken and Jane Laudon.

Furthermore, I want to gratefully acknowledge all the companies that have participated to the research interviews, case studies, and surveys. In particular, for the financial institutions: Banca Mediolanum, Banco Popolare, Banca Popolare dell'Emilia Romagna, Banca Popolare di Milano, Banca Popolare di Sondrio, Banca Popolare di Vicenza, Barclays, BCC Roma, BNL-BNP Paribas, Carige Group, Cariparma Credit Agricole, Cassa di Risparmio di Firenze, Cedacri, Che Banca!, Compass, Credito Emiliano, Deutsche Bank, Dexia, HypoVereinsbank,

ICBPI, ING Direct, Intesa Sanpaolo Group, IREN, Mediobanca, MPS Group, Poste Italiane Group, SEC, Société Européene de Banque, UBI Banca, Unicredit Group, Veneto Banca and WeBank. For the insurance sector: Allianz, Ergo Previdenza, Generali Group, Groupama, Poste Vita, Sara Assicurazioni, UGF Group and Vittoria Assicurazioni. For all other sectors: Acea, Aci Informatica, Amplifon, Anas, Angelini, ArcelorMittal, Armani, ATAC, ATM, Auchan, Autogrill, Autostrade per l'Italia, Avio, Baglioni Hotels, Barilla, Brembo, Chiesi Farmaceutici, CNH Industrial, Coca Cola HBC, Coop Italia, Costa Crociere, Danone, De Agostini, Diesel, Dimar, Dolce & Gabbana, Ducati, Edipower, Edison, Eni, Enel, ERG, Fastweb, Ferrari, Ferrero, Ferrovie dello Stato Group, Fiat Group, Finmeccanica Group, GlaxosmithKline, Grandi Navi Veloci, Gruppo Hera, Gtech, H3G, Il Sole24Ore, Kuwait Petroleum, Lamborghini, LBBW, Levi's, L'Oreal, Loro Piana, Luxottica Group, Magneti Marelli, Mapei, Marcegaglia, Messaggerie Libri, Miroglio, Oerlikon Graziano, Perfetti, Pirelli, Prysmian, Rolex, Saipem, Snam, Sorgenia, Telecom Italia, Terna, Unilever, Vodafone and Wind. For the public sector: Agenzia per l'Italia Digitale, Comune di Milano and Consip.

I would especially like to acknowledge all the people that have supported me during these years with insights and suggestions. I learned so much from them, and their ideas and competences have inspired my work: Silvio Fraternali, Paolo Cederle, Massimo Milanta, Massimo Schiattarella, Diego Donisi, Gianluca Pancaccini, Giovanni Damiani, Gianluigi Castelli, Salvatore Poloni, Milo Gusmeroli, Pierangelo Rigamonti, Danilo Augugliaro, Elvio Sonnino, Massimo Messina, Mario Collari, Massimo Castagnini, Pier Luigi Curcuruto, Giuseppe Dallona, Gilberto Ceresa, Jesus Marin Rodriguez, Fabio Momola, Rafael Lopez Rueda, Eike Wahl, Ruediger Schmidt, Marco Cecchella, Maria-Louise Arscott, Antonella Ambriola, Giovanni Sordello, Andrea Rigoni, Giovanni Rando Mazzarino, Silvio Sperzani, Samuele Sorato, Alfredo Montalbano, Gloria Gazzano, Massimo Basso Ricci, Giuseppe De Iaco, Riccardo Amidei, Davide Ferina, Massimo Ferriani, Cristina Bianchini, Dario Scagliotti, Ruggero Platolino, Ettore Corsi, Luciano Bartoli, Marco Ternelli, Alessandro Cucchi, Carlo Felice Ferrarini, Marco Tempra, Luca Ghirardi, Francesca Gandini, Vincenzo Tortis, Agostino Ragosa, Sandro Tucci, Vittorio Mondo, Enzo Bertolini, Roberto Fonso, Mario Bocca, Marco Zaccanti, Fabrizio Lugli, Marco Bertazzoni, Vittorio Boero, Jean-Claude Krieger, Maria Cristina Spagnoli, Alessandra Testa, Anna Miseferi, Carlo Brezigia, Mirco Carriglio, Matteo Attrovio, Nikos Angelopoulos, Paul Thysens, Luciano Romeo, Roberto Burlo, Gennaro Della Valle, Massimo Paltrinieri, Pierantonio Azzalini, Enzo Contento, Marco Fedi, Fiore Della Rosa, Carlo Capalbo, Simone Battiferri, Carlo di Lello, Gian Enrico Paglia, Fabrizio Virtuani, Luca Verducci, Luca Falco, Roberto Scolastici, Nicoletta Rocca, Mario Breuer, Marco Lanza, Marco Poggi, Giambattista Piacentini, Francesco Mastrandrea, Mauro Minenna, Massimo Romagnoli, Nicola Grassi, Gianni Leone, Domenico Casalino, Paolo Crovetti, Alberto Ricchiari, Alessandro Musumeci, Matthias Schlapp, Ugo Salvi, Danilo Gismondi, Patrick Vandenberghe, Guido Oppizzi, Alessandro Bruni, Marco Franzi, Guido Albertini, Vincenzo Russi, Diego Donisi, Fabio De Ferrari, Mauro Ferrari, Massimo Amato, Nunzio Calì, Gianfilippo Pandolfini, Cristiano Cannarsa,

Davide Carteri, Luca Terzaghi, Christian Altomare, Pasquale Tedesco, Ottavio Rigodanza, Lorenzo Pizzuti, Marcello Guerrini, Fabio Cestola, Alberto Alberini, Umberto Stefani, Elvira Fabrizio, Dario Pagani, Marino Vignati, Giuseppe Rossini, Renzo Di Antonio, Armando Gervasi, David Alfieri, Roberto Andreoli, Vincenzo Campana, Piera Fasoli, Alberto Grigoletto, Riccardo Scattaretico, Marco Ravasi, Mauro Viacava, Salvatore Stefanelli, Marco Zaffaroni, Giuseppe Langer, Daniele Rizzo, Massimiliano Gerli, Fabio Oggioni, Luca Severini, Roberto Conte, Nazzareno Gregori, Alessandro Campanini, Gabriella Serravalle, Giovanni Pietrobelli, Pietro Pacini, Stefano Firenze, Dario Castello, Michela Quitadamo, Francois De Brabant, Luciano Dalla Riva, Paolo Pecchiari, Francesco Donatelli, Massimo Palmieri, Riccardo Pagnanelli, Pierluigi Berlucchi, Raffaella Mastrofilippo, Davide Casagrande, Luca Martis, Stefano Levi, Patrizia Ferrari, Massimiliano Baga, Marco Campi, Laura Wegher, Diego Pogliani, Alessandra Grendele e Gianluca Pepino.

I would especially like to gratefully acknowledge Gianluigi Viscusi at EPFL-CDM-CSI, Alan Serrano-Rico at Brunel Univeristy, and Nadia Neytcheva Head of Research at the Business Technology Outlook (BTO) Research Program who have provided me valuable suggestions and precious support in the coordination of the production process of this book. Furthermore, I acknowledge the support of Business Technology Foundation (Fondazione Business Technology) and all the bright researchers at Business Technology Outlook (BTO) Research Program that have supported me in carrying out interviews, surveys, and data analysis: Florenzo Marra, Alessandro De Pace, Alessandro Scannapieco, Matteo Richiardi, Ezechiele Capitanio, Giulia Galimberti, Arianna Zago, Giovanni Roberto, Massimo Bellini, Tommaso Cenci, Marta Silvani, Giorgia Cattaneo Puppo, Andrada Comanac.

A special acknowledgement goes to the memory of Prof Antonino Intrieri who provided precious comments and suggestions throughout the years.

Finally I acknowledge my family whose constant support and patience made this book happen.

Vincenzo Morabito

Contents

Part II   Digital Management Trends

Acronyms

ACID	Atomicity, Consistency, Isolation, and Durability
BM	Business Model
BMI	Business Model Innovation
BYOD	Bring Your Own Device
CEO	Chief Executive Officer
CFO	Chief Financial Officer
CIO	Chief Information Officer
CMMI	Capability Maturity Model Integration
COBIT	Control Objectives for Information and related Technology
COC	Cross Organizational Collaboration
CoP	Community of Practice
CRM	Customer Relationship Management
CSCW	Computer-Supported Cooperative Work
CSFs	Critical Success Factors
CxO	C-level Manager
DDS	Digital data stream
DMS	Document management system
ECM	Enterprise content management
HR	Human Resources
ICT	Information and Communication Technology
IPO	Initial public offering
IT	Information technology
ITIL	Information Technology Infrastructure Library
KPIs	Key Performance Indicators
NoSQL	Not Only SQL
R&D	Research and Development
SMEs	Small and medium enterprises
TOGAF	The Open Group Architecture Framework
VOIP	Voice over Internet Protocol

Part I
Digital Systems Trends

Chapter 1
Big Data

Abstract The role of this Chapter is to introduce the reader to the area of Big Data, one of the IT trends actually emerging as strategic for companies competing in current digital global market. The Chapter aims to clarify the main drivers and characteristics of Big Data, both at technical and managerial level. Furthermore, the Chapter aims at investigating management challenges and opportunities, identifying the main phases and actions of a Big Data lifecycle. Finally, the discussion of case studies concludes the Chapter, providing insights from practice on factors and strategic points of attention, suitable to support Big Data-driven decision making and operational performance.

1.1 Introduction

"Try to imagine your life without secrets" claimed the incipit of an article by Niv Ahituv appeared on the Communications of the ACM in 2001 [1]. The author preconized the advent of an Open Information Society as a consequence of higher costs of information protection, proliferation and diffusion of computer networks, unlimited access to information by individuals and organizations, no matter their being private or else public subjects. Once considered a futuristic vision, this change in society is actually a reality, at least for what concerns the availability and the volume of data archived, stored, and exchanged as a consequence of the

V. Morabito, *Trends and Challenges in Digital Business Innovation*,
DOI: 10.1007/978-3-319-04307-4_1, © Springer International Publishing Switzerland 2014

information diffused, produced, and consumed through social networks and digital infrastructures.[1] However, we are facing a radical change, with a new breed of potential business leaders, users and consumers.

As pointed out by Bruce Horovitz on USA Today "the still-forming generation of young folks whose birth dates roughly begin around 1995, will be the technically savviest ever. Naming it, however, will require an unusual combination of science, art and, perhaps, luck" [2]. This Generation Z, as Horovitz called it [2], is made up of digital natives (born after 1995) who literally live and breathe of the information flows in social networks and potentially see the world as a big data repository to be exploited, adapted, and aggregated depending on their current needs. Digital Artifacts such as, e.g., Wii, iPad, iPod, among others, represent an artificial extension of their human being, allowing a seamless integration of the virtual world of social networks and playground as part of their own everyday life. They post everything on Facebook and they "makes a game out of everything" as said Brian Niccol chief marketing and innovation officer at Taco Bell, cited by Horovitz. Obviously, former generations make use of digital artifacts and social networks too, but they are not as dependent on them as a digital citizen may be, requiring code of conducts, rules, and right, likewise [3].

Generation Z represents the source and the target for what the Economist called a Data Deluge [4], and they are worth to be considered in order to clearly understand actual and future business challenges of the phenomenon called Big Data, a core component of the information infrastructure upon which our society is building its own open environment.[2]

---

[1] In the following we use *data* when we refer to raw, unstructured facts that need to be stored and processed by an information system, in order to be meaningful and useful for an agent (being human or else a machine). Whereas we call *information* the useful and meaningful output of information systems, being the data processed, organized, structured, and presented. Thus, adopting the General Definition of Information (GDI) we could define information "data + meaning" [35]. It is worth noting that computer based information systems are a specific type of information system and not exhaustive [36]. For a systematic survey on the different definitions, meanings and use of information we kindly refers the reader to [35, 37].

[2] Using an iPhone app to request money from a nearby Automatic Teller Machine (ATM), scanning the phone to retrieve the bill. This is an example of a Generation Z like evolution of ATM design towards a convergence with online and mobile banking, with a consequent change in the volume and variety of data to be managed by banks and financial services providers. Furthermore, it shows how, e.g., finance sector competition is facing the challenge of PayPal and Google Wallet diffusion and adoption by digital natives. "We think we'll attract a new client base, 35 and under, we didn't cater to before" said Thomas Ormseth, Senior Vice President of Wintrust Financial in an article appeared in July 2013 on Bloomberg Businessweek [38].

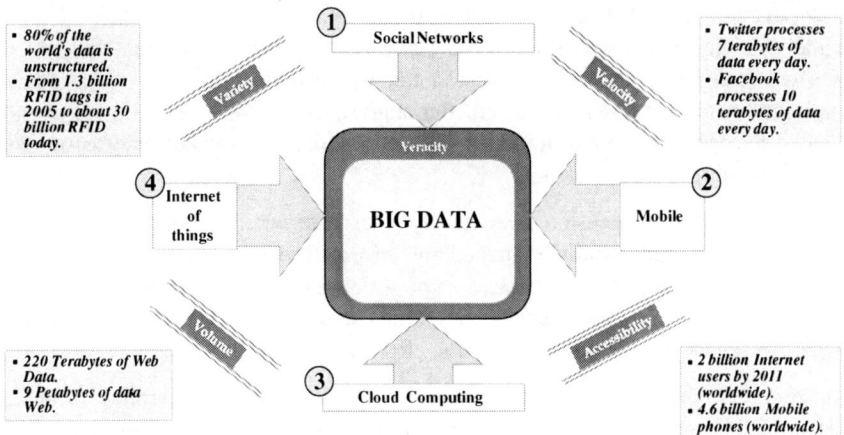

Fig. 1.1 Big data drivers and characteristics

1.1.1 Big Data Drivers and Characteristics

The spread of social media as a main driver for innovation of products and services and the increasing availability of unstructured data (images, video, audio, etc.) from sensors, cameras, digital devices for monitoring supply chains and stocking in warehouses (i.e., what is actually called *internet of things*), video conferencing systems and voice over IP (VOIP) systems, have contributed to an unmatched availability of information in rapid and constant growth in terms of volume. As a consequence of the above scenario, the term *"Big Data"* is dubbed to indicate the challenges associated with the emergence of data sets whose size and complexity require companies adopt new tools, and models for the management of information. Furthermore, Big Data require new capabilities [5] to control external and internal information flows, transforming them in strategic resources to define strategies for products and services that meet customers'needs, increasingly informed and demanding.

Thus, Big Data call for a radical change to business models and human resources in terms of information orientation and a unique valorization of a company information asset for investments and support for strategic decisions. Nevertheless, as usual with new concepts, also Big Data ask for a clarification of their characteristics and drivers. Figure 1.1 represents them, providing figures and examples, likewise.

At the state of the art the following four dimensions are recognized as characterizing Big Data [6–8]:

Volume: the first dimension concerns the unmatched quantity of data actually available and storable by businesses (terabytes or even petabytes), through the internet: for example, 12 terabytes of Tweets are created every day into improved product sentiment analysis [6].

Velocity: the second dimension concerns the dynamics of the volume of data, namely the time-sensitive nature of Big Data, as the speed of their creation and use is often (nearly) real-time. As pointed out by IBM, examples of value added exploitation of data streams concern the analysis of 5 million daily trade events created to identify potential fraud, or 500 million daily call detail records in real-time to predict customer switch.

Variety: the third dimension concerns type of data actually available. Besides, structured data traditionally managed by information systems in organizations, most of the new breed encompasses semi structured and even unstructured data, ranging from text, log files, audio, video, and images posted, e.g., on social networks to sensor data, click streams, e.g., from internet of things.

Accessibility: the fourth dimension concerns the unmatched availability of channels a business may increase and extend its own data and information asset.

It is worth noting that at the state of the art another dimension is actually considered relevant to Big Data characterization: *Veracity* concerns quality of data and trust of the data actually available at an incomparable degree of volume, velocity, and variety. Thus, this dimension is relevant to a strategic use of Big Data by businesses, extending in terms of scale and complexity the issues investigated by information quality scholars [9–11], for enterprise systems mostly relying on traditional relational data base management systems.

As for drivers, *cloud computing* is represented in Fig. 1.1, besides the above mentioned social networks, mobile technologies, and internet of things. It is worth noting that a priority number is associated to each driver, depending on its impact on one of the Big Data characteristics. As pointed out by Pospiech and Felden [7], at the state of the art, cloud computing is considered a key driver of Big Data, for the growing size of available data requires scalable database management systems (DBMS). However, cloud computing faces IT managers and architects the choice of either relying on commercial solutions (mostly expensive) or move beyond relational database technology, thus, identifying novel data management systems for cloud infrastructures [12, 13]. Accordingly, at the state of art *NoSQL* (Not Only SQL)[3] data storage systems have been emerging, usually not requiring fixed table schemas and not fully complying nor satisfying the traditional ACID (Atomicity, Consistency, Isolation, e Durability) properties. Among the programming paradigms for processing, generating, and analyzing large data sets, *MapReduce*[4] and

---

[3] Several classifications of the NoSQL databases have been proposed in literature [39]. Here we mention *Key-/Value-Stores* (a map/dictionary allows clients to insert and request values per key) and *Column-Oriented databases* (data are stored and processed by column instead of row). An example of the former is *Amazon's Dynamo;* whereas *HBase, Google's Bigtable*, and *Cassandra* represent *Column-Oriented databases*. For further details we refer the reader to [39, 40].

[4] MapReduce exploit, on the one hand, (i) a *map function*, specified by the user to process a key/value pair and to generate a set of intermediate key/value pairs; on the other hand, (ii) a *reduce function* that merges all intermediate values associated with the same intermediate key [41].

the open source computing framework Hadoop have received a growing interest and adoption in both industry and academia.[5]

Considering *velocity*, there is a debate in academia about considering Big Data as encompassing both data "stocks" and "flows" [14]. For example, at the state of the art Piccoli and Pigni [15] propose to distinguish the elements of *digital data streams* (DDSs) from "big data"; the latter concerning static data that can be mined for insight. Whereas *digital data streams* (DDSs) are "dynamically evolving sources of data changing over time that have the potential to spur real-time action" [15]. Thus, DDSs refer to streams of real-time information by mobile devices and internet of things, that have to be "captured" and analyzed real-time, provided or not they are stored as "Big Data".

The types of use of "big" DDSs may be classified according to the ones Davenport et al. [14] have pointed out for Big Data applications to information flows:

- *Support customer-facing processes*: e.g., to identify fraud or medical patients health risk.
- *Continuous process monitoring*: e.g., to identify variations in costumer sentiments towards a brand or a specific product/service or to exploit sensor data to detect the need for intervention on jet engines, data centers machines, extraction pump, etc.
- *Explore network relationships* on, e.g., Linkedin, Facebook, and Twitter to identify potential threats or opportunities related to human resources, customers, competitors, etc.

As a consequence, we believe that the distinction between DDSs and Big Data is useful to point out a difference in scope and target of decision making, and analytic activities, depending on the business goals and the type of action required. Indeed, while DDSs may be suitable to be used for marketing and operations issues, such as, e.g., customer experience management in mobile services, Big Data refer to the information asset an organization is actually able to archive, manage and exploit for decision making, strategy definition and business innovation [8].

Having emphasized the specificity of DDS, that will be further considered in the Chapters of this book dedicated to mobile services and social listening, we now focus on Big Data applications.

As shown in Fig. 1.2 they cover many industries, spanning from finance (banks and insurance), e.g., improving risk analysis and fraud management, to utility and manufacturing, with a focus on information provided by sensors and internet of things for improved quality control, operations or plants performance, and energy

---

(Footnote 4 continued)

MapReduce has been used to rewrite the production indexing system that produces the data structures used for the Google web search service [41].

[5] See for example how IBM has exploited/integrated Hadoop [42].

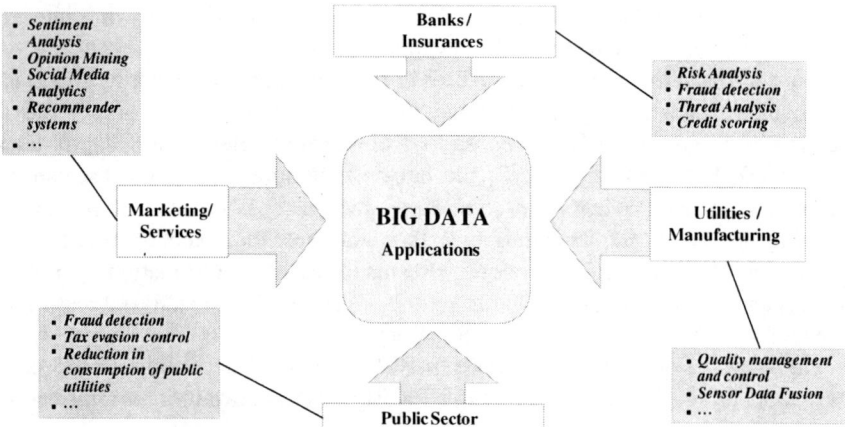

Fig. 1.2 Big data applications

management. Moreover, marketing and service may exploit Big Data for increasing customer experience, through the adoption of social media analytics focused on sentiment analysis, opinion mining, and recommender systems (for details we refer the reader to the Chap. 4).

As for public sector, Big Data represent an opportunity, on the one hand, e.g., for improving fraud detection as tax evasion control through the integration of a large number of public administration databases; on the other hand, for accountability and transparency of government and administrative activities, due to i) the increasing relevance and diffusion of *open data* initiatives, making accessible and available large public administration data sets for further elaboration by constituencies [16, 17], and ii) participation of citizens to the policy making process, thanks to the shift of many government digital initiatives towards an open government perspective [18–21].

Thus, Big Data seem to have a strategic value for organizations in many industries, confirming the claim by Andrew McAfee and Erik Brynjolfsson [8] that data-driven decisions are better decisions, relying on evidence of (an unmatched amount of) facts rather than intuition by experts or individuals. Nevertheless, we believe that management challenges and opportunities of Big Data need for further discussion and analyses, the state of the art currently privileging their technical facets and characteristics.

In the following Section, we actually would try to provide some arguments for understanding Big Data value from a business and management point of view.

Table 1.1 Big data perspectives and related actions

Perspectives	Types	Actions
Technical-data-provisioning	Technological	Storage
Technical-data-utilization	Technological	Use
Functional-data-provisioning	Business	Management
Functional-data-utilization	Business	Use

Elaboration from [7]

1.1.2 Management Challenges and Opportunities

In the Sect. 1.1.1 we have provided a set of drivers and characteristics actually identifying Big Data and their target applications. However, they do not allow yet a clear understanding of the specific actions required for exploiting their research and business value with regard to traditional information management problems. Indeed, on the one hand, as pointed out by Pospiech and Felden [7], Big Data seems to be yet another *brick in the wall* in the long discussion in the information systems field on information supply to decision makers and operations in enterprise. On the other hand, Big Data change the rules of the game, asking to change the overall *information orientation* [22] of an organization (from the separation of stocks and flows, to the need for paying an integrated and real-time attention to them).

Thus, Big Data are different because they actually prompt a rethinking of assumptions about relationships and roles of business and IT, moving information management and analytics from IT units to core business [14]. Accordingly, Big Data change decision making and human resources with regard to *capabilities* satisfying it, integrating programming, mathematical, statistical skills along with business acumen, creativity in interpreting data and effective communication of the results [5, 8, 14]. Therefore, Big Data challenges can actually be addressed by actions asking a technological/functional or else a business perspective, depending on the skills required by the specific task to be held. As for these issues, Pospiech and Felden [7] identified clusters of the main perspectives resulting from a state of the art analysis on, e.g., information systems and computer science, among other fields, contributions to Big Data research. In Table 1.1 we classify these perspectives with regard to their type and we associate actions they may be suitable to support in Big Data value exploitation.

Considering, the technological type of perspective, the *Technical-Data-Provisioning* classification mainly concerns *storage* related actions with regards to database management systems performance, in particular, as for scalability and query performance. On the contrary, the *Technical-Data-Utilization* classification addresses computational complexity issues related to both *provision* and *use* actions. As for the business type of perspectives, it is worth noting that they provide the management complement to challenges and actions that technological perspective is faced with. Whereas the *Functional-Data-Provisioning* one, mainly concerns approaches for the management of the data "deluge" [4], leading to an advanced information demand analysis and improved information supply [7].

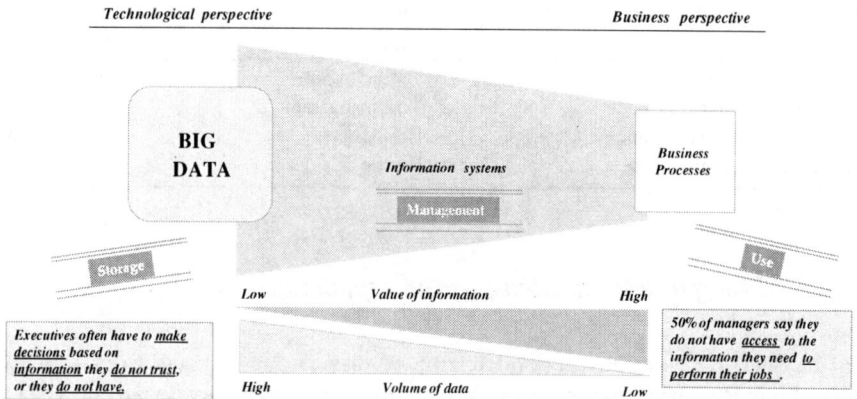

Fig. 1.3 Big data management challenges. Adapted from [7]

Thus, this may be seen as a management of information systems perspective, governing the overall lifecycle from Big Data storage to use. Nevertheless, the latter is suitable to be addressed with a *Functional-Data-Utilization* perspective, exploiting lessons learned and experience in the usage of Big Data from state of the art in various disciplines such as, e.g., social sciences, finance, bioinformatics, and climate science, among others [7].

Considering now the actions required for exploiting Big Data value, Fig. 1.3 provides a summary of the priority ones together with the related perspective (being technological, business, or information system oriented), and the management challenges they have to provide answers and solutions. Priority actions in Fig. 1.3 structure a lifecycle, starting from the (continuous) *storage* of data from the outer and inner flood involving today's organizations. Here, the challenge concerns the fact that executives often argue that they have to make decisions based on information they do not trust or they do not have. As pointed out by Tallon [23], managers have insights on value of data for their organization from profits, revenues, recovery costs derived by critical data loss or inaccessibility. As a consequence they have to assess their information asset to decide about retaining, searching, acquiring new data and to invest on storage technology. Indeed, the value of data and information they allow to produce in the information lifecycle curve, change depending on its currency and the usefulness in business processes and decision making [23, 24].

As shown in Fig. 1.3, the value of information augments with the positive impacts it has on business processes. In this case, the volume of data is reduced to a limited view on the asset actually stored in databases. Thus, having a very large volume of data does not imply that it provides valuable information to an organization's business processes or to decision making. Besides storage, companies need actions for Big Data management for (i) valuing information asset, (ii) understanding costs, (iii) improving data governance practices to extract the right data [23], (iv) providing useful information to demanding business processes and decision making.

Table 1.2 Data governance enablers and inhibitors

Factors	Enablers	Inhibitors
Organization	Highly focused business strategy	Complex mix of products and services
	IT/Strategy alignment	IT/Strategy misalignment
	Centralized organization structure	Decentralized organization structure
Industry	Regulations	Regulations variance by region (US, EU, etc.)
	Predictable rate of data growth	Absence of industry-wide data standards
Technology	Culture of promoting strategic use of IT	Data hoarding
	Standardization	Weak integration of legacy IT systems

Adapted from [23]

As for data governance, several approaches have been proposed in the literature for Data Quality Management (DQM) to face strategic and operational challenges with quality of corporate data [25]. Accordingly, scholars in the research areas of information systems and information quality have identified a set of enabling and inhibiting factors for effective data governance. In Table 1.2 we show the ones highlighted by Tallon [23] for implementing data governance practices suitable to support valuable Big Data management.

The factors considered in Table 1.2 act at organization, industry, and technology level, showing the enabling role of alignment, centralization, standardization, and strategic use of IT orientation. Nevertheless, these enablers being quite recognized in theory and practice as a good management of information systems target, on the other hand, they look as by far challenging, due to the distributed nature of Big Data and the unpredictable dynamics of the digital environment producing them. Furthermore, they often require business process management and optimization to get the target performance levels [26].

Thus, it is worth to be considered the advice by Awargal and Weill [27] that due to the increasing volatility of business environment, by building strategy around business process optimization issues, organization may fail to exploit Big Data. Indeed, optimization often leads to rigidity and inflexibility of business processes, instead of the agility expected by dynamic information flows.

Accordingly, we believe that a useful approach to management and use of Big Data is what Awargal and Weill [27] called *softscaling*, requiring three core capabilities for companies and their IT units to act as enabling factors for an "empatic" use of information for value creation. Softscaling allows companies to rely and exploit Big Data to develop flexible strategy and business models, thus, anticipating and responding to volatility of market and customer needs, while having efficient and sustainable business processes. Figure 1.4 shows these capabilities, i.e.:

- *optimizing business processes* and technology for operational excellence;
- *creating emotional ties* and connections for an improved focus on customer needs and experience;

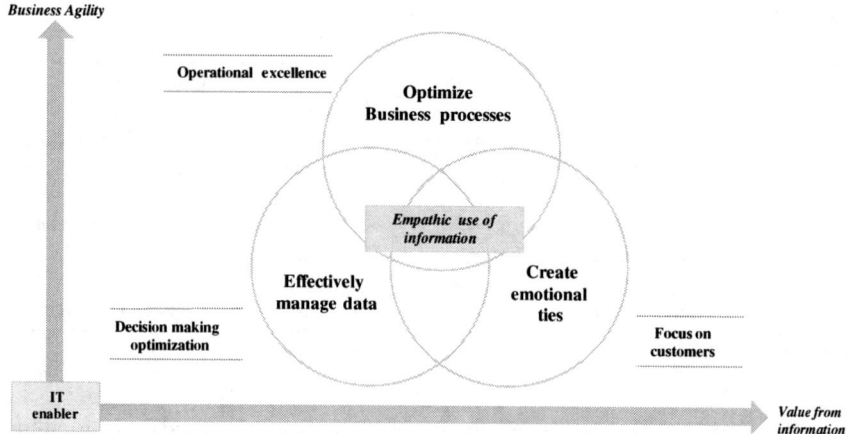

Fig. 1.4 Empathic use of information for value creation: actions and targets of IT as enabling factor

- *managing effectively data*, supporting time-to market and evidence-driven decision making.

Furthermore, companies aiming to exploit the opportunities offered by Big Data have to connect business agility to information value (axes in Fig. 1.4), through informed empathy. The latter meaning to contextualize data sources, improving data access to customers, employees, and value-chain partners, further cultivating emotional connections [27]. An example, is the case described by Awargal and Weill [27] of the use of demographics made by Hero MotoCorp. This New Dehli based manufacturer of motorcycles and scooters integrated its Customer Relationship Management (CRM) with contextual data on young women customer experience entering India's workforce. Thus, Hero MotoCorp has been able to promptly answer to their local concerns about shopping and driving moto scooters, by designing new products and initiatives, such as, e.g., showrooms staffed by women, with private curtain where trying the scooters and judge how they look on them.

The above arguments and cases lead us to the third Big Data lifecycle challenge. As for their *use*, as seen above, companies has to rely on new data management technologies and analytics to get evidence of facts rather than intuition by experts or individuals. However, as shown by Lavalle et al. [28] in a research on more than 3,000 business executives in 108 countries and more than 30 industries, top performing organizations use analytics both to guide future strategies (45 % vs. 20 % of low performers) and day-to-day operations (53 % vs. 27 % of low performers).

In particular, low performers resulted more oriented towards the use of intuition than top performers in customer service, product research and development, general management, risk management, customer experience management, brand management, and workforce planning and allocation. Furthermore, Lavalle et al. [28] pointed out that among the impediments to becoming data driven, companies answer the following main issues:

- lack of understanding of how to use analytics to improve the business;
- lack of management bandwidth;
- lack of skills internally in the line of business.

Accordingly, organizations involved in the Lavalle et al. [28] survey expected that *data visualization* techniques are worth to become the most valuable in the next years, when combined with analytics applied to business processes. Notwithstanding these techniques support a better understanding of how to use analytics to improve the business, we believe that the actual lack of skills require, first, a change in human resources and talent management towards an information orientation of the overall organization capabilities, and a consequent internal diffusion of data scientists among the employees [5].

In addition, it is worth noting that data were not considered by interviewees among the main impediments to a full exploitation of Big Data opportunities to business value. However, managers considered as a priority or mandatory premise for their organization to have their data asset characterized by high degree of integration, consistency, standardization and trustworthiness. Thus, we can summarize the main challenges and IT actions of Big Data for business value as follows:

- **Convergence of information sources**: IT in the organization must enable the construction of a "data asset" from internal and external sources, unique, integrated and of quality.
- **Data architecture**: IT must support the storage and enable the extraction of valuable information from structured, semi-structured as well as unstructured data (images, recordings, etc.).
- **Information infrastructure**: IT must define models and adopt techniques for allowing modular and flexible access to information and analysis of data across the enterprise. Furthermore, organizations must commit human resources in recruiting and empowering data scientist skills and capabilities across business lines and management.
- **Investments**: The IT and the business executives must share decisions on the budget for the management and innovation of information assets.

Taking these issues into account, we can now provide a comprehensive representation of the factors and actions described in previous section to support the maintenance, exploitation, and evolution of Big Data as key part of the digital asset of today's organizations.

To this end, Fig. 1.5 shows how digital asset components, i.e., IT portfolio and the data asset of an organization, actually are also determined by external data, applications, and services due to the growing relevance of social networks, mobile services, and technology/paradigms such as cloud computing (we provide further details on each of them in Chaps. 2, 3 and 4, respectively).

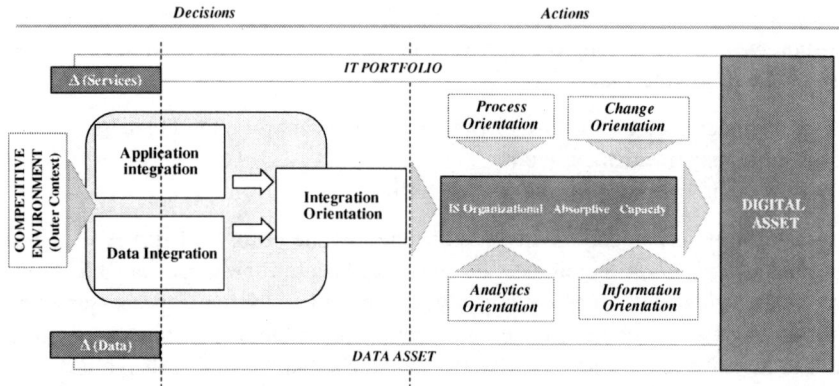

Fig. 1.5 A framework for managing digital asset

As a consequence, the competitive environment and the outer context both represent the main Big Data sources, alimenting in a volatile and dynamic way the digital asset of an organization, which has to be managed by internal information systems likewise. As shown in, Fig. 1.5, both business decisions and actions rely on the digital asset of an organization, although requiring different types of orientation in managing the information systems (IS). As for decisions, *integration orientation* seems to be required for satisfying the needs for optimization and effective data management of Big Data. Indeed, the greater the integration of a company's information system, the faster the overall planning and control cycles [29].

Applying to Big Data issues the SIGMA model, that we have proposed in a previous work to improve strategic information governance modeling and assessment [29], we argue that integration orientation refers to IS integration and is determined by two variables, *application integration* and *data integration* (see also [29, 30]). Accordingly, integration orientation constitutes a fundamental lever of both analytic, information, and process orientation, facilitating the absorption and transformation of information and knowledge into evidence-driven actions, helping managers decision making and employees perform their work.

Thus, integration orientation is one of the determinants of organizational absorptive capacity, which, in turn, is theorized to affect business performance [29, 30]. Indeed, *absorptive capacity* measures the ability of an organization to complete a learning process as coping with IT complexity or in our case with Big Data management and use by businesses. As a consequence, moving from decisions to actions call for an organization to improve *IS absorptive capacity* [29, 30] in terms of the set of key orientations considered in the above mentioned SIGMA approach: analytics, information, process, and change orientation. Considering these issues, we point out that the framework in Fig. 1.5 is suitable to provide a systemic and integrated "working" representation of factors and drivers involved in managing digital assets, which aim to exploit the opportunities of Big Data for business performance and value.

Table 1.3 Factors, recommendations, and strategy points for big data lifecycle phases

Lifecycle phase	Factors	Recommendations	Strategy points
Storage	Technology	Consolidate corporate databases (internal) and integrate new information sources (internal/external)	Completeness
Storage	Technology	Identify and store relevant data from all information sources (internal/external)	Relevance
Management	Technology	Adopt analytics appropriate to the volume, variety, and velocity of data (real-time)	Timeliness and accuracy
Management	Industry/ Organization	Establish clear goals and articulate a vision coherent with market opportunities, effectively engaging customers, employees and other relevant stakeholders	Leadership
Management	Organization	Investments in human resources with a mix of new analytical skills and business	Talent management
Management	Organization	Implement a decentralized approach, and diffuse collaborative and transparent use of information	Organizational culture
Use	Technology	Adopt data visualization tools and manipulate data with real-time tools	Timeliness/ Simplification
Use	Organization	Ensure access to information and an appropriate level of decision-making autonomy at all levels of the company	Accountability

Taking all the contributions discussed in this section into account, Table 1.3 summarizes a set of strategy points and recommendations for managerial actions in building what we call a *Big Data intelligence agenda*. It is worth noting that a relevant factor and challenge has to be considered as the background to the agenda and to most of the issues considered in this book: *privacy* and *identity* management for businesses and individuals as well.

Nonetheless, due to their extensiveness, we have decided to treat these issues in Chap. 7 dedicated to Digital Business Identity. Finally, in conclusion of this Chapter we would like to submit to the attention of the reader a set of case studies, providing him with insights from practice as well.

1.2 Case Studies

In this Section we discuss fact-sheets of case studies, which illustrate at a glance how strategy points for Big Data lifecycle phases in Table 1.3 have been addressed in practice, emphasizing point of attention and insights for managers.

The first case study shows the relevance of having a clear business strategy aligned with IS strategy for Big Data exploitation from social media. The case has been discussed by Moses et al. [31] and concerns The Minnesota Wild, an ice hockey team based in St. Paul, Minnesota, United States, members of the Central Division of the Western Conference, of the National Hockey League (NHL). The Minnesota Wild Hockey Club has developed a social media strategy strongly aligned with its business strategy, focused on three key objectives: to increase sales of subscriptions, to promote the sale of tickets among casual fans, and to increase advertising revenue.

In 2010, the club has launched its social program, using mainly Facebook and Twitter, and the ability of these platforms to provide data that can translate user choices in demographic information valuable to achieve marketing and communications initiatives, thus, maximizing the involvement of consumers and therefore the interest of sponsors.

> **POINT OF ATTENTION**: Hockey Club has managed to build and transform a wide and varied volume of digital interactions in satisfactory results in terms of market share and profit.

The second case study has been analyzed by Sharma et al. [32], and shows the relevance of having a clear strategy aimed to consolidate and integrate internal and external data sources through appropriate storage and data warehouse technologies. Bahrti Airtel operates in the Indian mobile market characterized by constant growth. In such a context, to remain competitive, companies must implement strategies geared to reach and engage a broad spectrum of potential customers with lifestyle, culture and income very different between them. Indeed, for all groups of consumers, even the most mature (concentrated in large cities and industrial areas), the locus of competition has shifted from the price of the service to the satisfaction of the specific needs of customers: time to market is critical to respond quickly to consumer trends, satisfying the needs of differentiated groups of consumer. Thus, data are the main asset for evidence-driven decision making.

The claim *"Our objective is to have one version of the truth!"* by Rupinder Goel, CIO of Bharti Airtel Limited, summarize the need for a single set of data that include finance, marketing, customer service, as a way to know its customers 'needs, experience, and lifestyles.

> **POINT OF ATTENTION**: Using Big Data should be enhanced and supported by a business strategy focused and shared by the overall company functions and processes. The analysis and the production of reports have to be outsourced with caution and should not be bound by formal standards that might reduce its effectiveness in the short and long term.

As a consequence, Baharti Airtel, to manage the evolution of the market, has created an IT infrastructure, including data warehouse systems aimed at the collection and subsequent analysis of data from various corporate activities. The production and use of information reports were introduced gradually in the company, up to in-house solutions aimed at the production of ad hoc reports for strategic value.

The third case study, based on a Cloudera case history [33], focuses again on the relevance of consolidation and integration for retrieving valuable information from Big Data, with a specific attention to data base technologies. The case analyzes how Nokia, the Finland based global telecommunications company, has faced with these challenges. Indeed, effective collection and use of data is strategic to Nokia for understanding and improvement of users' experiences with their phones and other location products/services. Nokia leverages data processing and analytics to build maps with predictive traffic and layered elevation models, information on points of interest around the world, and to monitor and assess the quality of its mobile phones, among other issues.

Considering the case study, Nokia aimed to have a holistic view on people interactions with different applications around the world, requiring an infrastructure that could support daily, terabyte-scale streams of unstructured data from phones in use, services, log files, and other sources. The challenge has been to integrate its silos of applications, enabling a comprehensive version of truth from data captured at global level. Furthermore, Nokia had to face the cost of capturing petabyte-scale data using relational databases. As a consequence, the choice has been to build an information infrastructure based on a technology ecosystem, including a Teradata enterprise data warehouse, Oracle and MySQL data marts, visualization technologies, and Hadoop at the core of Nokia's infrastructure.

POINT OF ATTENTION: Big Data ask for a clear understanding of both IT Portfolio and data asset, for identifying relevant data from all information sources (internal/external) to be stored, and for a savvy and sustainable choice of the right mix of technologies to consolidate corporate databases (internal) and integrate new information sources (internal/external).

As reported by Cloudera [33] the centralized Hadoop cluster actually contains 0.5 PB of data. The resulting infrastructure allows data access to Nokia's employees (more than 60,000), and efficiently moving of data from, for example, servers in Singapore to a Hadoop cluster in the UK data center.

Nevertheless, Nokia faced also the problem of fitting unstructured data into a relational schema before it can be loaded into the system, requiring extra data processing step that slows ingestion, creates latency and may eliminates important elements of the data. The solution has been found in Cloudera's Distribution that includes Apache Hadoop (CDH), bundling the most popular open source projects

in the Apache Hadoop stack into a single, integrated package. In 2011, Nokia put
its central CDH cluster into production to serve as the company's information
core.

Finally, we present a case study that shows how a Big Data strategy can be
implemented in a specific industry. The case is based on a Consultancy case
history [34] and shows how General Electric Co. (GE), the US based utility
corporation, is building Big Data and analytics capabilities for an "Industrial
Internet".

In 2011, GE announced $1 billion investment to build software and expertise
on Big Data analytics, launching a global software center in San Ramon, California. GE charged William Ruh from Cisco Systems to lead the center, developing software and data science capabilities for GE's Big Data domain of interest
('the industrial Internet').

> **POINT OF ATTENTION**: Big Data require top management commitment
> and investments, in particular, on human resources to be focused on data
> scientist capabilities. Furthermore, talent management and employees reten-
> tion have to be considered as a core target for the success of a Big Data strategy.

As argued by Consultancy [34], GE envisions Big Data as a $30 trillion
opportunity by 2030, using a conservative 1 % savings in five sectors that buy its
machinery (aviation, power, healthcare, rail, and oil and gas), estimating the
savings from an industrial Internet for these sectors alone could be nearly
$300 billion in the next 15 years. In particular, Big Data is strategic for a growing
percentage of GE's business related to services, such as, e.g., supporting its
industrial products and helping customers use GE's machines more effectively and
efficiently. Indeed, the GE assesses the success of software and analytics by their
enabling a new portfolio of compelling service offerings, helping, e.g., airlines,
electric utilities, hospitals to exploit GE's Big Data expertise, generating big
savings, likewise. Thus, human resources and talent management are key issues to
GE Big Data strategy.

The center has a staff of about 300 employees (most of them, characterized as
"hardcore data scientists"), located in San Ramon and around the globe, as well
(Bangalore, New York, and Cambridge), reporting into the center. The center
organizes employees into reference disciplines, such as, e.g., machine learning,
statistics, and operations research, among others. Furthermore, centralization of
the staff is motivated by three factors: an acute shortage of talent, having in-depth
data science and deep analytics capabilities; a consequent need for employee
retention; reusability in technology.[6]

---

[6] *"The reason is you can't find the talent, you can't maintain it, and so on. We believe this idea
of reuse is going to differentiate the winners from the losers."* Ruh, reported by Consultancy
(2013).

1.3 Summary

In this Chapter, we have discussed the business challenges of Big Data as a core component of the information infrastructure upon which our society is building its own open environment. Often referred as an IT trend, the Chapter has clarified the main drivers and characteristics of Big Data, both at technical and managerial level, emphasizing their differences with regards to, e.g., *digital data streams* (DDSs); the latter referring to streams of real-time information by mobile devices and internet of things, that have to be "captured" and analyzed real-time, provided or not they are stored as "Big Data". Furthermore, we have investigated management challenges and opportunities, identifying the main phases and actions of a Big Data lifecycle. As for these issues, the Chapter has pointed out the relevance of "softscaling" approaches, balancing optimization issues, such as, e.g., integration and standardization of the information infrastructure, and an attention to experience and contextual needs for an empathic exploitation of Big Data as a digital asset.

Finally, the Chapter has discussed a set of case studies, confirming the importance of a clear and shared Big Data strategy together with investments and focus on human resources for capabilities, suitable to support Big Data-driven decision making and operational performance.

References

1. Ahituv N (2001) The open information society. Commun ACM 44:48–52. doi:10.1145/376134.376158
2. Horovitz B (2012) After Gen X, Millennials, what should next generation be? In: USA today. http://usatoday30.usatoday.com/money/advertising/story/2012-05-03/naming-the-next-generation/54737518/1. Accessed 5 Jul 2013
3. Saltman D (2011) Turning digital natives into digital citizens. Harv Educ Lett 27(5)
4. The Economist (2010) Data, data everywhere. Special report on information management
5. Davenport TH, Patil DJ (2012) Data scientist: the sexiest job of the 21st century data scientist. Harv Bus Rev 90(10):70–76
6. IBM (2013) What is big data? http://www-01.ibm.com/software/data/bigdata/. Accessed 9 Jul 2013
7. Pospiech M, Felden C (2012) Big data—a state-of-the-art. In: Americas conference on information systems (AMCIS 2012)
8. McAfee A, Brynjolfsson E (2012) Big data: the management revolution. Harv Bus Rev 90(10):61–68
9. Wang RY, Strong DM (1996) Beyond accuracy: what data quality means to data consumers. J Manag Inf Syst 12:5–33
10. Madnick SE, Wang RY, Lee YW, Zhu H (2009) Overview and framework for data and information quality research. J Data Inf Qual 1:1–22. doi:10.1145/1515693.1516680
11. Huang KT, Lee Y, Wang RY (1999) Quality, information and knowledge. Prentice-Hall Inc, New Jersey

12. Agrawal D, Das S, El Abbadi A (2010) Big data and cloud computing: new wine or just new bottles? Proc VLDB Endow 3:1647–1648
13. Agrawal D, Das S, Abbadi A (2011) Big data and cloud computing: current state and future opportunities. In: Proceedings of extending database technology (EDBT), ACM. March 22–24, Sweden, pp 530–533
14. Davenport TH, Barth P, Bean R (2012) How "Big Data" is different. MIT Sloan Manag Rev 54:43–46
15. Piccoli G, Pigni F (2013) Harvesting external data: the potential of digital data streams. MIS Q Exec 12:143–154
16. Zuiderwijk A, Janssen M, Choenni S (2012) Open data policies: impediments and challenges. In: 12th European conference on e-government (ECEG 2012). Barcelona, Spain, pp 794–802
17. Cabinet Office UK (2012) Open data white paper—Unleashing the potential
18. Nam T (2012) Citizens' attitudes toward open government and government 2.0. Int Rev Adm Sci 78:346–368. doi:10.1177/0020852312438783
19. Feller J, Finnegan P, Nilsson O (2011) Open innovation and public administration: transformational typologies and business model impacts. Eur J Inf Syst 20:358–374. doi:10. 1057/Ejis.2010.65
20. Di Maio A (2010) Gartner open government maturity model
21. Lee G, Kwak YH (2012) An open government maturity model for social media-based public engagement. Gov Inf Q. doi:10.1016/j.giq.2012.06.001
22. Marchand DA, Kettinger WJ, Rollins JD (2000) Information orientation: people, technology and the bottom line. MIT Sloan Manag Rev 41:69–80
23. Tallon PP (2013) Corporate governance of big data: perspectives on value, risk, and cost. IEEE Comput 46:32–38
24. Tallon BPP, Scannell R (2007) Information life cycle. Commun ACM 50:65–69
25. Weber K, Otto B, Österle H (2009) One size does not fit all—a contingency approach to data governance. J Data Inf Qual 1(1):1–27, Article 4. doi:10.1145/1515693.1515696
26. Vom Brocke J, Rosemann M (2010) Handbook on business process management 1. Springer, Heidelberg
27. Awargal R, Weill P (2012) The benefits of combining data with empathy. SMR 54:35–41
28. Lavalle S, Lesser E, Shockley R, Hopkins MS, Kruschwitz N (2011) Big data, analytics and the path from insights to value. MIT Sloan Manag Rev 52(2):21–32
29. Morabito V (2013) Business technology organization—managing digital information technology for value creation—the SIGMA approach. Springer, Heidelberg
30. Francalanci C, Morabito V (2008) IS integration and business performance: the mediation effect of organizational absorptive capacity in SMEs. J Inf Technol 23:297–312
31. Moses J, Bapna R, Chervany N (2012) Social media strategy for the MINNESOTA wild, Carlson School of Management
32. Sharma N, Subramanian S, Bapna R, Iyer L (2008) Data warehousing as a strategic tool at Bharti Airtel—Case No. CS-08-001
33. Cloudera (2012) Nokia: using big data to bridge the virtual & physical worlds
34. Consultancy T (2013) Big data case study: how GE is building big data, software and analytics capabilities for an "Industrial Internet." http://sites.tcs.com/big-data-study/ ge-big-data-case-study/. Accessed 20 Jul 2013
35. Floridi L (2010) Information: a very short introduction. Oxford University Press, Oxford, pp 1–43
36. Avison DE, Fitzgerald G (1999) Information systems development. In: Currie WL, Galliers RD (eds) Rethinking management information systems: an interdisciplinary perspective. Oxford University Press, Oxford, pp 250–278
37. Floridi L (2011) Semantic conceptions of information. In: Zalta EN (ed) Stanford encyclopaedia of philosophy

38. Kharif O (2013) ATMs that look like iPADs. Bloom Businessweek, pp 38–39
39. Han J, Haihong E, Le G, Du J (2011) Survey on NoSQL database. In: Proceedings of the 6th international conference on pervasive computing and applications, pp 363–366
40. Strauch C (2010) NoSQL databases. Lecture notes on Stuttgart Media, Stuttgart, pp 1–8
41. Dean J, Ghemawat S (2008) MapReduce: simplified data processing on large clusters. Commun ACM 51:1–13. doi:10.1145/1327452.1327492
42. IBM, Zikopoulos P, Eaton C (2011) Understanding big data: analytics for enterprise class hadoop and streaming data, 1st edn. McGraw-Hill Osborne Media, New York

Chapter 2
Cloud Computing

Abstract During the last decade, the Information and Communication Technology (ICT) industry has been transformed by innovations that fundamentally changed the way we use computers, how we access information, how businesses derive value from ICT and how consumers live their daily lives. This fast evolution made the ICT able to cover more areas in business and other fields. It can be used to reduce costs by keeping accurate records of all the transactions that are happening in the company, which enables better stock controlling by using Electronic Point of Sales (EPOS), Electronic Data Interchange (EDI) and Electronic Funds Transfer at Point of Sale (EFTPOS), and allows improved automation of the production process by using computer controlled machines. Moreover, marketing has benefited from ICT in many ways such as analyzing the results of market research in more effective ways by utilizing the capabilities of Business Intelligence (BI), ICTs have important role in improving communications between the different departments and branches within the same company, among other firms by using mobile phones, emails, intranet, internet, and faxes, and between the business and its customers. One important new development in the ICT field is the cloud computing, which will be investigated in details in this Chapter.

2.1 Introduction

The development of cloud computing started years ago with the emergence of grid computing. Grid computing can be explained as the allocation of several computer systems in a parallel structure to solve one problem [1]. Cloud computing is similar to Grid but differs in the sense it aims to provide on demand access to a specific service or pool of services over the network through virtualized IT servers such as data centers and specialized software applications [2]. It is the latest development in the computing models that performs computing functions on multi-level virtualization and abstraction by integrating many IT resources. The key features of cloud computing can be summarized in the following list [1]:

V. Morabito, *Trends and Challenges in Digital Business Innovation,*
DOI: 10.1007/978-3-319-04307-4_2, © Springer International Publishing Switzerland 2014

1. *On demand self-service*. Defined as the process that enables the user to utilize computing capabilities, such as server using time and data storage, automatically and without human interaction.
2. *Broad network access*, which enables the user to access the cloud computing resource from different platforms, such as mobile phones, laptops or PDAs.
3. *Improved accessibility*, by providing the ability for the employees to access work applications and files from everywhere.
4. *Resources pooling and allocation*, which enables the service provider to serve multiple customers as the same time by smartly allocating its resource to them [3].
5. *Agile structure*, which is complementing characteristics for the previous feature and enables the cloud computing structure to comply with the user's demands.
6. *Measured and controlled service*. This feature is important for both, the service provider and the consumer, since it provides transparency and clarity to their relation.
7. *Reduced total cost of ownership*, which is achieved by sharing the same infrastructure by several clients.
8. *Quick deployment* of the cloud computing structure in comparison with traditional information systems implementations.

2.1.1 Cloud Computing: Service Models

Dhar [4] defines cloud computing as the structure that provides the ability to the users to utilize the hardware, software, and networking infrastructure over the Internet. From this definition, three levels of cloud computing can be defined (see Fig. 2.1). The first level is the *Software as Service* (*SaaS*). In this layer, the applications such as office and enterprise systems are used over the network. This level is considered as the highest level of abstraction on the cloud. The second level is the Platform as a *Service* (*PaaS*), which is considered as the next level of abstraction and provides essential application infrastructure services such as computation, connectivity and emails access.

The last layer is the *Infrastructure as a Service* (*IaaS*), in which the client will have full ownership over the service provided such as virtual servers, memory and storage devices. These layers are also called the application layer, the platform layer and the infrastructure layer respectively in which each one of them is loosely coupled with the layers above and below and are illustrated in more details in Fig. 2.2 [5].

In addition to these, a new abstraction level in cloud computing has emerged recently and called Network as a Service (Naas). This layer provides customers with the ability configure the network on the cloud, which gives them access to virtual network functions such as network-aware VM placement, real time network monitoring, diagnostics and management. It aims to support scalability and availability on highly dynamic networks [6].

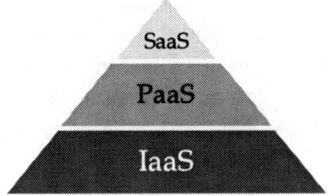

Fig. 2.1 The *three layers* of cloud computing. Adapted from [4]

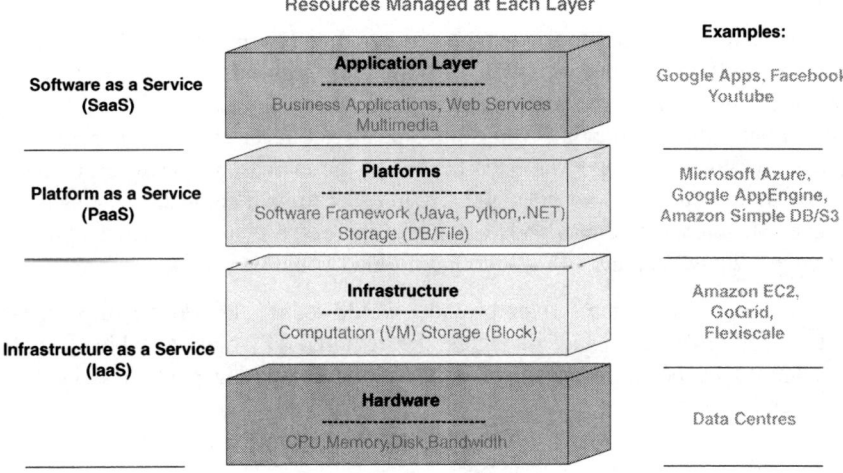

Fig. 2.2 Cloud computing architecture. Adapted from [5]

2.1.2 Cloud Computing Service Providers

In this section, examples of the main names in cloud computing will be introduced. The first example is Amazon EC2 which allows users to rent virtual computers on which to run their own computer applications. It runs over HTTP, using REST and SOAP protocols. It gives the subscribers the ability to launch and manage server instances in data centers using APIs. The second one is Microsoft Windows Azure platform, which is composed of three components. The first component which is Windows Azure provides Windows based environment to enable users to run applications and store data in data centers. The second component which is SQL Azure provides data services in the cloud using SQL server. The last component which is .NET services facilitates the creation of distributed applications. The last example of cloud computing service provider is Google, which uses its own infrastructure that contains three independent but cooperated systems. The first one is Google File System, which is a proprietary distributed file system that is developed by Google to provide efficient, reliable access to data using large clusters of commodity servers. The second one is the Big Table, which is a model-simplified large-scale distributed database. Finally, the last one is the Map\Reduce[1] programming model that can be modified according to the characteristics of the applications that Google is running on its servers. The previous three systems represent data storage, data management and programming models respectively [5].

2.2 Strategic and Managerial Challenges and Opportunities

The decision of whether to implement the cloud computing project by the organization itself or to outsource it to a third party depends on the abilities and strategic objectives of the implementing company. For instance [4] argues that outsourcing cloud computing would have positive effects on the management to achieve its goals such as to take the benefit of the increased globalization and to deploy the products and services globally in order to gain competitive advantage, to generate higher revenues and to achieve increased consumer satisfaction. In summary, the advantages of outsourcing a cloud could be seen as:

1. *Lower costs*, since the service provider would reduce the direct and overhead costs of developing and managing the required IT solution, which can be achieved by better management of the cloud computing pooling services to several clients.
2. *Faster development cycle*, which can be achieved by getting the advantage of delivering the product to customers.
3. *Performance assurance and quality*, which would be achieved by the vendor by utilizing better technologies and employing more experienced consultants in this field, which would have a better response time for the future emerging demands.
4. *Professional and geographically dispersed service*, which can be achieved by the vendor by providing the service 24/7 over the diverse geographical areas.
5. *Creative and structured leases*, that can be provided by the cloud computing service provider, which allows the company to transfer the risk of failure to the vendor, especially when the company does not have the required experience and the core competence in this field. The agreement between the implementing organization and the cloud computing service provider can be flexible enough to benefit both parties and to comply with supply and business demand.

---

[1] See also Chap. 1 of this book for details on Map\Reduce and Big Data.

2.2.1 Challenges Accompanying Cloud Computing

Businesses across industries have come to a consensus about the inherent business value of cloud computing and are increasingly transitioning to the cloud. However, despite all these trends, there are many challenges that face the research and evolution in this field. For example, [5] argued that these new issues are emerging from the industry as a result for the new demands for new applications and new requirements, and are summarized in the following points:

1. *Automated service provisioning.* One of the key advantages for cloud computing is its ability to provide its service to several businesses simultaneously by acquiring and releasing the resources on-demand and as needed. This feature enables the service provider to allocate and de-allocate resources from the cloud to satisfy the cloud's service level objectives. However, it is not clear how to automate the mapping between the business requirements and the low level resources requirements such as CPU and memory in order to fulfill all demands. The automated service provisioning has been researched in the past and one of the solutions for this problem is to periodically predicting the demand and to automatically allocate the resources that meet the requirements.

2. *Virtual machine migration.* Virtualization can be important for cloud computing by enabling virtual machine migration to balance the load throughout the data center. Virtual Machine (VM) migration enables robust and highly responsive provisioning in data centers. As a result, it can be concluded that the major benefit of VM migration is to avoid hotspots; however, this is not straightforward. Currently, detecting workload hotspots and initiating a migration lacks the agility to respond to sudden workload changes. Moreover, the in-memory state should be transferred consistently and efficiently, with integrated consideration of resources for applications and physical servers.

3. *Server consolidation.* Server consolidation is an approach to the efficient usage of computer server resources for the sake of cost and electricity savings [7]. However, despite the benefits of this approach, server consolidation, bear many problems that have to be considered. One example of these problems is resource congestion when VM changes its footprint on the server, which could happen as a result of maximally consolidating a server. Thus, it is crucial to monitor the fluctuations of VM footprints in order to best mange server consolidation. In addition, the system has to quickly response to resource congestion when they occur.

4. *Energy management.* Energy efficiency and environmental considerations are very important factors in cloud computing that have to be well-thought-out in designing its architecture. Those requirements can be met by adopting different solutions. One example is the usage of energy efficient hardware architecture that allows better utilization of hardware resources such as CPU and memory. Also, energy-aware job scheduling and server consolidation are two other ways to reduce power consumption by turning off unused machines.

5. *Traffic management and analysis*. The importance of the analysis of the data traffic is faced by many challenges in cloud computing. These challenges stem from the difficulties in calculating, measuring and predicting the traffic to the data centers, especially when they are composed of several hundreds of servers.
6. *Data security*. The infrastructure provider tries to achieve best data security by meeting the following two objectives (1) *confidentiality*, for secure data access and transfer, and (2) auditability, for attesting whether the security settings of the application have been altered or not. However, this factor forms big challenge for all stakeholders in cloud computing. This happens because of the structure of the cloud computing when the VMs can dynamically migrate from location to another, which creates difficulties in using remote attestation. In this case, it is critical to build trust mechanisms at every architectural layer of the cloud.
7. *Software frameworks*. The main objective behind the cloud computing is to provide a platform to host and run large-scale data intensive applications. These applications use the MapReduce frameworks such as Hadoop for scalable and fault-tolerant data processing. However, modeling the performance of Hadoop tasks (either online or offline) and the adaptive scheduling in dynamic conditions form an important challenge in cloud computing.
8. *Storage technologies and data management*. The concerns that can arise here come from the compatibility issues between the Internet-scale file systems that host the software frameworks such as MapReduce on one hand, and the legacy applications that are required to run on these file systems from the other hand. These issues are based on the differences in storage structure, access pattern and application programming interface.

2.2.2 Advantages and Risks in Cloud Computing Outsourcing Projects

Cloud computing is like any other new development in IT, since it has advantages and risks. According to [8], there are many benefits for utilizing a third party cloud computing service provider for the implementing company. Those benefits are presented and explained in the following section:

1. The company will have the ability to manage the income and the expenditures, since the cloud pricing model is clear and is less affected by the expenditures of the electricity, because of the savings on energy costs, which would result in overall costs savings.
2. Participating successfully in the implementation of this project would improve the status of the management and support engineers in the implementing firm.
3. Increased satisfaction of the support engineers by focusing on more important IT issues.

4. It gives the opportunity for the employees from different departments to develop their experiences about cloud computing support and management. Also, it gives them the opportunity to explore the interaction with this new technology.
5. Finally, sales and marketing staff will have the chance to participate more actively in creating new products and services.

Chang et al. [9] also suggest that shaping the right business strategies for cloud computing transformation would enhance the organizational sustainability. Moreover, another study by Gai and Li [10] added more advantages that can be gained by transforming to cloud computing such as high expandability, friendly utilisation and environmental protection. Finally, the users can use cloud resources to scale-up or down and the providers of this service can maximize the performance of the servers and other resources to comply with the business needs. On the other hand, and in spite of the tempting advantages of utilizing cloud computing in the business, [8] suggests there are s number of risks when adopting cloud computing services. These risks are summarized as follows:

1. The *customer service quality* at the company might be affected with this change, which could happen because the support managers and engineers become mode dependent upon the cloud service provider because their knowledge about the cloud service is limited.
2. The *staff responsible about the supporting the service* may lose interest and satisfaction about their roles, since the work may shift from hands-on technical experience to reporting and following up the service provider to solve the emergent problems.
3. The *IT department* would possibly lose some of its staff due to the fact that many of them are not necessary any more, since the service provider will be in charge of their jobs of providing software and hardware support.
4. Based on the last point, there will be a possibility of losing the *expert employees*, which would create a problem for the company in case it wanted to bring the old systems back due to the insufficient performance by the cloud service provider.
5. There will be doubt about the new technology and whether it should be provided as an *in-house service* or to be *outsourced* by a third party.
6. There might be an unnatural *growth in the size of some department* to cope with the new technology in the business environment.

The risks and impact of IT outsourcing also have to be considered. Gai and Li [10], for example suggest that security problem could arise because of poorly executed protocols and authentication process as well as the lack of security standards that govern cloud computing. The importance of the security issues is also addressed by many other authors such as Srinisvasan et al. [11]. In their research they classify the concerns about the security into two main categories:

A. *Architectural and Technological Aspects*, and includes the following points:

1. *Logical storage segregation and multi-tenancy security*

This risk might happen when some clients and their own competitors share the same physical storage location, which could result in private data exposure. In such a case, the Cloud Service Provider CSP should ensure proper data isolation to handle such sensitive situation.

2. *Identity management*

As the traditional identity and access management is still facing challenges from different aspects such as security, privacy, provisioning of service as well as VMs, etc., hence, more considerations should thought of when considering it for cloud computing, since it needs to be more secure and sophisticated. This is especially necessary when considering the 'pay as you use' feature of the cloud.

3. *Insider attacks*

This risk can be very dangerous based on the fact that the provider does not reveal information such as, e.g., how it grants employees access to physical and virtual assets, how it monitors these employees, or how it analyses and reports on policy compliance and the little or lack of visibility into the hiring standards and practices for cloud employees. This risk can lead to situations like financial impact, brand damage and productivity loss.

4. *Virtualization issues*

Virtualization is very important in the cloud computing to achieve its goal of sharing resources. This can be accomplished by using hypervisor, which also called Virtual Machine Monitor (VMM). It is a platform that allows multiple OS and related applications (called Virtual Machines VMs) to run on a cloud machine concurrently to facilitate sharing of cloud resources. Virtualization of enterprise servers introduces considerable security concerns. Associating multiple servers with one host removes the physical separation between servers, increasing the risk of undesirable cooperation of one application (of one VM) with others on the same host. Also, if an attacker gets the root to access the hypervisor, then it brings significant threats to the holistic view of cloud computing.

5. *Cryptography and key management*

The need for appropriate and, up-to-date cryptography systems with efficient key management will be the main objective for any CSP with highly sensitive customer information. The following are the possible weak components of the cloud environment:

- communication channel between the customer and the CSP;
- storage areas that are specified for customers' data;
- hypervisors;
- cloud mapping services.

B. *Process and regulatory-related aspects*, and includes the following points:

6. *Governance and regulatory compliance gaps*

The well-developed information security governance processes should exhibit the following characteristics:

- scalable;
- repeatable;
- measurable;
- sustainable;
- defensible;
- continually improving;
- cost-effective.

7. *Insecure APIs*

The Applications Programming Interface (APIs) are the software interfaces that document how to communicate with the concerned software. The CSP publishes those API to allow users to discover the available features of the cloud computing. However, insecure APIs would invite attackers' attention to know the architecture of the CSP and internal design details which would lead to major security concerns for CSP as well as customers like cyber-attacks and illegitimate control over user accounts.

8. *Cloud and CSP migration*

Transforming to the cloud or moving from one CSP to another involves two levels of migration:

- *Level 1: Data (and Application) migration*, which will happen during the change to the cloud computing model and comprises risks related to data security and portability.
- *Level 2: Cloud migration*, which will happen during the change from one CSP to another and comprises risks about data migration security and about making sure that the old CSP, will delete customer's data on its cloud servers.

9. *Service Level Agreement and trust management gaps*

Service Level Agreement (SLA) is the document that details the agreed minimum performance provided by the cloud provider. This document should aim to clarify customer's needs, simplify complex issues, manage conflictions and eliminate unrealistic expectations. Therefore, the following SLA Security Qualities (SSQs) are important for any customer who wants to transform to cloud computing service model:

- logical segregation of customer data;
- accessibility and auditability of the customer and CSP;
- guaranteed data deletion when customer is no longer with the CSP;
- 24/7 availability of the service;

- agreements on security related issues;
- up-to-date technology improvement by the CSP;
- governance and regulatory compliance maintenance with respect to the country(s) bound of the deployed application.

Other examples of the risks include the low controllability over the service, data ownership and loss of data since it is provided by a third party service provider, which can result in weak auditing ability of the service [12].

The previous mentioned risks and challenges have to be considered by the transforming company which needs to be able to deal with them by having backup plans in case of a disaster. Also it has to prepare better plans for its employees training and development in order for them to be able to cope with changes associated with the coming IT transformation. Moreover, it has to establish well governing policies that would control the relationship with the service provider regarding the security issues. Finally, they have to ensure that the contract will have the provider involved in dealing and covering the problems that could emerge such as security issues [13]. On the other side, [14] suggests that the service supplier can enhance the quality of the service it provides by using an execution log to register the correct execution of a business process, which can be checked regularly by the client in order to check the correct transactions.

2.2.3 Managing Changes and Organizational Issues

Outsourcing the cloud computing services can be considered as a very important step on the road of having agile and efficient business, since business agility is defined as the ability to adapt to the market trends and changes. These changes need to be closely managed, since losing control over the variations in the business may have a bad impact over the business in general. Several factors that are related to change management need to be well-thought-out in order to have smooth change. One example is the resistance for change that may arise during the transformation to the cloud computing services [15]. Dealing with the issues related to change management is very important, since imposing changes would not have a good impact on employees performance; therefore, careful change management techniques should be applied in such a situation in order to ease the new changes. The opposition of the employees needs to be addressed and carefully dealt with, which can be achieved by examining the reasons for the resistance and dealing with them such as the fear from more work and more responsibility [15]. These reasons can be alleviated by clearly explaining all the issues are related to the coming change. In other words, managing changes requires more effective communications and employee development which can be achieved by additional training [16]. Moreover, and most importantly, top management support should be guaranteed at all time during the change process [17].

Khajeh-hosseini et al. [8] also suggests that the organization implementing cloud computing has to consider the socio-technical factors that concern with interaction between the people and technology in the work environment, and that affect its intention behind this transformation. Some examples of these factors are, organization climate, IT support, perceived relative advantage, perceived compatibility, perceived complexity and the intention to encourage knowledge sharing. These main factors include sub factors such as top management support, the usage of electronic storage devices, team workers performance and the policies that govern the way the business work [18]. All the previous factors have to be properly managed in order to have smooth transition to cloud computing services.

2.3 Deployment Models (Private, Public, Community and Hybrid)

Cloud services can be deployed in different ways, depending on the organizational structure and the provisioning location. Four deployment models are usually distinguished, namely public, private, community and hybrid cloud service usage [11]. Table 2.1 shows how each model infrastructure is managed, owned, located and accessed or its services are consumed.

As for infrastructure characteristics described in the columns of Table 2.1, it is worth noting that *management* (first column of Table 2.1) includes governance, operations, security, compliance, etc. Furthermore, infrastructure implies *physical assets* (second column of Table 2.1) such as facilities, compute, and network and storage equipment. However, infrastructure *location* is both physical and relative to an organization's management umbrella and speaks to ownership versus control.

Finally, as for infrastructure *accessibility and consumption* issues, trusted consumers of service are those who are considered part of an organization's legal/contractual/policy umbrella including employees, contractors and business partners. Whereas, untrusted consumers are those that may be authorized to consume some/all services but are not logical extensions of the organization. In the following we provide further details for each model.

Private Cloud is for the sole use of a single organization and its customers. The chief advantage of this model is that the enterprise retains full control over corporate data and security and system performance. However, private cloud is usually not as large-scale as public cloud, which affects its economical outcome. This is a common model for governments and large enterprises, when there are concerns about security and data sovereignty. In contrast to previous model, the *public cloud* is open for use by the general public i.e., individuals or organizations. From the technical point of view, there is no difference between public and private cloud architecture, however, security concerns may be considerably different for the cloud services such as applications, storage, and other resources that are made available by a service provider for public access and when communication is happening over a non-trusted network.

Table 2.1 Cloud computing deployment models

	Infrastructure managed by	Infrastructure owned by	Infrastructure located	Accessible and consumed by
Public	3rd party provider	3rd party provider	Off-premise	Untrusted
Private / Community	Organisation or 3rd part provider	Organisation 3rd part provider	On-premise Off-premise	Trusted
Hybrid	Both organisation and 3rd Provider	Both organisation and 3rd provider	Both on and off premise	Trusted and untrusted

Adapted from [11]

Considering the *Community Cloud* model, the cloud computing environment is not dedicated to a single organization. This model used when organizations from the same community and with similar requirements share a cloud infrastructure, and it can be seen as a generalization of a private cloud. In this model, the costs are shared among the participating organizations. The main advantages in this model are 1) sharing the common practice among the companies which would result in a better performance for the cloud, and 2) since this model is larger than the private one, then, there will be more effective utilization of the cloud resources. Finally, *Hybrid Cloud* setup is a combination of two or more distinct and unique cloud setup such as private, community, or public, that remains as unique entities but are bound together, offering the benefits of multiple deployment models. This model is suitable for enterprises in which the transformation to full outsourcing is already done, for instance, to combine community cloud services with public cloud services.

Taking the above issues into account in what follows we provide and discuss guidelines and recommendations to support decisions on outsourcing and project implementation life cycle.

2.4 Guidelines and Recommendations

2.4.1 Choosing a Cloud Computing Service Provider

Choosing the cloud computing service provider is considered as a strategic decision for any organization, since it would have important implications on its future strategies. Therefore, according to authors such as, e.g., Low and Chen [19], companies who consider making this transformation have to study issues about the possible provider such as interoperability, flexibility, Service Legal Agreements (SLAs), security standards, backup strategies, customer support, downtime history and pricing policy. Thus, this choice has to be built upon a careful decision and a set of criteria [19]. Although Low and Chen focused their research on the healthcare sector, the guidelines they proposed could be generalized to other sectors, as they are based on commonly used frameworks for multi-criteria decision-making problems.

The first framework is the *Fuzzy Delphi Method* (FDM), which is used to decide the important factors for decision making. FDM is a combination of the Fuzzy Logic, which is an approach for computing that is based on degrees of truth rather than the usual true or false symbolized by (1) or (0) that represents the Boolean logic on which the modern computer is based, and Delphi Method, which is a type of a collective decision-making method [20], with several rounds of anonymous written questionnaire surveys conducted to ask for experts' opinion [21]. FDM has the following properties:

1. *Anonymity*: The experts involved with the prediction process do not see each other, remain anonymous and don't know how many experts are involved. This helps to prevent them from influencing and encourages objectivity.
2. *Feedback*: The survey feedback gives the participants an idea about the main ideas in the group. They can then draw from it information relevant to them, make a new judgment, and then submit it to the group again.
3. *Statistical*: The expert opinions are processed statistically and a splines graph produced with the expert opinion frequencies arrayed chronologically. The top is the majority consensus (50 % experts) representing the prediction team's opinion. The top and bottom quarter percentile (each representing 25 % of the experts) represent the prediction deviation.
4. *Convergence*: Through multiple reverse feedback make the final prediction results converge.

The purpose of the Delphi Method is to achieve a consensus among the experts on the subject being evaluated. When used with one-to-many objectives, multi-principle, multi-proposal and multi-participant decision-making problems, the method not only serves to draw on a large body of opinion but also meets the requirement for independence in the experts' judgment [21].

The second one is the *Fuzzy Analytic Hierarchy Process* (FAHP), which is used to calculate the weights of the chosen criteria by FDM. The Analytic Hierarchy Process (AHP) is a structured technique for organizing and analyzing complex decisions. Rather than prescribing a correct decision, the AHP helps decision makers find one that best suits their goal and their understanding of the problem. It provides a comprehensive and rational framework for structuring a decision problem, for representing and quantifying its elements, for relating those elements to overall goals, and for evaluating alternative solutions. However, despite of its popularity, this method is often criticized for its inability to adequately handle the inherent uncertainty and imprecision associated with the mapping of the decision-maker's perception to exact numbers. Therefore, the fuzzy logic is used to provide more accuracy in making judgments and solves the problems exist in AHP [22].

Figure 2.3 illustrates the supplier selection hierarchy, which can be used by the transforming firm. This hierarchy studies five main criteria categories that include other sub factors that have to be considered during the decision making process.

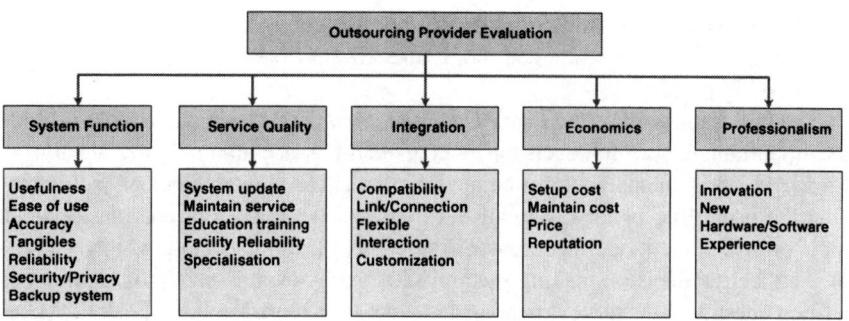

Fig. 2.3 Cloud computing supplier selection. Adapted from [19]

The top level of the hierarchy represents the research goal, and the second level is consisted of five main provider selection dimensions: system function, service quality, integration, economics, and professionalism.

At the third level, these criteria are decomposed into several sub-criteria that may influence an organization's choice of an appropriate cloud computing service provider. The criteria in this three-level hierarchy are the ones that can be weighted in the approaches mentioned above to decide its importance for the concerned stakeholders [19].

2.4.2 Cloud Computing Project Implementation Life Cycle

Conway and Curry [12] propose an implementation life cycle for cloud computing depicted in Fig. 2.4.

This cycle is divided into four major phases: architect, engage, operate and refresh, which they are further subdivided into 9 steps: investigate, identify, implementation strategy, business design, select, negotiate, operational roll-out, manage the supply chain, and review. The following sections provide a brief explanation about these phases and steps.

Phase 1: Architect

This stage is about investigation and planning of the cloud project. Also, it gives the company an indication whether it should continue with a full-scale project or not. This stage is composed of four steps, which are:

1. *Investigate*. To determine the goals and expectations of moving to cloud computing and includes the activities and outputs shown in Table 2.2. This step provides an understanding of the needs of the implementing organization and how the transformation to the cloud computing model would help to meet those

Fig. 2.4 Cloud computing
life cycle. Adapted from [12]

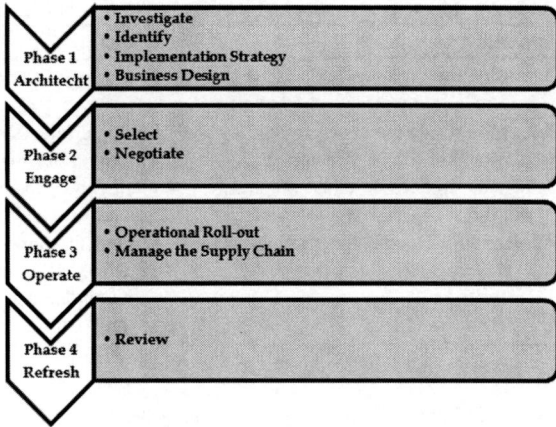

Phase 1
Architecht
- Investigate
- Identify
- Implementation Strategy
- Business Design

Phase 2
Engage
- Select
- Negotiate

Phase 3
Operate
- Operational Roll-out
- Manage the Supply Chain

Phase 4
Refresh
- Review

necessities. This step faces some challenges such as satisfying the new requirements within the existing or new budget, resistance for this change because of the lack of the financial control over the pay as you go model and the need for fund for investigating the different cloud options.

2. *Identify.* To identify which areas of the business are qualified to be moved to the cloud computing and includes the activities and outputs shown in Table 2.3. In this step, the implementing company objectively assesses which departments or functional units are suitable to be transformed to the cloud service model. This is done by comparing their current state with the desired future state and measuring the impact on cost, infrastructure and stakeholders.

This step faces two important challenges which are defining the enterprise architecture which can be a time consuming task, and investigating the impact with the concerned users and IT department employees, whose jobs will be altered or removed.

3. *Implementation strategy.* To define the long term implementation strategy and risk assessment and includes the activities and outputs shown in Table 2.4.

In this step, a strategic planning will be done for the services that will be affected with the cloud computing transformation. This includes critical decisions such as staffing, communication, organizational rules and risk assessment. This step faces challenges such as clearly defining business and technical requirements and to fully ensuring stakeholders' engagement and collaboration.

4. *Business design.* To design how the services will look like and behave and includes the activities and outputs shown in Table 2.5.

In this step, there will be a planning for how the future state will be after transforming to the cloud computing service model. This planning will detail the new service, how it will be managed, how it interfaces to the existing/remaining

Table 2.2 Phase 1, activities and outputs of the *Investigate* step

Activities	Outputs
Determine the organization's IT objectives and its alignment with the business	IT strategy for cloud computing
Determine what role cloud computing will play within the IT strategy	Strategic intent of moving to the cloud and how it progresses the business objectives
Gather intelligence on cloud service offerings	Intelligence document on cloud service offerings and providers
Validate with cloud subject matter experts	Documented understanding of what will be achieved by comparing the strategic requirements with the available services and providers

Table 2.3 Phase 1, activities and outputs of the *Identify* step

Activities	Outputs
Determine what services will be outsourced to the cloud, and consider impacts on the service, people, cost, infrastructure, and stakeholders	A list of services to be outsourced to the cloud, with documented understanding on impacts to service, people, cost, infrastructure, and stakeholders
Decide what type of cloud outsourcing model will be used, and why it is suitable	A cloud outsourcing model, with documented justification
Document the current and future states of the IT infrastructure	Documented current and future states of the IT structure

Table 2.4 Phase 1, activities and outputs of the *Implementation strategy* step

Activities	Outputs
Determine the roll-out approach and how the program will be managed	A program roll-out strategy
Detail how the program will be staffed and reported	A communication strategy
Decide how cloud suppliers will be engaged, selected and managed	A strategy to manage staff impacted by the migration to cloud

Table 2.5 Phase 1, activities and outputs of the *Business design* step

Activities	Outputs
Detail the service offering you wish to tender for clearly define negotiable/non-negotiable issues around contracts, service-level agreements (SLA), and pricing model	Detailed and clear tender documents for cloud suppliers

systems, and how it will be monitored and reported. The challenges for this step are providing a clear definition of the existing and desired interfaces and defining the relationship with the stakeholders.

Phase 2: Engage

In this stage, the company would select the service provider that would be able to meet its requirement, goals and objectives identified in the previous stage. Many organizations would choose to stop at this point if they cannot find an appropriate provider that would be able to satisfy their needs. This stage is composed of two steps, which they are:

5. *Select.* To select best supplier depending on the defined requirements and includes the activities and outputs shown in Table 2.6.

This step will select the best supplier based on the defined requirements and [12] criteria such as value, sustainability and quality. This step will face some challenges such as balancing requirements between what functionality is available now, with what will be available in the future, backup plans and satisfying the overall strategic intent without making compromises.

6. *Negotiate.* To agree on all issues and to sign contracts and includes the activities and outputs shown in Table 2.7. This step is about selecting, finalizing and signing the contracts with the chosen supplier. This step faces some challenges such as resisting last minute changes that can be imposed by the supplier, having clear and solid backup plans in disaster situations and having clear contract get-out clauses and making sure there is enough time to move cloud services in-house, or to an alternative cloud supplier.

Phase 3: Operate

This stage is about the actual implementation and the day-to-day management of the cloud service. This stage is composed of two steps, which they are:

7. *Operational Roll-out.* To assign the team that will be responsible about the transformation and includes the activities and outputs shown in Table 2.8.

In this step, the assigned project team will accomplish some important tasks such as the transition of the service, the management of the staff impacted, the management of the communication to all stakeholders, knowledge retention/ transition and acceptance sign off. This step faces challenges such as complying with the schedule, accessing similar successful case studies and resisting the temptation to compromise on quality in order to maintain the schedule.

8. *Manage the Supply Chain.* To manage the relationship with the cloud supplier and it includes the activities and outputs shown in Table 2.9.

This step is about managing the relationship with cloud supplier as efficiently and effectively as possible, which will require effective monitoring and controlling in order to resolve the arising issues, variations and disrupts to satisfy both parties. This step faces some challenges as the integration of the cloud service with

Table 2.6 Phase 2, activities and outputs of the *Select* step

Activities	Outputs
Define the tender/bid process	A tender process
Select and staff an evaluation team	Evaluation criteria
Invite bids/tenders	A shortlist of suitable suppliers with caveats
Evaluate suppliers against the defined criteria	A due diligence report
Shortlist the supplier(s)	
Carry out due diligence	

Table 2.7 Phase 2, activities and outputs of the *Negotiate* step

Activities	Outputs
Define the negotiation strategy	A negotiation strategy
Select and staff the negotiation team	Results of the negotiation
Carry out negotiations	Signed final documents: contract, SLA and pricing document
Select the preferred cloud supplier	
Get internal approvals and sign the contract	

Table 2.8 Phase 3, activities and outputs of the *Operational Roll-out* step

Activities	Outputs
Finalize and publish transition plans	A roll-out plan
Select and staff the transition team	Progress updates
Agree and publish acceptance criteria	A signed acceptance document
Carry out the transition	
Communicate progress	
Conduct knowledge transfer	
Manage staff (directly and indirectly) impacted	

Table 2.9 Phase 3, activities and outputs of the *Manage the Supply Chain* step

Activities	Outputs
Manage and report at cloud service operational level	Day-to-day cloud service performance metrics
Capture and manage issues, variations and disputes	Status on issues, problems, variations, and disputes
Manage the supplier relationship	Supplier meeting minutes
Change management	A change management report
Continuous improvement	Audit reports
Assess and validate how the cloud service is performing	

existing support and reporting structures and achieving a smooth transition in the IT department from managing their own internal staff to managing the cloud supplier and the interfaces.

Table 2.10 Phase 4, activities and outputs of the *Review* step

Activities	Outputs
Gather intelligence on the relevant market segment, cloud service technology trends, and supplier offerings	An intelligence report for next generation cloud service offerings
Audit cloud supplier performance and compare to alternatives	Cloud supplier audit results
Understand and assess how other changes in the organization impact on the existing cloud service arrangement	A business case for any proposed changes
Based on the above inputs, regularly reassess and review requirements	
Make and present a business case for any significant change to the current cloud service arrangement in order to get approval to start	

Phase 4: Refresh

This stage is about the continuous review of the cloud service. There is one step in this stage, which it is *Review*. The activities and outputs of this step are shown in Table 2.10. The step entails to continuously review the performance of the service. Thus, this step is about managing the cloud service requirements based on: the cloud service itself, other changes within the business, changes within the supplier organization, or the need to change the supplier. The main challenge in this step is to prioritize and get approval to start a new cloud service transformation project cycle.

2.5 Case Studies

In this section we investigate some cloud computing related case studies and we provide explanation about cloud computing outsourcing and its role in the strategic business change.

The first case study is about a UK based SME firm that provides IT services and solutions for Oil and Gas industry with offices in UK and in the Middle East area and it shows the implication of the cloud computing transformation on the IT department in the implementing organization. In this case study, Khajeh-hosseini et al. [8] argues that the costs will be 37 % less over the 5 years period resulting of transforming an in-house data center to Amazon EC2, benefiting from the (IaaS) that Amazon has. They also argue that there will be 21 % less supporting calls after completing the proposed transformation. Moreover, Khajeh-hosseini et al. [8] highlight the importance of considering the socio-technical factors and the risks accompany this migration before the firms transform their IT system to the cloud.

POINT OF ATTENTION: It is import for any company that consider to transform its IT systems to the cloud, to ponder the benefits that will be gained as well as the risks that are inherited in this transformation.

The second case study, which is presented by Levine and White [23], is about a furniture manufacturing company, Hafford, who suffered from a devastating natural disaster: a hurricane that hit and destroyed the company's operations including its entire IT infrastructure and data storage. In response for this situation, the Vice President of Information Technology suggested using cloud computing to move the company's Business Information Systems (BIS), which includes Executive Information System (EIS), a Management Information System (MIS), a Decision Support System (DSS), an Accounting Information System (AIS), a Transaction Processing System (TPS), and a Supply Chain Management (SCM) system, to the cloud to cut internal information technology costs. With a cloud computing solution, the IT department would be reduced from twelve people to six. IT infrastructure (servers, hardware, programs, processing) would be done by a vendor ("the cloud"), although responsibility for information technology would be retained by the company.

As the case unfolds, the authors explained that proper oversight was neglected; rash decisions were made; and a crisis developed. The president took matters into his own hands, and without following proper protocols, selected a vendor that later went bankrupt and forced the company into dire circumstances. The cloud service provider's processing capability and personnel were not able to deal with the increased customer demands, which created a bottleneck that caused many sales orders to be lost or never received. As result, the company's sales performance was poor.

POINT OF ATTENTION: The strategic decision of selecting the cloud computing service provider is very important for the success of this IT transformation project and for the transforming company.

The third case study, which is analyzed by Lee and Kim [24], is about building cloud-based IT environments for Korean central governmental agencies (K-Cloud Centres) in order to improve service delivery in the public sector and reduce the cost of the government operations. This project will be achieved by leveraging cloud computing technologies in the government data centers of the National Computing and Information Agency (NCIA). This agency is consisted of two huge data centers that contain thousands of computer systems for about 47 organizations and department, including the Ministry of Education, Science and Technology, the Ministry of Public Administration and Security, Korea Customs Service, Ministry of Construction and Transportation, the National Tax Service, and the National Police Agency. However, despite this centralized operation, there is no integration between the computer systems.

This situation triggered the move to the cloud environment, in which the Korean government can obtain a number of benefits. First and most important benefit is the reduction of the large IT related costs. Second, is the ability to have a green IT implementation, which will reduce the costs of the government operations and energy consumption by consolidating various redundantly operated information systems. Third, it provides an environment that can respond to user requests promptly via an automatic provisioning process based on on-demand operation. Fourth, the government will have a possibility of more efficient management and arrangement of personnel resources.

> **POINT OF ATTENTION**: Careful analysis of the benefits, opportunities and risks are very important in the transformation to the cloud computing environment. This situation is even more imperative when the transition is happening in the governmental sector that deals with very sensitive information.

Last, less human errors will result in a more stabilized status of system resources and IT services, since various accidents caused by human error and inadequate operating conditions can be prevented in a cloud-based infrastructure.

The fourth case study is about introducing the cloud computing technologies to the Indian education system to overcome deficiencies, and is discussed in [25]. For example, there is no centralized system for the government to check and monitor the educational institutes and the results achieved every year. Another example is the lack of distribution of resources and teaching tools.

> **POINT OF ATTENTION**: The limitations and restrictions that might affect the cloud computing transition project and the actual usage of the system are as important as the benefits that might gained from it, therefore they must be well thought of before starting this strategic transformation to the cloud computing.

However, despite the promising benefits of this transition, the authors of [25] presented several limitations that would affect the outcomes of this project. The first limitation is that not all applications run on the cloud. The second is about to the risk related to the data protection and security, which is a very important factor that needs to be considered. The third barrier is related to the organizational support that is needed from each and every organization that is involved in this project such as the education and communication ministries. Guaranteeing the full support from the concerned parties is very important for the success of this project.

The last restriction is related to the Internet speed that might hinder the entire system especially that the system will target the rural areas of India.

2.6 Summary

In this Chapter, detailed explanations about the concept of cloud computing, its characteristics, different service models and available deployment models have been described. Additionally, this Chapter provided a set of guidelines on how to choose the service provider as well as an implementation life cycle for the cloud computing transformation project.

Cloud computing is simply about an innovative IT model for providing an on-demand network access to a shared pool of configurable computing resources such as networks, servers and software applications. It allows people to access the applications and software they need over the internet and without any limit. Also, it provides many benefits and advantages to the implementing companies. Cloud computing helps organizations to adapt quickly to market changes and to add flexibility to companies' current IT infrastructure and to replace legacy systems which will result in a better performance, agile business processes and reduced operational costs.

However, there are many considerations that are related to the strategic decisions that concern the outsourcing and implementation of this service and these issues have to be well thought-out before commencing with these types of projects. This Chapter provides a description about the risks accompanying cloud computing and how to manage them. Also, it highlighted the importance of change management and socio-technical aspects that have to be considered during the implementation life cycle.

Finally, the Chapter has discussed case studies, confirming the importance, benefits and risks associated with cloud computing. These case studies show that many issues have to be considered before commencing with the transition to this new technological platform.

References

1. Song J, Junfeng Y, Chengpeng W (2011) Cloud computing and its key techniques. In: Proceedings of 2011 international conference on electronic and mechanical engineering and information technology, vol 1, pp 320–324. doi:10.1109/EMEIT.2011.6022935
2. Carroll M, Van Der Merwe A, Kotzé P (2011) Secure cloud computing benefits, risks and controls. In: IEEE, pp 1–9
3. Mohan NRR, Raj EB (2012) Resource allocation techniques in cloud computing—research challenges for applications. In: 2012 fourth international conference on computational intelligence and communication networks, pp 556–560. doi:10.1109/CICN.2012.177

4. Dhar S (2011) From outsourcing to cloud computing: evolution of IT services. In: IEEE, pp 434–438
5. Zhang Q, Cheng L, Boutaba R (2010) Cloud computing: state-of-the-art and research challenges. J Internet Serv Appl 1:7–18. doi:10.1007/s13174-010-0007-6
6. Raghavendra R, Lobo J, Lee K (2012) Dynamic graph query primitives for SDN-based cloud network management. In: Proceedings of the first workshop on hot topics in software defined networks, pp 97–102
7. Corradi A, Fanelli M, Foschini L, Elettronica D, Deis S (2011) Increasing cloud power efficiency through consolidation techniques.In: IEEE symposium on computers and communications, pp 129–134
8. Khajeh-hosseini A, Greenwood D, Sommerville I (2010) Cloud migration: a case study of migrating an enterprise IT system to IaaS Ian Sommerville. Inf Syst J abs/1002.3:450–457
9. Chang V, De Roure D, Wills G, Walters RJ (2011) Case studies and organisational sustainability modelling presented by cloud computing business framework. Int J Web Serv Res 8:26–53. doi:10.4018/JWSR.2011070102
10. Gai K, Li S (2012) Towards cloud computing: a literature review on cloud computing and its development trends. In: 2012 international conference on multimedia information networking and security, pp 142–146. doi:10.1109/MINES.2012.240
11. Srinivasan MK, Sarukesi K, Rodrigues P, Manoj M, Revathy P (2012) State-of-the-art cloud computing security taxonomies—classification of security challenges in the present cloud. In: Proceedings of international conference on advanced computing and communications and informatics, pp 470–476
12. Conway G, Curry E (2010) Managing cloud computing: a life cycle approach. In: 2nd international conference on cloud computing and services science CLOSER 2012, pp 198–207
13. Bublitz E (2010) Catching the cloud: managing risk when utilizing cloud computing. Natl Underwrit P C 114:12
14. Alsouri S, Katzenbeisser S, Biedermann S (2011) Trustable outsourcing of business processes to cloud computing environments. In: 2011 5th international conference on network and system security, pp 280–284
15. Atkinson P (2005) Managing resistance to change. Manag Serv 49:14
16. Proctor T, Doukakis I (2003) Change management: the role of internal communication and employee development. Corp Commun An Int J 8:268–277. doi:10.1108/13563280310506430
17. Maurer R (2005) Taking stock of change management. J Qual Particip 28:19
18. Hsiu-Fen L, Gwo-Guang L (2006) Effects of socio-technical factors on organizational intention to encourage knowledge sharing. Manag Decis 44:74–88
19. Low C, Chen HY (2012) Criteria for the evaluation of a cloud-based hospital information system outsourcing provider. J Med Syst 36:3543–3553. doi:10.1007/s10916-012-9829-z
20. Linstone HA, Turoff M (1975) The Delphi method: techniques and applications. Addison-Wesley Educational Publishers Inc.
21. Ho Y-F, Wang H-L (2008) Applying fuzzy Delphi method to select the variables of a sustainable urban system dynamics model. In: 6th international conference of the system dynamics society, pp 1–21
22. Vahidnia MH, Alesheikh A, Alimohammadi A, Bassiri A (2008) Fuzzy analytical hierarchy process in GIS application. Int Arch Photogramm Remote Sens Spat Inf Sci XXXVII:593–596
23. Levine K, White B (2011) A crisis at Hafford furniture: cloud computing case study. J Cases Inf Technol 13:57–71
24. Lee H-O, Kim M (2013) Implementing cloud computing in the current IT environments of Korean government agencies. Int J Softw Eng Its Appl 7(1):149–160
25. Bhatia G, Lala A (2012) Implementation of cloud computing technology in Indian education system. ICCCNT12 26th_28th July 2012, Coimbatore, India

Chapter 3
Mobile Services

Abstract In this Chapter we discuss the main implications of mobility for digital business. In particular, we introduce the reader to the drivers and the enablers that impose mobility as the characterizing feature of digital services, depending on and made possible by the convergence and the resulting dependencies between contents, devices, networks, and social activities. Furthermore, the Chapter provides the reader an introduction to frameworks related to the Technology Acceptance Model (TAM) academic research stream. The discussion is suitable to provide useful insights and conceptual tools for increasing the understanding of the behavioral intention to accept and adopt a mobile technology as well as the related services and applications. Then the Chapter focuses on how IT managers and executives interested in digital innovation of services through mobile can face challenges related to the lifecycle of such initiatives: from development and integration with enterprise information systems, to a secure supply to the final users, through a constant control and performance monitoring. Finally, the discussion of case studies concludes the Chapter, providing insights from practice on factors and strategic points.

3.1 Introduction

"The battle for your body is about to begin". This is how starts an article on InfoWorld by Caroline Craig on "wearable computing" [1], reviewing among others the hot topics of the The Wall Street Journal's AllThingsD's D11 conference.[1] Since 2003 the event aims to highlight innovation, and bringing conversations with the most influential figures in media and technology. Indeed, in the days when mobile devices such as smartphones and tablets have overtaken the role of Personal Computers (PCs) and their leadership in terms of market-share, a new breed of technologies seem ready to take their place in a few years. As pointed out

---

[1] http://allthingsd.com/category/d/d11/

V. Morabito, *Trends and Challenges in Digital Business Innovation*,
DOI: 10.1007/978-3-319-04307-4_3, © Springer International Publishing Switzerland 2014

by Mary Meeker[2] and Liang Wu in the annual "InternetTrends" report by venture capital company Kleiner Perkins Caufield Byers, in two Computing Cycles (i.e. smartphones, and tablets cycles respectively) we are entering, faster than before, a third Computing Cycle of "Wearables/Drivables/Flyables/Scannables" devices [2]. Considering smartphones and tablets, as reported by InfoWorld [3], in 2013 a research company such as, e.g., IDC has predicted that tablet shipments will hit 229.3 million units in 2013, further expecting they will exceed PC shipments by 2015.

This phenomenon can be related to other changes always noticed by Mary Meeker and Liang Wu for relevant players in the digital business, such as, e.g.:

- the rise of Groupon North America Transactions Completed on mobile (45 % of total transactions) [2];
- the role of mobile in helping drive Facebook users and revenue [2].

Moreover, analysts has placed in 2013 mobile applications and development among the top priorities of CIO and IT budget [11] (considering Europe, nearly 2 % of total expenditure, according to ComputerWeekly [12]). Thus, the convergence of digital devices and networks seems to have contributed to a consolidation, perhaps an overcoming, as well as a transformation of the global economy towards a service economy, through a consequent change in IT innovation for service management, as claimed by Rai and Sambamurthy [4].

Table 3.1 shows the main *digital enablers* that Rai and Sambamurthy [4] consider having significant implications for innovation of service management capabilities, in terms of description and discovery, design, and orchestration of services for enhanced accessibility and dynamic offerings. Furthermore, it should be noted that Rai and Sambamurthy [4] point out the relevance of analytics for a better understanding of service performance and quality, against a richer and detailed knowledge of customers' needs and experiences.

In order to understand the role and the implications of digital enablers for innovation of service management it is useful to introduce the difference between digitizing and digitalization as outlined by Tilson et al. [13]. On the one hand, *digitizing* is *"the process of converting analog signals into a digital form, ultimately into binary digits (bits)"* [13]. Thus, considering services, it refers to the conversion into bits of analog functionalities (e.g., from listening music on a vinyl to reproduce it on an mp3).

On the other hand *digitalization* requires the convergence of digital devices and networks, fostering digital communication, processing, and storage of diverse types of information as a service. Accordingly, Tilson et al. define digitalization as "a *sociotechnical process* of applying digitizing techniques to a broader social and institutional contexts that render digital technologies infrastructural" [13]. As a

---

[2] As argued by Michael V. Copeland senior editor at WIRED: *"Every year (sometimes twice), longtime tech analyst turned venture capitalist Mary Meeker drops her state of the internet presentation. It's that time of year again, and here it is"* [36].

Table 3.1 Digital enablers of service management capabilities

Service management capabilities	Digital enablers
Description, discovery, and reuse	• Semantic web languages and technologies [5] for representing service resources • Universal Description Discovery and Integration (UDDI) for implementing registries of web services [6] • Standards-based solutions for reuse, interoperability, and composition of services [7] • XML-based protocols for accessing services and exchange messages, such as, e.g., the Simple Object Access Protocol (SOAP) [8]
Design	• Service oriented architectures [9] characterized by: - Standardized interfaces - Service invocation independent of technology - Decoupled and loosely coupled interactions - Synchronous interactions between providers and customers - Event messaging for services coordination
Orchestration	• Business process modeling [10] • Standard executable languages for specifying actions within business processes as web services, such as, e.g., the Business Process Execution Language (BPEL) [10] • Usage models based service invocation
Analytics	• Mining of event-stream data • Real-time execution of business rules

Adapted from [4]

consequence, digitalization requires the above mentioned digital enablers for service management capabilities have to be coupled with a key technology, thus, acting as service enablers (see Table 3.2).

Actually, the convergence of, e.g., social networks, smart mobile communications, cloud computing, high bandwidth telecommunication networks contribute to create digital infrastructures for service provision, that are more than a simply conversion of functionalities of existing "analog" services, but rather a radical transformation having impact on lifestyle, work, as well as on markets structures, business strategy and customer experience.

Indeed, digital infrastructures enable organizations and individuals to co-create services at local and global level, enforcing a wider participation [13]. As a consequence, they make indistinct the boundary of organizations, and enable new sourcing models, such as, e.g., *crowdsourcing*, lowering production costs. Furthermore, they contribute to create *multi-sided markets*[3] where the business focus is on networking benefits for value creation, asking for new business models and pricing strategies, likewise. Thus, *mobility* as the characterizing feature of digital

---

[3] Multi-sided markets create value by enabling direct interactions between distinct types of affiliated customers [37, 38]. Multi-sided markets challenges governance and digital business models innovation [38]. For further details on digital governance we refer the reader to Chap. 8 of this book.

Table 3.2 Key technology service enablers (adapted from Schwarz et al. [14].)

Key technology service enablers	Examples
Social networking	• Facebook, Twitter, Google, etc.+
Smart mobile communications	• iPhone, iPAD, Android OS Smartphones and tablets
Cloud computing	• Amazon, dropbox, Google, Salesforce.com, Windows Azure, etc.
High bandwidth telecommunication networks	• Comcast, AT&T, Verizon, etc.
Big data	• Amazon's Dynamo, HBase, Google's Bigtable, Cassandra, Hadoop, etc.
Ultra-fast, low latency switches	• Cisco Networks, etc.
High density, low cost chips	• IBM, Intel, AMD chips

service depends on and is made possible by the convergence and the resulting dependencies between contents, devices, networks, and social activities [13]. As for these issues, the increasing diffusion and advancement of mobile applications (or *apps*) plays a relevant role in changing the market impact and business value of mobile services and devices; for example, consider the growing importance of location-based application on mobile devices for marketing activities and social sensing (discussed in detail in the following Chap. 4) [15].

The above discussion provides a preliminary interpretative framework to understand "digital" services, and the mobility characterizing them, as emergent from and enabled by underpinning and evolving digital infrastructures. In Sect. 3.2 we are going to focus on mobile services and applications, eliciting their drivers, challenges, and opportunities.

3.2 Mobile Services Drivers and Challenges

Mobility is currently one the main characteristics of today digital information infrastructures. However the diffusion of mobile devices, such as, e.g., smartphones and iPads or tablets, does not entail a consequent success of no matter services provided through them and accessible to a correspondent wide audience. Furthermore, also the adoption of the above technologies may still find resistance by final users and the current business model adopted by a given company may not always sustain the service design and delivery, thus requiring constant updates as well as revisions. As a consequence, in this section we consider some of the main drivers and challenges related to mobile services. In particular, we first focus on the acceptance by users as a key issue, analyzing the factors that make up the *Technology Acceptance Model (TAM)* [16–18] one among the most important and studied ones in the management of information systems research field [19, 20]. Once briefly introduced the main constructs of the TAM we will identify the way these can be or have been instantiated for the case of mobile services.

As pointed out by Bagozzi [20], TAM is characterized by a "parsimony" in the number of basic constructs influencing the user intentions towards the usage of a technology. However, they are defined as follows in the original article by Davis [18], introducing the model [19], and inaugurating what is currently named the TAM research stream:

- *perceived usefulness (PU)* is the "degree to which a person believes that using a particular system would enhance his or her job performance" [18][4];
- *perceived ease of use (PEOU)* is "the degree to which a person believes that using a particular system would be free of effort" [18].[5]

It is worth noting that theses constructs were theorized by Davis as determinants of system use in a "white collar" organizational context, thus under an internal oriented perspective on a company information system. Thus, the origins of the model do not consider a complex digital ecosystems as the one acting in today market scenarios, smoothing the organizational boundaries. However, also from the original on-the-job perspective, the above constructs resulted too parsimonious.

As a consequence, and considering the contributions from a constantly growing literature, authors such as, e.g., Venkatesh and Davis [22] have introduced further determinants for *perceived usefulness* (*subjective norm, image, job relevance, output quality, result demonstrability*), and two moderators (*experience* and *voluntariness*), thus, extending TAM to what have been called TAM2. The extended model presented two types of explaining processes for the new constructs, the one referring to *social influence* (for *subjective norm* and *image*) and *cognitive instrumental* processes (for *job relevance, output quality*, and *result demonstrability*), the latter related mainly to information systems characteristics.

Taking these issues into account, being *perceived ease of use* considered among the determinants of perceived usefulness, Venkatesh [21] further studied how it forms and changes over time. Accordingly, the analyses of [21] have been based on *anchors* and *adjustments* related to individuals' general beliefs regarding a technology (in that case computers) and its use. In particular, Venkatesh [21] identified anchors related to constructs for individual control beliefs, motivation, and emotion, as shown in Table 3.3. As for the adjustments, Venkatesh [21] pointed out the relevance of *perceived enjoyment* and *objective usability* for perceived ease of use after individuals become acquainted and experienced with the new system.

The TAM 2 have been further developed by Venkatesh and Bala [17] in the TAM 3 shown in Fig. 3.1. The main points of the new version of the model

---

[4] Davis points out that the definition follows from the word *useful* as "capable of being used advantageously" [18].

[5] Davis points out that the definition follows from the word *ease* as "freedom from difficulty or great effort" [18].

Table 3.3 Constructs and related anchors for perceived ease of use, elaborated from [21]

Constructs	Anchors
Control	Computer self-efficacy
	Perceptions of external control or facilitating conditions
Intrinsic motivation	Computer playfulness
Emotion	Computer anxiety

concerned the following issues and new relationships (the latter represented by dotted arrows in Fig. 3.1):

- *absence of crossover effects*, that is determinants of perceived usefulness do no influence perceived ease of use and vice versa;
- *perceived ease of use influence* on perceived usefulness and on behavioral intention, when moderated by experience;
- *computer anxiety influence* on perceived ease of use, when moderated by experience.

As said above the research of TAM has produced a vast literature, whose detailed discussion is out of the scope of this Chapter and for which we refer the reader to [16, 19, 20]. However, we think is important to provide a quick summary of the main concepts, constructs, and issues of the TAM related contributions to point out their relevance for practitioners willing to understand how to deal with the acceptance of external users and costumers of digital services provided by "new" mobile technologies and devices. As pointed out above, TAM focused mainly on an inner organizational context, whereas the new challenges concern the outer context of a company.[6] Nevertheless, due the central role of behavioral intention also in the adoption and use of mobile services and technologies, the TAM constructs are yet a core asset for the development of models, aiming to identify key drivers supporting IT as well as business executives decision making. As for these issues, Fig. 3.2 provides a representation of current efforts towards a framework for identifying mobile services behavioral intention and adoption drivers. In particular, the figure aims to summarize contributions such as the one of Hong and Tam [23], integrating it with constructs resulting from other interesting findings, such as, e.g., the ones from López-Nicolás et al. [24].

Hong and Tam [23] questioned the application of TAM, seen as a traditional organization-centric IT model, to mobile data services having an ubiquitous nature and an impact on individuals' lifestyle. In particular, they focus on devices designed to provide the users heterogeneous types of information, such as, e.g., data, video, and pictures, thus providing a suite of utilitarian and hedonic functions. Apart from traditional core constructs of TAM (such as *perceived ease of*

---

[6] With a "feedback" effect also on the internal portfolio of technologies, due to the adoption of personal devices by employees for work, as we are going to see in Chap. 5 on the IT Consumerization phenomenon.

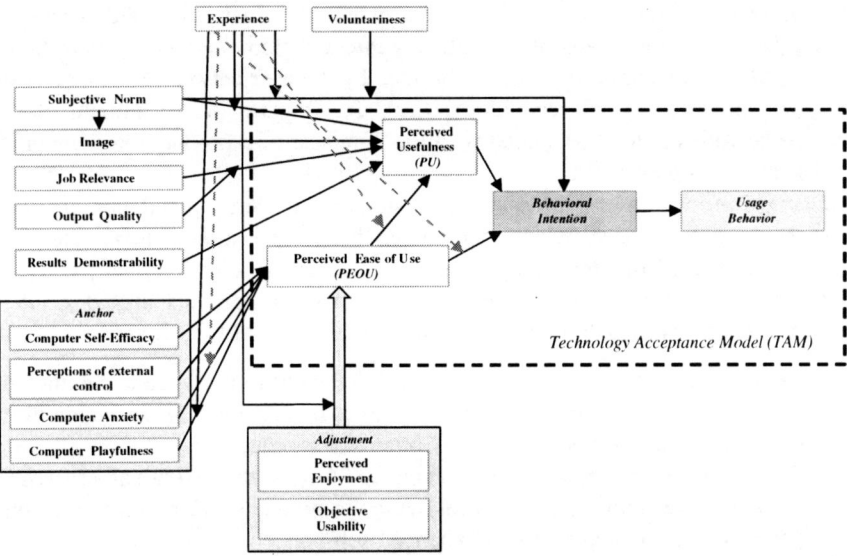

Fig. 3.1 Technology acceptance model 3 (TAM3). Adapted from [17]

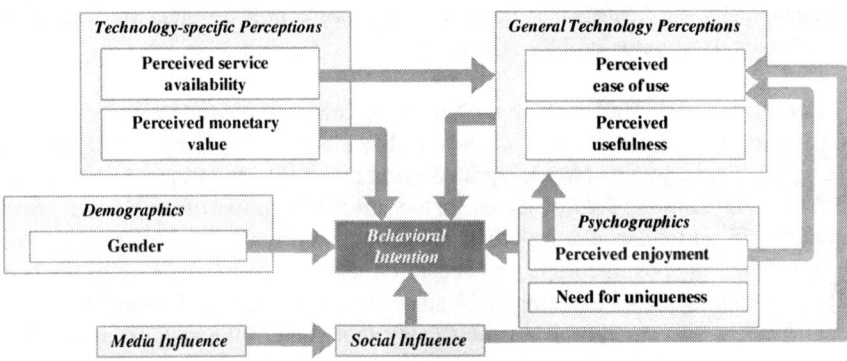

Fig. 3.2 Mobile services behavioral intention drivers. Adapted from [23] and [24]

use and *perceived usefulness*), classified as "general technology perceptions", Hong and Tam [23] consider the following four more clusters of determinants of mobile services behavioral intentions (see Fig. 3.2, starting from the top left hand side):

- *Technology-specific perceptions*, encompassing the unique features of the mobile technology as IT artifact and its usage contexts. This cluster includes the following determinants of behavioral intentions:

- *perceived service availability* as the extent to which a mobile service is perceived as being able to provide anytime and from anywhere connections;
- *perceived monetary value* as the balance by the user between the usage costs and the price of the technology: thus, an indicator of the amount of the perceived sacrifice associated with the purchase of a product/service and its perceived quality.
- *Demographics* concern information about the considered population of users such as, e.g., *gender*, which determines behavioral intentions towards the adoption of a mobile technology and related services.
- *Psychographics* concern the user personality, values, opinions, attitudes, interests, encompassing determinants considered also in TAM, such as:

  - *perceived enjoyment* as the extent to which the use of a mobile technology or the access to one or more mobile services is perceived to be enjoyable in its own right, without considering any other consequences;
  - the *need for uniqueness* (close to *image* in TAM) as the individual's search in the mobile technology/services (as symbolic products) for an increased self-perceived social status and an enhanced self-concept.
- *Social influence:* as discussed above for the TAM perspective, this construct is related to the belief by the user about the approval or disapproval by the group he belongs for his behavioral intention to adopt/use a mobile technology/service. Furthermore, as also shown in recent studies by Kim et al. [25] on user's mobile engagement, e.g., with smart phones, social motivation significantly influences their perceived value and satisfaction.

Concerning social influence in mobile technology/services adoption, it is worth considering the contribution of studies such as, e.g., the one by López-Nicolás et al. [24]. These authors have integrated TAM and diffusion of innovations theory [26] for analyzing the role of social factors on the adoption of mobile advanced services.[7] In particular, among other interesting results, the study has shown, on the one hand, the positive impact of social influence on perceived ease of use (see Fig. 3.2), that is one of the core TAM antecedents of behavioral intention; on the other hand, it has emerged from their study that social influence resulted determined by media (see the two constructs at the bottom of Fig. 3.2), and in particular by the mass media perception. These results seem to confirm, even if indirectly, the role of marketing as a key partner of IT in the design and development of digital innovation initiatives, in particular for mobile services and technologies.

Considering now again demographics, while gender (see Fig. 3.2) received a certain attention by scholars as a dimension influencing at a certain degree behavioral intention towards the adoption of mobile solutions and services, Hong et al. [27] claim the relevance of *age*. They point out, however, that this dimension

---

[7] The research and analyses were based on a sample of 542 Dutch consumers.

has received limited attention, in particular, in the information systems research field [27]. Indeed, considering the ageing phenomenon at global level and the inedited parallel presence and divide between digital natives and last century generations, Hong et al. [27] focus on an interesting point: the tendencies of older individuals to feel younger than they are and the question about the diversity of factors influencing information technology acceptance between the latter and the individuals that in a sense accept their actual age. Thus, the point concerns the influencing factors for people having a different or the same *cognitive age* with respect to their actual *chronological age*, with a specific focus on the self-perception by the user.

The results of this interesting research show that for the people feeling younger than they actually are (in particular, the 30 and 40 years old ones) dimensions such as perceived usefulness, perceived ease of use, and perceived enjoyment have a worth mentioning role in their IT acceptance decisions; whereas for the people with a self-perceived correspondence between cognitive and chronological age are more relevant the perceived ease of use and subjective norms[27].

Studies such as, e.g., the one carried out by Hong et al. [27] are important for pointing out the potential relevance of constructs as the above mentioned cognitive age for innovating marketing methods, in current digital business context. Indeed, they provide useful insights for innovating them towards an improved social listening (see the following Chap. 4), questioning the appropriateness of, e.g. the uncritical adoption of the chronological age as dimension in the customer segmentation, which may lead to incorrectly identify the needs for customers having actually a cognitive age different from their chronological one.

The above claims and research results about the need for different constructs and dimensions influencing technology acceptance, in particular, referring to mobile devices, applications, and services have to be related to other research streams investigating, e.g., the difference of usage behavior between mobile phones and personal computers. In particular, it is worth mentioning the work by Ghose et al. [28] which explores the difference in economics between the two settings, focusing on the relevance of *ranking* and *distance effects*. Considering the specific characteristics of mobile phones (reduced screen size, etc.) and the consequent search costs and constraints, e.g., to browsing, the study focuses on a specific microblogging context, identifying a higher importance of ranking in mobile context (what we could call a *first link advantage*) as well as of the proximity, e.g., of stores promoted or resulting from the user querying/browsing (what we could call a *contiguity advantage*).

Having clarified the main drivers and challenges also related to the difference of mobile applications and services, compared with, e.g., the desktop or personal computer ones, in the following Section we are going to discuss which digital management solutions can be considered and adopted for an efficient and effective implementation of mobile technology enabled service initiatives.

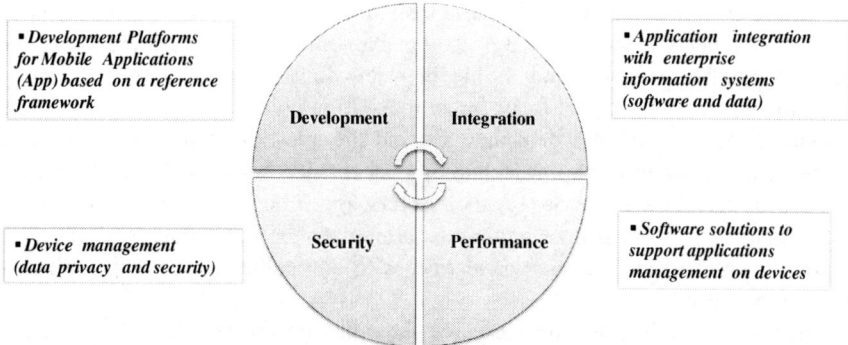

Fig. 3.3   Digital management solutions

3.3 Digital Management Solutions

As we have seen in the previous section, several dimensions and perspectives impact on mobile services and technologies acceptance and adoption by users (internal as well external to an organization). However, IT managers and executives interested in digital innovation of services through mobile have to face challenges related to the lifecycle of such initiatives from development and integration with enterprise information system, to a secure supply to the final users, through a constant control and performance monitoring.

Accordingly, Fig. 3.3 shows in detail the lifecycle challenges which require appropriate digital management solutions. They can be summarized as follows:

- *Development*, entailing, among other issues, the choice of platforms for producing mobile applications.
- *Integration*, facing the issue of the alignment and adaptation to enterprise information systems, at software as well as data level.
- *Performance*, encompassing the need for monitoring and control of applications on the different devices hosting or using them.
- *Security*, strictly connected to performance issues, but focused on the challenges of guarantying the privacy of data and the trustworthiness of mobile applications and services interactions.

We now provide a discussion of each of the above issues, identifying the different available solutions and selection criteria, when multiple options exist, then outlining their benefits and drawbacks, likewise.

As for *development*, the diversity of devices and the consequent scalability of development platforms pose significant challenges to applications management with regard to costs of functionalities, user experience, and data security. Taking these issues into account, we overview the main characteristics of three types of development models, native, hybrid, and web-based, that we adopt to summarize the diversity of the ones available at the state of the art.

The *native development model* is specific for a single device and allows to integrate all the features of the device itself (e.g. camera, gps, Wi-Fi), working online as well as offline. The selection criteria for this model require an organization to carry out the following actions:

- *Define* a priori reference device(s).
- *Choose* the preferred device(s).
- *Exploit* any internal skills already acquired on a particular technology suitable to be adopted for the mobile applications development on the chosen device(s).
- *Develop* the requirements of usability of the mobile applications, according to the degree of use of the native features of the selected device.

As for the *web-based development model*, it focuses on applications using the web browser already installed on the devices. It is worth noting that due to the highly standardization required by this model, the applications may not exploit the characteristics of each specific device. The selection criteria for this model require an organization to carry out the following actions:

- *Evaluate* whether the standard technologies adopted for development are already available and developed in the company.
- *Deploy* the application through a leaner channel (Web vs. EAS—Enterprise Application Systems).

Finally, we consider a *hybrid development model*. This is a combination of the previous ones, which built applications using web technologies that ensure portability, however, integrating them with specific characteristics of the different devices. In this case, the selection criteria for this model require an organization to carry out the following actions:

- *Identify* if the context of implementation of the application presents a peculiarity, fitting to a native development model or else to a web-based one.
- *Consider* the business impacts of the benefits related to a reduction of time and realization costs, allowing the development of a pilot application with tight deadlines.

After having chosen an appropriate model and the associated development platforms, an organization faces management decisions concerning their *integration* with its own enterprise information systems (see Fig. 3.3). Indeed, the adoption of a strategy of *Enterprise Mobility* highlights some critical issues in terms of management of' the infrastructure, which must support the applications, often interfacing different preexisting platforms and heterogeneous databases.

To solve the above issues, managers can follow an *integrated* or else a *best-of-breed approach* (benefits and drawbacks for each of them are shown in Table 3.4). In the former, the integration of the technological components of the mobile application in the company's management system is carried out in a simultaneous way per "suite of products" (namely, considering tools for application development, device management, monitoring of applications and systems integration of the data).

Table 3.4 Management approaches for mobile applications integration: benefits and drawbacks

Approaches	Benefits	Drawbacks
Integrated	• Decrease of the likelihood that problems arise at the interface between the different components of the system • Simplification of the management of the relationships with vendors	• The analysis phase requires a careful assessment of the impacts of the management of applications and devices on the legacy systems
Best-of-breed	• The option to acquire progressively on the market the needed functionalities mitigates the risk of relying on a single vendor	• The approach while providing a better matching of the solutions to the needs of specific target users, may require a careful monitoring of the market and an evolutionary design of the architecture of the solution

Table 3.5 Types of application stores

Types of store	Description
Consumer application store	• These stores are managed at global level by manufacturers of mobile operating systems (Apple, Samsung, Google, Microsoft, RIM), thus with a degree of freedom and control over the application depending on the policies of the owner of the store itself
Business application store	• This type of store adapts the logic typical of Consumer Application Stores to provide custom apps supporting business processes • However, in such a store are available almost exclusively applications supporting business processes • It is generally required a direct contact with the developers to modify or customize the applications according to the specific needs of the buyer
Private enterprise application store	• These environments have a restricted access, typically managed by the IT organization, dedicated to the employees of a company and/or business partners • This type of store aims to deploy applications for specific internal users based on their business role (executives, middle management, sellers, maintainers, retailers, and other mobile workers) • These stores are generally managed as a repository of enterprise applications

Whereas the best-of-breed approach introduces progressively the different functionalities, following a trial and error perspective. Accordingly, the latter approach reduces switching costs and facilitates the measurement of the benefits that basically arise from implementing first and progressively simple application solutions with reduced functionalities.

Considering now performance issues (see Fig. 3.3), these are strictly related to the distribution channel, through which the applications are made available to the final users. Indeed, the choice of which is the "store" for mobile applications, and

Table 3.6 Solutions suitable to enable device security management

Solutions	Benefits	Drawbacks
Mobile device management	• Simple to install • Provide centralized management of the devices used by the user	• Manage only devices, so the IT department of a company has to define policies to regulate the practices of users
Application streaming	• The data is not directly stored on the device as well as a part of the application code, ensuring greater safety	• Typically, the solutions delivered in streaming are native desktop ones, usually not always user friendly for mobile, thus, not guaranteeing fast delivery of the service
Mobile device virtualization	• The device can be used safely, even for personal purposes, without being subject to corporate policies	• Solutions not always mature and in some case still in a testing phase. • Require investment in infrastructure to ensure the effectiveness of the solution

services has an impact as well on the efficiency and effectiveness of their management, use and updating. The main "store" solutions may be classified as shown in Table 3.5, depending on their consumer, business, or else private orientation.

Finally, ensuring the security of the data (see Fig. 3.3) is by far one of the most critical issues in the field of development and management of mobile applications and services. Accordingly, security can be addressed through the adoption of different types of enabling solutions. We discuss them in what follows, referring the reader to Table 3.6 for a list of benefits and drawbacks for each of them.

Considering *Mobile Device Management* solutions, they facilitate the management of devices deployed across different mobile operators or service providers, ensuring the safety of sensitive data access, user profiling as well as compliance with corporate policies. To this end, these solutions provide protection through a control of the settings and configuration for all mobile devices (company-owned as well as employee-owned) in the network of a given company. In summary, they focus on risks and challenges for company data privacy and security by Bring Your Own Device (BYOD) and IT Consumerization emergent phenomena (see for details the Chap. 5 of this book).

As for *Application Streaming* solutions, they can be considered a kind of application virtualization. Indeed, they are basically an on-demand service distribution, which kept applications on corporate servers with only core parts or a subset of an application's code installed on the device, making the other packages available in streaming on the user's mobile device, when eventually required by a given specific application context.

Finally, *Mobile Device Virtualization* solutions are a kind of hardware virtualization, allowing, e.g., the use of two or more operating systems on the same mobile device. These solutions, on the one hand, provide the user with a certain degree of freedom in the choice of the device and operating systems; on the other hand, they improve security and control, ensuring the virtual separation of personal and business data as well as operating systems (the former managed by the mobile operators, the latter by the IT department of the company where the user is actually working).

Taking the above issues into account, as a tentative conclusion and recommendation, we can say that regardless of the technology chosen for supporting the digital management of mobile application and services, it is necessary to adopt practices that focus on increasing user awareness about the privacy, and security related, e.g., to the access and unauthorized disclosure of corporate data as well as the sharing of personal sensitive data.

3.4 Case Studies

In this Section we discuss fact-sheets of case studies, which illustrate at a glance how mobile initiatives have been addressed in different industries at global level.

Toyota, among the global leaders in the automotive industry by number of vehicles sold per year, has carried out mobile initiatives at retail level. In particular, Toyota has promoted in 2010 the development of a mobile application with the intent of increasing the Customer Experience also in its stores (dealers and dealerships), making more and more accessible information also at the time of negotiation. To this end, the adopted solution should have been able to operate on different mobile devices, regardless of operating system, without losing the native capabilities, and synchronize with the corporate CRM and Inventory management systems [29, 30].

Among the solutions available on the market, Toyota has chosen the Kony's[8] *Write Once, Run Everywhere*, enabling the development of a single app, compatible with different operating systems (OS), such as, e.g., iOS, Android, Blackberry, WinMobile), as well as facilitating the updates by the users [29, 30]. Thus, the Kony solution have been selected to deliver Toyota's Mobile Shopping Tool application, including the mLot™ features [29, 30], allowing the different users to:

- compare the different car models, e.g., by rotating a vehicle to view all its features;
- refer to the availability of the cars at the factory (for dealers);
- customize the car configuration;
- locate the closest dealer to request a quote and obtain personal information on the vehicle via barcode;

---

[8] Kony is a United States based global company, leader in mobile application development and platform with over 350 customers in 45 countries, including more than 70 Fortune 500 companies (http://www.kony.com/about).

- use the customers' own device's camera to take a picture of a vehicle, capturing information such as, e.g., the Vehicle Identification Number (VIN);
- save and share on social networks or via e-mail, the "Favorites" vehicles against other Toyota models, or against other comparable on the market;
- streaming instructional videos.

> **POINT OF ATTENTION**: Mobile services initiatives have to consider integration with existing back-end systems without the need to rewrite the application for multiple types of OS, among the key issues for obtaining substantial savings from enhanced Customer Experience.

We now consider another case study on mobile innovation in the automotive industry, focusing on a country experience instead that a global one.

Sodicam is a subsidiary of Renault Italy specialized in the sale of spare parts, accessories and products to post-sale, thus, dealing with their supply to the network of authorized dealers and repair shops by Renault/Dacia. Before 2012, the acquisition and processing of the orders were carried out on paper forms or by personal computer (which, however, required an active connection at the time the order). Furthermore, among other useful information to the sales force, the vendors also did not have access to:

- data on previous purchases of a given customer;
- the types of orders typically performed by a given customer;
- the discounts, which were not recorded.

Thus, in 2012 Sodicam has designed and implemented with Vodafone a Sales Force Automation mobile app for iOS based tablets (iPad). The goal of the solution was to provide more useful information to sellers to increase the effectiveness of the sales (historical data on the customer, complete catalog, real time inventory, etc.) [31, 32]. Thanks to the optical scanning of product codes, using the camera of the tablet, and the access to historical cases of sales, the process of acquisition of orders has been streamlined, likewise. The solution resulted in a reduction of the time of data entry, increased personal productivity, and a reduction of errors at order entry. Furthermore, the solution reduced operating costs by approximately 15 % without affecting productivity with an estimated 18 months payback period of the investment [31].

> **POINT OF ATTENTION**: Mobile services initiatives applied to supply chain activities and sales provide increased productivity, improved data quality, and knowledge on customers' behavior and history.

The following case is based on a Datalogic success story [33] and concerns the convergence of mobile services and sensors devices.[9] Habasit AG, headquartered in Switzerland, is a worldwide leader in the production of conveyor belts, plastic chains, timing belts, sliding profiles and guides, for different industries including Food, Textile, Logistics and Automotive.

The process of storage and picking of goods in the warehouse was particularly slow and problematic, because the comparison with data from the company's management system took place only in the final balance, without the ability to guide the action of the operators with the sampling of real time updates.

> **POINT OF ATTENTION**: The adoption of a convergent approach, combining mobile applications and, e.g., "rugged" devices results in a reduction of errors and processing times, optimizing the operating performance of workers, also offering real-time production data with a higher precision.

To solve these issues, Habasit has implemented a solution based on the development of a mobile application and the purchase of rugged devices[10] that, once combined, has allowed to speed up and streamline the processes in the warehouse. Indeed, goods receipts have been then carried out automatically with Kyman™ by Datalogic Mobile Wireless Handheld Computer and Barcode Scanner. Besides technology issues, the investment in this solution has covered also a set of training activities by the staff. Indeed, the operators have to be able to scan the barcode using the optical drive of the tablet supplied, thus, synchronizing the data on the availability of the product in a purchase order system by SAP®. Then, the Warehouse Management Software (WM) SAP® directly has to indicate where the scanned unit must be stored. Subsequently, the process has been applied to the logistics, increasing the traceability of goods in transit and at delivery. As a result, Habasit has streamlined the process of storage and picking, reducing time, increasing productivity and efficiency through the use of tablets and mobile applications development.

The last case study shows the relevance of mobile services for marketing and advertising activities, acting as a bridge towards the topics of the next Chapter, which discusses in detail social listening as well as social sensing. The case is based on an experience from Optism [34, 35], a permission mobile advertising solution from Alcatel-Lucent, and a partner of mobile operators in over 130 countries. It is worth noting the multidisciplinary nature of the Optism team, including advertising as well as mobile marketing experts.

---

[9] For further details on the impacts of sensor technologies on business innovation, we refer the reader to the discussion on social sensing in Chap. 4.

[10] Mobile devices designed to survive demanding environments, harsh conditions, rough handling, providing ergonomics that reduce operator effort. They can meet military standards, e.g., for dust, rain, humidity, strong shocks, repetitive tumbles and temperature extremes.

> **POINT OF ATTENTION**: Mobile services and applications need for a strong support by advanced marketing perspectives, focused on a continuous and appropriate listening to social networks as well as supported by multidisciplinary competencies, enabling an effective and as close as possible attention to the different contexts and populations adopting the mobile solution.

In 2012, the mobile provider Etisalat Nigeria, the fastest growing one in Nigeria, publicised the deployment of a permission and preference-based mobile advertising service, in collaboration with Alcatel-Lucent enabled by Optism. The service, called EasyAdz, at its launch in the beginning of 2012 had more than 800,000 subscribers and was then adopted from businesses such as, e.g., Nigerian Breweries, British Council, and Coca-cola [35]. As for Coca-Cola, the company used the service for their mobile 'Open and Win' campaign to drive consumer awareness on it and encourage participation through viral and social media actions such as, e.g., forwarding the campaign link. According to Optism [34], the campaign results in nearly 200,000 messages delivered in a 12 h period, with over 41,000 responses. In particular, the campaign response rate of 21 % was characterized by a significant engagement from the 18-25 age group, and an equal responsiveness by men and women [34].

3.5 Summary

In this Chapter, we have discussed the business challenges of mobility for digital business. In particular, we have analyzed the drivers and the enablers that impose mobility as the characterizing feature of digital services. Accordingly, we have shown the role of media convergence for the current relevance and diffusion of mobile services and applications, resulting from the infrastructural dependencies between contents, devices, networks, and social activities. Furthermore, the Chapter has outlined the importance to understand the users' behavioral intention to accept and adopt mobile technology as well as the related services and applications. To this end we have introduced the reader to the main constructs and frameworks related to the Technology Acceptance Model (TAM) academic research stream and how they change when focused on mobile solutions.

Furthermore, we have provided insights to IT managers and executives on the options they have when facing challenges related to the lifecycle of mobile initiatives, from development and integration with enterprise information system, to a secure supply to the final users, through a constant control and performance monitoring.

Finally, the discussion of the case studies has provided insights from practice on key factors and strategic points. In particular, they have shown that mobile services initiatives have to consider the integration with existing back-end systems and a focused application to supply chain and sales activities, among the key issues for obtaining increased productivity, improved data quality, knowledge on customers' behavior, and consequent substantial savings from enhanced customer experience. Furthermore, the case studies have shown the importance of the convergence of mobile services and sensors technologies as well as social listening activities (that will be discussed in detail in the following Chapter). As for the former, the adoption of a convergent approach, combining mobile applications and, e.g., "rugged" devices, results in a reduction of errors and processing times, leading improved performance of workers. As for social listening, the considered case study has shown that mobile services and applications need for a continuous and appropriate listening to social networks as well as the involvement of multidisciplinary competencies to enable an effective knowledge for implementing mobile solutions and services in different contexts, fitting the needs of various populations of users adopting them.

References

1. Craig C (2013) Beyond Google Glass: get ready for more wearable computers. InfoWorld
2. Meeker M, Wu L (2013) Internet trends D11 conference
3. Samson T (2013) IDC: PC shipments worse than predicted, tablet shipments get better. InfoWorld
4. Rai A, Sambamurthy V (2006) Editorial notes—the growth of interest in services management: opportunities for information systems scholars. Inf Syst Res 17:327–331
5. Antoniou G, van Harmelen F (2008) A semantic web primer, 2nd edn. MIT Press, Cambridge
6. UDDI.org (2001) UDDI technical white paper
7. Papazoglou M (2007) Web services: principles and technology. Prentice Hall, Englewood Cliffs
8. Shuler JA (2001) XML, UDDI, and SOAP: the "verbs" and "nouns" of "semantic electronic government information": edited by John A. Shuler. J Acad Librariansh 27:467–469
9. Papazoglou MP, Heuvel W-J (2007) Service oriented architectures: approaches, technologies and research issues. VLDB J 16:389–415. doi:10.1007/s00778-007-0044-3
10. Weske M (2012) Business process management-concepts, languages, architectures, second. Springer, Heidelberg
11. Gartner Executive Programs (2013) Hunting and harvesting in a digital world—insights from the 2013 Gartner CIO Agenda Report
12. Goodwin B (2013) IT budgets to rise despite downturn. CW Europe, pp 4–5.
13. Tilson D, Lyytinen K, Sørensen C (2010) Digital infrastructures: the missing IS research agenda. Inf Syst Res 21:748–759
14. Schwarz S, Durst C, Bodendorf F (2012) Service innovation—a roadmap for practitioners. Serv Sci Manag Res 1:8–16
15. Brynjolfsson E, Hu YJ, Rahman MS (2013) Competing in the age of omnichannel retailing. MIT Sloan Manag Rev
16. Venkatesh V, Morris MG, Davis GB, Davis FD (2003) User acceptance of information technology: toward a unified view. MIS Q 27:425–478

17. Venkatesh V, Bala H (2008) Technology acceptance model 3 and a research agenda on interventions. Decis Sci 39:273–315. doi:10.1111/j.1540-5915.2008.00192.x
18. Davis FD (1989) Perceived usefulness, perceived ease of use, and user acceptance of information technology. MIS Q 13:319–339
19. Lee Y, Kozar KA, Larsen KRT (2003) The technology acceptance model: past, present, and the future. Commun AIS 12:75280
20. Bagozzi RP (2007) The legacy of the technology acceptance model and a proposal for a paradigm shift. J Assoc Inf Syst 8:244–254
21. Venkatesh V (2000) Determinants of perceived ease of use: integrating perceived behavioral control, computer anxiety and enjoyment into the technology acceptance model. Inf Syst Res 11:342–365
22. Venkatesh V, Davis FD (2000) A theoretical extension of the technology acceptance model: four longitudinal field studies. Manage Sci 46:186–204
23. Hong S-J, Tam KY (2006) Understanding the adoption of multipurpose information appliances: the case of mobile data services. Inf Syst Res 17:162–179
24. López-Nicolás C, Molina-Castillo FJ, Bouwman H (2008) An assessment of advanced mobile services acceptance: Contributions from TAM and diffusion theory models. Inf Manag 45:359–364. doi:http://dx.doi.org/10.1016/j.im.2008.05.001
25. Kim YH, Kim DJ, Wachter K (2013) A study of mobile user engagement (MoEN): engagement motivations, perceived value, satisfaction, and continued engagement intention. Decis Support Syst. doi:http://dx.doi.org/10.1016/j.dss.2013.07.002
26. Rogers EM (1995) Diffusion of innovations, 4th edn. The Free Press, New York
27. Hong S-J, Lui CSM, Hahn J, Moon JY, Kim TG (2013) How old are you really? Cognitive age in technology acceptance. Decis Support Syst. doi:http://dx.doi.org/10.1016/j.dss.2013.05.008
28. Ghose A, Goldfarb A, Han SP (2013) How Is the mobile internet different? Search costs and local activities. Inf Syst Res 24:613–631
29. Kony (2010) Kony powers Toyota's cutting edge mobile shopping tool application. Application offers enhanced customer service, social networking and exclusive mLotTM shopping feature. Kony Press Releases, 07 Dec 2010. http://www.kony.com/content/kony-powers-toyotas-cutting-edge-mobile-shopping-tool-application. Accessed 9 Nov 2013
30. Butcher D (2010) Toyota launches mobile shopping tool app for customer service. Mobile Commerce Daily (16 Dec 2010). http://www.mobilecommercedaily.com/toyota-launches-mobile-shopping-tool-application-to-enhance-customer-service. Accessed 10 Nov 2013
31. Todorovich P (2013) Renault Italia, un'App per vendere ricambi. In: Wirel. 4 Innov. http://www.wireless4innovation.it/business-case/renault-italia-un-app-per-vendere-ricambi_43672151570.htm. Accessed 10 Nov 2013
32. Renault (2013) La app "Vodafone saleforce solution" per Renault è tra le finaliste del "Mob App Award Business" a Smau Roma 2013. Press Release. http://media.renault.com/it/it–it/dacia/Media/PressRelease.aspx?mediaid=45368. Accessed 10 Nov 2013
33. Datalogic (2012) Mobile computers connected to SAP®: wireless inventory and warehouse management for Habasit
34. Optism (2013) Case study/Coca Cola: boosting soft drink purchases in Nigeria
35. Alcatel-Lucent (2012) Etisalat Nigeria introduces permission-based mobile advertising to over thirteen million customers using Alcatel-Lucent's OptismTM. News Releases. http://www3.alcatel-lucent.com/wps/portal/!ut/p/kcxml/04_Sj9SPykssy0xPLMnMz0vM0Y_QjzKLd4x3tXDUL8h2VAQAURh_Yw!!?LMSG_CABINET=Docs_and_Resource_Ctr&LMSG_CONTENT_FILE=News_Releases_2012/News_Article_002688.xml. Accessed 16 Jan 2014
36. Copeland MV (2013) Bullish on wearable tech: Mary Meeker's annual state of the internet presentation. WIRED
37. Eisenmann TR, Parker G, Van Alstyne MW (2006) Strategies for two-sided markets. Harv Bus Rev October:1–12. doi:10.1007/s00199-006-0114-6
38. Sambamurthy V, Zmud R (2012) Competing in digital markets. Guid. Digit. Transform, Organ

Chapter 4
Social Listening

Abstract This Chapter aims to discuss the key issues raised by social networks and 2.0 technologies for companies competing in a digitalized market. In particular, the Chapter provides an overview of the main characteristics that marketing intelligence activities assume when they become more and more a means to carry out social listening initiatives. Considering them as a core marketing driver for digital business value, the Chapter discusses the main approaches and tools for sentiment analysis and opinion mining, as well as a model for market monitoring. In addition the Chapter introduces the reader to social sensing as a specific configuration of social listening, emerging from the convergence of sensors and social network technologies.

4.1 Introduction

The 2.0 technologies development and the worldwide social network diffusion ask for new, agile, and flexible strategies for digital business. As a consequence, companies face unprecedented challenges in terms of marketing perspectives and Customer Relationship Management (CRM) vision, actually redefined in terms of Customer Experience Management (CEM). Adopting a brand new CEM perspective means that firms have to reconsider, on the one hand, their current Digital Business Models [1–4]; on the other hand, they have to innovate their CRM systems, often asynchronous in their descriptive and predictive functions and highly influenced by the implicit limit that characterizes their analytic models and representations (usually built inside the organization and literally projected on customers). This kind of evolution, would actively participate in creating a CRM system able to support the Customer Experience Management through what is nowadays defined as Decision 2.0 [5, 6]. As already said, a highly innovative vision grows out of the specific Web 2.0 technologies current configuration, producing unpredictable information accessibility, and the consequent need of transforming this huge information volume in applied strategic knowledge.

V. Morabito, *Trends and Challenges in Digital Business Innovation*,
DOI: 10.1007/978-3-319-04307-4_4, © Springer International Publishing Switzerland 2014

In literature, this new configuration and the related types of applications has been defined *"Collective Intelligence"* [6]. As argued, e.g., by Gregg Dawn, collective intelligence applications differ from Web 2.0 applications because they can be custom applications designed for small highly specialized domains instead of the larger Web audience [7]. Furthermore collective intelligence applications have the following characteristics [7], that is they:

- have *task specific* representations;
- are *data centric*;
- are designed to *collect and share data* among users;
- enable the *user access and intervention* to add and modify the data;
- have an improved *usefulness through different devices*.

Thus, there are several situations in which these solutions, based on new digital business models, have been implemented supporting decision making processes in different fields such as, e.g., R&D, market research and analysis, and customer services (relevant results have been achieved in terms of increased number of solved problems, problems identification, better use of emotional and expressive skills during "face to face" and virtual interactions). As highlighted by Eric Bonabeau, Icosystem corp. CEO, on MIT Sloan Management Review, the collective intelligence systems represent a support able to create added value in generating and evaluating new products and services, playing a complementary role sideways with all the traditional analytic tools used for previsions [5].

4.2 Marketing Analysis as Social Listening

According to a research by Universal McCann (http://umww.com) conducted in July 2009, 32 % of the 200 million worldwide active bloggers used to write comments and opinions about products and brands, while 71 % of the 625 million active internet users used to read blogs. Moreover, 78 % of people usually trusted other consumers, while 57 % was more comfortable with traditional advertisement forms and 34 % preferred web advertisement [8]. In this scenario, the marketing intelligence has evolved and further focused on what we can call *social listening*, facing the new strategic challenges of social media analytics [9]. As a consequence, the goal of marketing intelligence as social listening is to create and sustain a competitive advantage in terms of products and services' differentiation. The main questions here are:

- *How to identify, e.g., blogs and social media in which the focus is both on searched product and relevant concepts?*
- *Once identified, how to identify the most influential users?*
- *How to distinguish relevant matters from other "false positives" or "false negatives?"*

The first step has to be the *boundaries definition*, trying to extrapolate, e.g., the websites, blogs or social media that really talk about the products or issues we are actually looking for. In this context tools have been developed in order to support advanced activities of marketing intelligence: *text-based* and *network-based* mining. The former evaluates the *significance* of the information or the source only relying on textual content (i.e. using key words or classifying systems), the latter uses links between, for example, blogs or wikis as content similarity indicators. Usually these tools are used simultaneously, trying to be as accurate and automated as possible. The second step is to identify the most *influential users*, such as, e.g., bloggers, whose opinions are usually considered as the most important. Nowadays is becoming highly strategic for firms to keep this type of users always up to date and involved.

Moreover, advanced *social network analysis* techniques [10, 11] support the creation and maintenance of maps of influence based of available links; for example, a blog's importance can be evaluated measuring how it contributes to the information diffusion process (*Flow Betweeness*) or calculating how many blogs contained a link for the considered one (*PageRank*). Other important metrics that have to be considered at the state of the art are the *Degree centrality* (for example which blogs, tweets or posts on facebooks receive more links, retweets, or "like"), *Closeness centrality, and Betweeness centrality,* that allow to define the influence on specific arguments. Nevertheless, it is important to underline that not always, e.g., bloggers include their sources' link; for this reason, a better indicator of influence could be the number of users that read the blog, a tweet, a post on Facebook, even if is often difficult to measure it accurately. However, to read and evaluate all the huge amount of materials generated by, e.g., bloggers or tweets creates the first challenge that has to be overcome. In addition to that, it is demonstrated that bad opinions and comments usually has a diffusion rate higher than the others. For these reasons, it became strategically relevant to have systems that make the reader able to recognize bad opinions on blogs and social media, monitoring the overall trend of opinions about a specific matter or event [12]. With this aim, systems able to interpret the overall opinion on a blog, website, or social media have been developed, thus, supporting *sentiment analysis* or *opinion mining* as the key activities to find and monitor in real time authors of specific contents across different (social) media [12–14].

Notwithstanding the difficulty and complexity of the task, nowadays it is strategic to understand the overall evolution of some specific arguments, for example identifying the most used sentences or expression. This analysis can be even more sophisticated if we look at the frequency by which those key expressions have been used together. As an alternative, could be an idea to create sources' clusters that talk about the same matter and only then choose the most representative one or, again, to use a *multi-document summarization* tool in order to have a global summary. However, the most valuable thing is to identify new relevant arguments; this goal could be achieved creating new documents clusters, underlining that these have to be different from the previous ones. To summarize, it is worth noting that in a review on the Communications of the ACM, Ronen Feldman focused on five specific problems of sentiment analysis [14]:

- *Document-level sentiment analysis*: the document is assumed to contain opinion expressed by the author.
- *Sentence-level sentiment analysis*: considering that a document may allow different opinions even about a same entity, the analysis moves to a more fine-grained view, thus, focusing on sentences.
- *Aspect-based sentiment analysis*; here the focus is on the many facets a given entity (for example, in a review about a hotel or a brand new smart phone) may have, and the goal is the recognition of all sentiment expressions and the aspect they refer to in a given document.
- *Comparative sentiment analysis*: in this case the focus is on users that do not provide direct opinions, but comparative or comparable ones, instead; as a consequence, the goal is to identify the sentences that contain the comparative opinions, thus, eliciting the preferred entity.
- *Sentiment lexicon acquisition*: in this case the goal is the production/creation of a domain-specific lexicon, to, e.g., understand the polarity (positive or negative) of adjectives.

Taking these issues into account, nowadays, algorithms for global evaluation are the most common methods used to identify opinion leaders online, without pointing out that usually they are considered opinion leaders only on specific fields [15–19]. In the last few years new weaknesses related to the mining techniques with key words have been pointed out, underlining that these techniques cannot fully understand some of the intrinsic aspects of the languages' complexity. In order to overcome this potential problem can be useful to enhance search engines' capabilities and mining tools with lexical integration through instruments such as, e.g., WordNet [20], reducing the potential threat described above. Under this point of view, *ontologies* enable Web documents annotation, making the process of *querying* formulation and reaching accurate results easier [21]. The annotation usually implies the creation of *metadata* in order to represent the specific entities recognized within the resources and, therefore, connect these metadata to the resource as its illustration. The research efforts are now focused on the supply of computerized or semi-computerized tools able to annotate documents (not only web documents) in different formats, from images and texts to more structured formats like those used in traditional relational database [21].

4.3 Information Growth and Market Opinion

The computerized text analysis has been traditionally focused on *facts* and only during the last few years started to consider *opinions* as well. This evolution was facilitated by the diffusion and growth of the volume of information produced, supplied and spread online or through the internet (see Chap. 1 of this book on Big Data issues). As already seen in previous Sections, new instruments such as, e.g., blogs, wikis, microblogging, and social media, changed the whole way to consider information diffusion and its impacts on businesses and everyday life. Before these tools and the 2.0 web technologies' spread, firms that wanted to understand consumers' opinions had to conduct long and costly market researches. Internet and its ability to share comments and opinions changed not only the way firms keep themselves posted on consumers' needs and preferences but also the way consumers inform each other about products and services, shaping their own decision process through worldwide shared knowledge and experiences. This new contest face marketing field in front of new challenges. They now have to find relevant content for their firm and to analyze huge amount of information, often qualitative and only sometimes presented in a structured way. As mentioned in previous section, *sentiment analysis* software (or *opinion mining*) try to monitor all the relevant matters discussed online. Even though is not easy to create an accurate and reliable system, the research is now focusing on sentiment analysis systems to understand the potential value that these applications can have on firms' strategies.

Together with this evolution, new frontiers related to the usage of online market opinions have been opened, nowadays represented by the so called *Opinion Search* [12]. As well as a search engine allows searching information through websites, an opinion search engine can easily find judgments and evaluations about the argument the users are looking for. In this context, it is important to underline Horringan [22] reported that out of 2000 American adults' sample in 2007[1]:

- 81 % of internet users looked for information about product using internet at least once, and 20 % does so regularly.
- Among those who read opinions about hotels, restaurants or other services, more than 73 % said that they have been highly influenced in their final choice.
- In some case, consumers are willing to pay from 20 to 99 % more for products rated with five stars with respect to products with a rating of four stars.
- 32 % gave its evaluation about products or services through online rating systems at least once, and 30 % wrote comments or reviews online.

Furthermore, according to this research [22], even if most of the users considered their own experiences with online searches positively, 58 % of them claimed that they had to face cases of:

- lack of information;
- lack of reliable or valuable information;
- information overload (too many information can make the decision process harder for the end users).

---

[1] According to [22] data were gathered through telephone interviews conducted by Princeton Survey Research Associates between August 3, 2007 and September 5, 2007, among a sample of 2,400 adults, aged 18 and older.

Therefore, it seems to be very important to create organized, clear and user-friendly systems able to really help consumers in their online decision making processes.

4.3.1 Text Mining and Conversation's Analysis

The developing potential about text mining for sentiment analysis and opinion mining represents an extension and evolution of the traditional researches about text mining. In particular, sentiment analysis means the computerized analysis of opinions, sentiments and emotions expressed through a text, although at different level of analysis, as seen above [14]. In simple terms, the aim is to transform not-structured and qualitative data, coming from, e.g., online comments, posts or tweets, into a well-structured data set through which quantitative analysis can be done. Once achieved this goal, it is easier to reach shorter information, such as *feature buzz* (indicating the relative frequency with which people used to talk about a specific product's characteristic) and *object buzz* (indicating the relative frequency with which people talks about competitors' products). The time evolution of the analysis' results is showed by the so-called *trend tracking*. Thus, according to Pang and Lee [12] a *sentiment analysis* software has to be able to:

- *Identify* relevant posts and texts classified by their argument.
- *Recognize* which sentences contain only "facts" and which opinions and sentiments.
- *Define* if the comment has positive, negative or neutral meaning.
- *Create* reports with the most relevant comments, identifying points of agreement and disagreement and classifying communities of users on the base of their preferences.

However, current systems use different methods to identify and count words commonly used with positive (good, excellent, nice, etc.) or negative (awful, terrible, uncomfortable, etc.) meaning, establish a syntactic structure and consider potential denials or contradictions. Taking these issues into account, in the following section we are going to focus on methods and technologies used in order to *classify* different messages and texts (including in the classification also *regression* and *ranking*).

4.3.2 Classification and Analysis Methods and Solutions

As social listening is expected to provide business value in terms of time-to-market, offering differentiation, and increasing customer experience, several issues related to the marketing intelligence activities can be expressed as questions about classification, regression, and ranking of textual units. That is the reason why is so important to underline the role of classification process; for example, according to Pang and Lee [12] the strategic actions in the classification process are shown in Table 4.1.

Taking these issues into account, Table 4.2 shows the main classification typologies with the associated objectives. To better understand them, in the following we provide some useful examples taken from the industrial and academic literature (we refer the reader also to [12, 14]).

Looking at the first classification (i.e. *sentiment polarity*), most of the related activities have been conducted in the context of the reviews [12]. However, many others may require it, being the process much more complex such as, e.g., evaluate a political speech trying to understand if it is in favor or against the discussed argument, or classify opinions from an electoral forum with the aim of predicting a result instead of another [23–25].

The second classification is related to the *degree of positivity*, through which is possible to define the polarity [26] of specific results such as, e.g., in the case of medical tests (i.e. improvement vs. death). Other difficulties can be associated with the interpretation of specific sentences such as *"the last model is more expensive than the previous one"* or *"I prefer the new model with respect to the old one"*, considered as important evaluation made by users or authors [27].

Finally, focusing on the third classification (*Subjectivity Detection and Opinion Identification*), it is actually possible to evaluate the subjectivity degree of a specific document or message. Indeed, in the last few years several methods and techniques have been developed in order to, for example, face the problem considering every single clause. In this context, it has to be pointed out that there is a difference between defining the subjective strength of opinions and making evaluation based on the methods described above. Classifying as *neutral* a text is different from considering it as objective: indeed, defining something *"so and so"* or *"mediocre"* gives a strong opinion but may be classified as neutral. Therefore, classifying texts by categories can be useful in order to identify the level of subjectivity [28].

Finally, the precision and the accuracy of the classification can be influenced by the domain of the elements in which it is applied. One of the main reasons is that the same sentence can have different meanings according to the contest in which it has been used.

4.3.3 Marketing Intelligence and Risk Analysis

Key words for new strategies such as "open solution", "information accessibility", "synchronicity of the provisional activities", mark the transition from closed firms in which external consumers were not considered as an involved part in the productive process, to open firms in which the end users is considered as a vital actor in the value creation process. This whole new strategic approach, as already mentioned, had been (and, will be) enabled by the diffusion of Web 2.0

Table 4.1 Classification process: strategic actions and key questions

Strategic actions	Key questions
Take decisions for a particular sentence or document	"How positive is it?"
Organize a series of data	"Are reviews classified on the basis of the positivity degree expressed?"
Give a single tag for a document collection	"How is ranked the text by this author in the range that goes from liberal to conservative?"
Categorized the relationship between two entities on a textual proof base	"Does the considered individual approve the actions from another individual?"

Adapted from [12]

Table 4.2 Main types of classification activities with related objectives

Classification activities	Objectives
Sentiment Polarity	Labeling a document on the basis of the evaluation of the opinion expressed regarded as completely positive or negative
Degree of Positivity	Assess through comparison the degree of positivity of achievements and phrases in their entirety
Subjectivity Detection and Opinion Identification	Assess the degree of subjectivity of a given document/message

Adapted from [12, 14]

technologies and social networks, as well as by the adoption of new service oriented technological architectures. In banking sector, for example, the spread of mobile banking services represent the first step of an evolution that will conduct, thanks to new technologies such as RFID (Radio Frequency Identification) and NFC (Near Field Communication), to a whole new way to consider costumers' experience. These new opportunities are rewriting the marketing strategies and forcing companies to constantly identifying new business models, reshaping all the back-end and front-end activities (we are going to detail some of these in challenges in the Section of this Chapter on *Social Sensing*).

Talking about 2.0 technologies, along with the already mentioned wikis, blogs, etc., several other technologies are yet available such as Mashup systems, RSS syndication, social bookmarking, Podcast and widget. These systems reshape the way social networking is considered, giving it a more dynamic and multi-sources perspective. However, the adoption of these technologies based on web applications is influenced by the ability to properly develop security policies. Thinking about mobile banking, it seems to be evident the potential threat related to security issues, considering, on the one hand, data interception; on the other hand, the possibility of losing the device by the user/costumer.

Moreover, in addition to web browsers, also web server software can be easily attacked by malware and other threats. In order to effectively react to these challenges is highly important to define security policies able to identify in advance any kind of vulnerability. These policies do not have to be general but they must be well-defined in advance according to the specific case or web application cluster, always considering the preferences, behaviors and habits of the end users, trying to be as customized as possible. However, even though a large number of firms recognize the importance of these policies for end users and stakeholders in general, not so many are now able to guarantee a suitable degree of attention on this matter. Moreover, in those firms that have structured plans in this sense, the IT function is often occasionally involved in the social network platforms identification, integration and management. Trying to manage the security issues actively, involving in an integrated way IT, Marketing and Human Resources functions, is necessary to have a set of technologies able to monitor a highly dynamic and complex system, in which huge amount of heterogeneous information are usually exchanged. The available solutions still do not provide the standard required in terms of trust, flexibility and configurability.

Therefore, the marketing intelligence approaches and technologies can play a crucial role in the risk analysis process (using, for example, sentiment analysis and opinion mining in order to forecast and identify specific arguments that are potentially dangerous for the organization). Using the results that come out from these analyses make it easier to improve products and services on the base of the highlighted weaknesses. Furthermore, the additional threat is that illegal behaviors such as "cyberbulling", "stalking", "phishing", "scam", "marketing spam", etc. use the same technologies and platforms that intelligence could potentially use for marketing activities. Furthermore, according to [29] a few attributes such as, e.g., {ZIP code, date of birth, gender} allow to identify 87 % of US citizens using public data base (as for gender, age, and location, see also [30]). Other researchers has shown the risk to privacy related to *vanity queries*, in which a user issues a query for his or her own name [31].

Approaches, methods and tools for marketing intelligence are therefore strategic if companies want to monitor, identify, evaluate and face the impact of external risks that rise up from social networks and 2.0 technologies. As shown in Fig. 4.1, an ex-ante marketing intelligence activity let the firms monitor external environment, identify potential threats, evaluate the impact and undertake initiatives in order to eliminate or reduce the potential threats. Precautionary actions (through marketing intelligence tools) can create the conditions through which firms can control the information flow and prevent damaging behaviors from external or internal actors, leading to losses in terms of profitability or, more in general, of resources.

In this context, in order to prevent and control risks through marketing intelligence tools, these have to use advanced and appropriate metrics. Nevertheless, even if several metrics have been developed in order to translate potential risks into quantified data, further efforts are required to design and develop frameworks and applications to recognize potential threats into a text. One of the most interesting approach could be the one described by [32], that is focused on the risks identification in messages or texts, trying to support the decision making process (this approach has been applied in the financial sector). In this specific case, a message is defined as *risky* every time it gives information that can influence investors' opinions or beliefs about the future of a firm.

Fig. 4.1 Risks areas and
factors

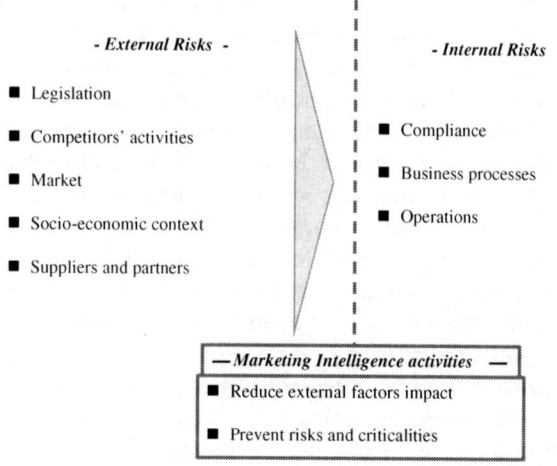

Fig. 4.2 Model for
recognize risks associated
statements. Adapted from
[32]

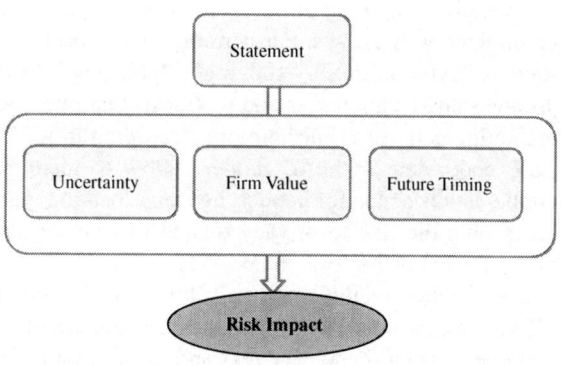

As shown in Fig. 4.2, three dimensions deserve to be considered in this definition: *firm value, future timing,* and *uncertainty*. First of all, messages that are not
focused on the firm value are not considered at all. Secondly, all the information
has to impact on the future in order to be valuable. Finally, one of the characteristic
of the risk is the uncertainty. This means that more than one result can occur. A
common way to represent uncertainty is to connect the possible results' proba-
bility. These probabilities are embedded in the investors' "cupboards" about the
future development of the firm. The three dimensions lead investors to recognize
risk associated statements or messages.

After this first step, the potential threats are classified on the base of their
impact (positive, negative or positive–negative). Examples of these two steps are
offered in Table 4.3. The approach described is structured in two core steps:

• identify and decide if one sentence is (or can be) associated to a risk;
• evaluate which kind of impact this risk can have.

Table 4.3 Statements and risk impact examples

Statements	Risk impact
"Although lots of analysts predicted that the defibrillator market would have increased by 20 % yearly, due to the population ageing most of the analysts now predict less than 10 % of increase yearly"	Negative
"Hitachi has returned to profitability during the third trimester thanks to the sales of digital products, such as crystal liquid display and hard drives, and the sales of its participations"	None
"… Alex. Brown and Sons raised the rating he gave to Qwest Communications International, supplier of telecommunication services in Denver"	Positive

Adapted from [32]

In order to facilitate the automatic learning activity, all the sentences are converted into a numerical representation, which can refer to single words, sentences with two or three words, or part-of-speech (POS) tags. POS are usually used in order to catch syntactic aspects, while for semantic aspects usually tools such as, e.g., General Inquirer have been used (http://www.wjh.harvard.edu/~inquirer/). Finally, statistical approaches are used for machine learning such as Support Vector Machines (SVM) and Elastic-net Logistic Regressions (ENETs).

The one we presented is just one of the rising models that use mining tools in order to predict potential risks, but it perfectly shows all the threats and challenges that the marketing intelligence has to face in order to be effective in the new competitive landscape.

4.4 Social Listening Challenges

Nowadays the techniques and technologies for sentiment analysis and opinion mining have several potential applications in support of marketing intelligence in the sphere of social networks and 2.0 technologies. In this section, we will briefly discuss some of the main implications that an access to information and services oriented led by opinion can have.

A first factor worth to be considered is that a marketing intelligence activity, trying to collect massive amount of information about people's preferences, can generate concerns about possible *privacy* violation. In fact, on the one hand, one can figure out or barely accept that companies analyze its own opinion about a product, looking at blogs and online comments; on the other hand, people rarely accept that their personal conversations are constantly checked, e.g., by the government in order to identify opinions or negative comments about a politician.

Closely related to the privacy issue is the *handling* of the users' opinions that can be enabled by the marketing intelligence tools. If the two issues described above can be classified as challenges for users, there are others that impact organizations as well. In particular, firms have to face the so called *opinion spam* [33], that is the generation of positive or negative comments and opinions by spiteful persons made in order to promote one product/service instead of another. This behavior can deceive users as well, and has already attracted the blogosphere and media attention. However, considering that an increasing number of persons and firms have their decision influenced by online opinion, it is easy to understand why the opinion spam can become a crucial issue. Therefore, it is highly important to find a way to reduce this threat before people lose their trust on online reviews. There are essentially three kinds of *opinion spam* [33]:

1. *Fake Opinions*: fake views that try to promote a specific product (*hype spam*) or damage a competitor's one (*defaming spam*);
2. *Brand Opinions:* reviews that are focused only on brands or companies without considering the specific product or services people are talking about;
3. *No Opinion:* general texts that do not actually express any form of opinion about a product/service (advertisement, not relevant texts, questions and answers, etc.).

The second and third kind of spam are usually easier to identify and eliminate through specific filters, while the first one is extremely difficult to identify because is usually (at least when is well done) mistakable with a normal opinion about products/services.

Another challenge related to the opinion spam is the ability to differentiate a spam from a useless opinion. If the first one, once identified, has to be denounced and deleted, the second one should just be considered as less relevant. In order to easily identify useful comments, lot of websites gives users the chance to rate comments, helping other users in their researches. Obviously this is only a partial solution because, on the one hand it cannot be used for the newest or not commented products and services and, on the other hand, also comments' rates can be spammed.

The above challenges are the other side of the benefits associated to the inedited volume and availability of information made possible, on the one hand, by social networks, 2.0 applications, and digital services; on the other hand, further scenarios are emerging from the convergence of different media and channels, enabled by the diffusion of mobile, smart phones, and tablets, likewise (as seen in Chap. 3). However, mobile technologies are only one of the several facets of what we have seen in previous Chapter as the emerging digital infrastructure; indeed, sensors as well are assuming a growing role in designing a *pervasive social context* [34], becoming an important asset for the evolution of social listening through *social sensing* [35, 36]. The latter is discussed in what follows.

4.5 Social Sensing

Social Sensing may be defined as the exploitation of social sensors, such as, e.g., the ones in mobile device, but also social networks, and web technologies to infer data about people preferences, activities, and their social environments [35]. According to this perspective, social sensing is an intelligence activity acting on

Table 4.4 Technological enablers of social sensing. Adapted from [36]

Enablers	Example
Miniaturized sensor Technology	The *spec mote*, which is a small sensor that can be embedded, e.g., in cloths, while remaining unobtrusive
Advanced smartphone technology	Devices containing, e.g., GPS, Bluetooth and Near Field Communication (NFC) functions
Increased bandwidth	Large wireless bandwidth required to transmit large amount of data in real time (for example, in forms of audio or video streams)
Increased storage	Hyperscale storage[a] for big data
Fast stream processing platforms	Platforms such as, e.g., IBM System S, storing and processing large volume of data streams in real time
Stream synopsis algorithms and software	Histograms and sketches for data stream computation problems (see [37] for a survey)

[a] According to [42] *Hyperscale storage* is a storage space measured in terms of petabytes, serve millions of users with often one or a limited set of applications, may lack redundancy, aiming to maximize the raw storage space and minimize the cost, focusing on a high degree of automation (see also Chap. 1 of this book for storage issues for Big Data)

what Schuster et al. [34] term as the *pervasive social context* of an individual, namely "the set of information that arises out of direct or indirect interaction with people carrying sensor-equipped pervasive devices connected to the same social network service" (p. 3).

This pervasive social context is characterized or better enabled by a set of technologies (see Table 4.4), spanning from miniaturized sensors, to smartphones, through an increasing and inedited capacity of bandwidth and storage, requiring empowered analytics for large volumes of real-time information or digital data streams (as outlined in Chap. 1, which we refer the reader for further details). Some authors have started to call this new breed of instruments and tools as *people analytics* [37], focusing on advanced wearable electronic sensing devices, such as, e.g., Sociometric® Badges, that provide the infrastructure to measure real-world social behavior, capturing face-to-face interactions as well as information providing social signals from speech and body movement.

Taking these issues into account, we believe that organizations interested into competing through digital business innovation should more and more rely on the information extracted from social sensing, integrating sensors with social networks data. This may definitely shift the meaning of what businesses mean time-to-market towards the capability of interpreting individual customer experience through real-time offerings.

However, the main question still concerns which domain is currently and in the near future suitable to enable the application of social sensing. To this end we have reported in Table 4.5 a list of applications and the related domain identified by Aggarwal and Abdelzaher in a comprehensive study of current challenges of social sensing [36]. It is worth noting that actually the main applications concern what in Table 4.5 is classified as "Crowdsourcing for user centered activities" with a prevalence of the convergence of localization features and social networks through

Table 4.5 Social sensing domains and applications

Domains	Applications(sample)
Crowdsourcing for user centered activities	*Location trends* • Google Latitude • Google Public Location Badge • Mobile Location used with Google + Hangouts • Navizon (http://www.navizon.com/) • iLocalis (http://ilocalis.com/) • CitySense (https://www.sensenetworks.com/products/ macrosense-technology-platform/citysense/) • MacroSense (https://www.sensenetworks.com/products/ macrosense-technology-platform/) *Grocery Bargain Hunting, Feedback/Product recommendation* • LiveCompare (http://www.intellicorp.com/livecompare.aspx) • Mobishop(http://www.mobishop.co/) • Yelp(http://www.yelp.com/) • Foursquare (foursquare.com) *Augmented Reality* • Wikitude (http://www.wikitude.com/app/)
Internet of Things	• Microsoft SensorMap • Radio Frequency Identification (RFID) embedded in objects for tracking commercial products, in large animals for tracing movement of, e.g., whales, or in patients to monitor their history
Vehicular Participatory Sensing	• CarTel (http://cartel.csail.mit.edu/doku.php) • GreenGPS System (http://green-way.cs.illinois.edu/GreenGPS. html) • Biketastic(http://biketastic.com)
Healthcare	• Enhanced Holter ECG • Wireless Respiratory and Audio Sensor (http://vivonoetics.com) • BodyMedia FIT(http://www.bodymedia.com/)

Adapted from [36]

mobile phones and tablets or iPAD. Always related to localization as a core feature, we point out the increasing relevance and interest into the applications of "Vehicular Participatory Sensing", in particular for the potential contribution to research and innovation areas such as, e.g., smart cities and urban mobility.

Other applications, such as the ones of the "internet of things" and "healthcare domains" are promising but require appropriate frameworks and new business models for overcoming the specific nature of their features and functions, moving from specializing domains towards a wider diffusions and adoption through the inclusion, e.g., in inedited bundles of services.

However, social sensing is still a promising perspective at business level, providing a wide spectrum of research challenges. Among others, as pointed out by Aggarwal and Abdelzaher [36] are worth to be mentioned, the following ones:

• *privacy sensitive techniques*, protecting personal data involved in real-time interactions and data streams;

- *new battery types* with longer life and the consequent trade-off between them and the applications continuity and goals;
- *compression techniques*, supporting the efficient process of large amounts of data or Big Data;
- *data quality techniques*, enabling, e.g., the trustworthiness, accuracy, and completeness of data collected through sensors which most of the time are not verified for their provenance;
- *dynamic and real-time* response for multiple and large volume of sensors data tracked at a given application transaction time.

The above discussion on the domain, application, and challenges for the use of social sensing technology can act as well as a bridge to the following section where case studies are further detailed for social listening as mainly focused on market signals.

4.6 Case Studies

As seen in previous Sections, the online social interaction has contributed in empowering marketing intelligence, thus, opening new opportunities in terms of market monitoring. Furthermore, the increase and the unprecedented growth of available information have also influenced the way market monitoring is considered by companies, moving it from a linear structure to a focus on at least three different key factors to be considered in the process:

- *new information sources* (i.e., social media, 2.0 as well as 3.0 applications and services, the latter usually related to semantic web [38]);
- *new market signals* that come out straight from end-users, by means, e.g., of sensor technologies;
- *collaboration* as discussions about the above mentioned market signals.

This extension of the monitoring process reconfigured the role of the marketing intelligence activities inside and outside the organization. In what follows we will discuss this important shift referring to some specific case studies. Figure 4.3 describes a marketing intelligence model proposed by [39]. This model aims to combine and integrate new sources of information, cooperative mechanisms and market signals in a whole new strategic way. The first way to take advantage from social media is to attract and maintain contacts and audience as a new source of potentially unlimited information. Platforms such as, e.g., Linkedin, Facebook, Twitter, and so on, provide information about competitors' actions, customers' tendencies, and other strategically relevant dimensions. However, it is important to consider also that the information retrievable from these platforms is based on an open discussion among people and, therefore, as we have seen, have to be considered as potentially unreliable.

Let's take now as an example the Outotec case, according to what reported in [39]. Based in Finland, Outotec is a worldwide leader in supplying processes'

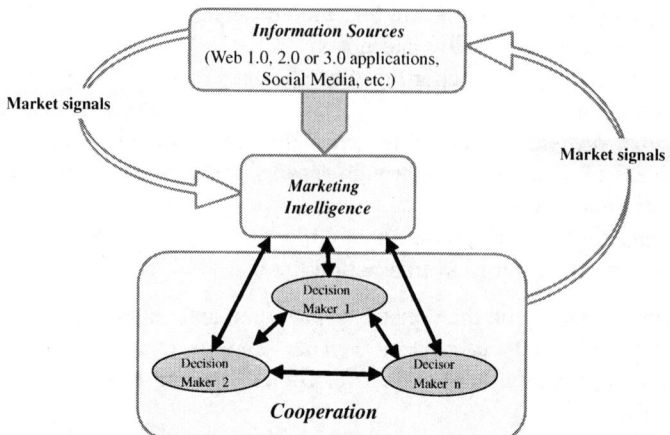

Fig. 4.3 An advanced model of marketing intelligence based on cooperation and new information sources exploitation in the decision making process. Adapted from [39]

solutions, technologies and services for extractions and the metallurgic field. The firm decided to enlarge its market monitoring process in order to extrapolate market signals from social media. After a series of analyses on blogs and forums straightly related to its own sector, Outotec found out that all these information could have significantly helped its business to grow. Therefore, the company decided to keep monitoring these sources, with the aim of providing new information about tendencies, preferences and opinions to decision makers.

> **POINT OF ATTENTION**: The extrapolation of market signals from social media by a company, when associated with a shared access by decision makers, may enable a virtuous circle, leading to the creation of new market signals from the ones formerly elaborated by the company decision makers.

The case shows that using marketing intelligence tools and approaches, combined with the information constantly provided by social sources, the decision making process can be intensely smoothed, making easier for decision maker to cooperate and to share information. Some distribution format, such as web interfaces or mobile services, can be easily integrated with instruments for users' interaction (comments, online discussions, rating mechanisms, etc.). These services can encourage decision makers to actively participate in the marketing intelligence process, providing additional information. Moreover, the shared access to market signals by those who have to take decisions can create a virtuous circle: through a continuous exchange of relevant information, this circle may lead to the production of new market signals that come from decision makers and go to the market itself.

Taking the above issues into account, it can be useful to analyze the case of Fujitsu [40], one of the biggest IT services supplier in the world. For many years, the European operation functions in Fujitsu developed their own market monitoring process with the aim of providing as much strategic information to the decision makers as possible. The team involved in the intelligence activities had to understand and transmit valuable information about both external signals and internal signals (i.e. from employees). With this scope, the team built up tools able to increase the participation, involvement and cooperation of end users in general (decision makers as well as other internal users). Thus, end users could foster the market signals while they received information from the monitoring process, enhancing the virtuous circle described above. All the instruments and tools enhancing and facilitating internal collaboration, such as comments or discussions about market signals, acted as endorsement mechanisms for original market signals, provided by different media, surveys or social media themselves. Even though all the signals were evaluated already during the sourcing phase, their value could have been increased through other evaluations and discussions during the delivery phase.

POINT OF ATTENTION: Rating and tagging mechanisms provide added value to market signals, enabling further evaluation and discussion between intelligence teams, decision makers, and internal users.

Abstracting from the case of Fujitsu, it is worth noting that this is one of the reasons why all the online services call for rating mechanisms. However, more interesting, and maybe useful for market monitoring applications, can be the so called *tagging* mechanism, that let decision makers to apply tag on single content elements such as potential threats, business opportunities, etc., adding, therefore, information about the competitive landscape.

Consider now, for example, the Cintas Corporation case study, adapted from [39]. The company, based in United States, plans, builds and implements facility programs for firms, providing uniforms, cleaning services, hygienic supplies, promotional products, security products, fireproof protection services, and document management services. Therefore, the strategic plan team has constantly to monitor and control all facets of a diverse entrepreneurial market, looking for new opportunities, likewise. The scope of investigation is therefore very broad and the opportunities can rise up in different business areas, probably not yet explored.

POINT OF ATTENTION: Social listening and marketing intelligence empower strategic planning for companies working in complex and variegate environments, allowing to monitor and control the whole entrepreneurial market, keeping record of all the competitive activities related to new potential strategic opportunities.

According to [39], trying to make this process as efficient as possible, Cintas has started to keep record of all the competitive activities related to new potential strategic opportunities identified during the monitoring process. With a marketing intelligence tool, the strategic plan team has been able to structure the strategy on the base of always up to date information from the involved actors. Taking these issues into account, it is worth noting that a monitoring model, such as the one described in Fig. 4.3, can lead companies like Cintas also to a brand new definition of the traditional benchmarking practices.

Under this point of view, it can be useful to consider the Nokia's case as discussed by [40]. Nokia works in the international telecomm market, producing mobile devices, providing services and solution for worldwide dynamics and evolving markets. Inside Nokia's organization, benchmarking is used in order to support and guide all the development and innovation activities in many sectors (i.e. logistic, R&D, human relationships, etc.). The benchmarking approaches involve also collaborative and competitive benchmarking, as well as bench-marking projects based on specific firms or topics. Considering social media, their diffusion opened new opportunities also in terms of benchmarking, enhancing collaborative relationships, creating new spaces for knowledge and information sharing, and therefore helping the strategic plan process in all its phases, from the preparation to the implementation. In particular, the external practitioners involved in projects, frequently used Linkedin, Facebook, and Twitter also for bench-marking analysis. Especially in the open source activities or in the development communities, the usage of social media and collaborative spaces has contributed to provide reliable source of information and platforms where people (and firms) can easily interact and share information useful for benchmarking activities.

POINT OF ATTENTION: Social media provide new opportunities for benchmarking activities, on the one hand, enhancing collaborative rela-tionships among employees, creating new spaces for knowledge and infor-mation sharing; on the other hand, opening the boundary of a company through the involvement of external stakeholders and users, likewise.

As a consequence, Nokia's employees were able to enhance their capabilities in sharing and finding useful information through social media, opening new con-versations about strategically or relevant arguments. In particular, the areas of interest involved the open source practices, the professional use of 3D elements, software development and open innovation. Among the instruments, blogs and wikis, forums for discussion, video services (YouTube and SlideShare), have provided dynamic and direct sources for interact and collect/share information. In summary, as shown in Nokia's case, social media can be proactively used in order to improve the benchmarking process.

4.7 Summary

This Chapter shows the main characteristics that marketing intelligence activities can assume in the current competitive environment, when the traditional value chain is opening thanks to social media and collective intelligence practices [5, 6], creating the so called *value constellation* [41]. Considering the social listening as a core marketing driver for digital business value, the main approaches and tools of sentiment analysis and opinion mining, in addition to advanced models for market monitoring, have been described as well. In this Chapter, we have further discussed social sensing as a specific configuration of social listening, emerging from the convergence of sensors and social network technologies. Here below, we provide the reader with guidelines for short term strategy actions:

- consider the social listening activities as *continuous, open* and *evolving*;
- involve also *internal users* in a proactive participation to the marketing intelligence process (helping and enhancing the monitoring and risk management performance);
- adopt procedures as *opened* as possible (less sequential);
- clearly define the *strategic requirements* and its *implementation mechanisms* also to the operational level;
- constantly monitor through *mining* and *intelligence* techniques the development and evolution of the company perception by inner and outer context users' opinions.

We believe that the companies' interest into social listening and sensing technologies and approaches will grow significantly in the next years. Thus, a consequent strategic focus on analytics and data management capabilities across the overall company functions and business processes is rising as one of the key factors and priorities for IT executives as well as for other CxOs (as also early emphasized in Chap. 1 on Big Data).

References

1. Weill P, Vitale M (2002) What IT infrastructure capabilities are needed to implement e-business models? MIS Q Exec 1:17–34
2. Osterwalder A, Pigneur Y, Tucci C (2005) Clarifying business models: origins, present, and future of the concept. Commun AIS 16:751–775
3. Overby E, Bharadwaj A, Sambamurthy V (2006) Enterprise agility and the enabling role of information technology. Eur J Inf Syst 15:120–131
4. Weill P, Malone T, D'Urso VT, Herman G, Woerner S (2005) Do some business models perform better than others? a study of 1000 largest firms. MIT Cent Coord Sci Work Pap 226
5. Bonabeau E (2009) Decision 2.0: the power of collective intelligence. MIT Sloan Manag Rev 50:44–52
6. Malone TW, Laubacher R, Dellarocas C (2009) Harnessing crowds: mapping the genome of collective intelligence. Work Paper 001

7. Gregg DG (2010) Designing for collective intelligence. Commun ACM 53:134–138. doi: 10. 1145/1721654.1721691
8. Melville P, Sindhwani V, Lawrence R (2009) Social media analytics: channeling the power of the blogosphere for marketing insight. In Proceedings of the Workshop on Information in Networks (WIN-2009), New York, September, 2009
9. Lawrence R, Melville P, Perlich C, Sindhwani V, Meliksetian E, Hsueh P, Liu Y (2010) Social media analytics. The Next Generation of Analytics-Based Marketing Seeks Insights from Blogs. Operations Research/Management Science Today, 26–30 (February)
10. Wasserman S, Faust KC (1994) Social network analysis: methods and applications. Cambridge University Press, Cambridge
11. Wasserman S, Galaskiewicz JC (1994) Advances in social network analysis: research in the social and behavioral sciences. Sage Publications, Thousand Oaks, Calif
12. Pang B, Lee LC-1454712 (2008) Opinion mining and sentiment analysis. Found Trends Inf Retr 2:1–135. doi: 10.1561/1500000011
13. Tsytsarau M, Palpanas T (2011) Survey on mining subjective data on the web. Data Min Knowl Discov 24:478–514. doi:10.1007/s10618-011-0238-6
14. Feldman R (2013) Techniques and applications for sentiment analysis. Commun ACM 56:82–89
15. Bodendorf F, Kaiser CC-1651448 (2009) Detecting opinion leaders and trends in online social networks. In: Proceeding 2nd ACM Work. Soc. web search Min. ACM, Hong Kong, pp 65–68
16. Li Y, Ma S, Zhang Y, Huang R, Kinshuk (2013) An improved mix framework for opinion leader identification in online learning communities. Knowl Based Syst 43:43–51. doi: http://dx.doi.org/10.1016/j.knosys.2013.01.005
17. Chenga CP, Laua GT, Lawa KH, Panb J, Jones A (2009) Improving access to and understanding of regulations through taxonomies. Gov Inf Q 26:238–245
18. Song X, Chi Y, Hino K, Tseng BL (2007) Identifying Opinion Leaders in the Blogosphere. CIKM'07
19. Zhou H, Zeng D, Zhang CC-1706490 (2009) Finding leaders from opinion networks. In: Proceedings 2009 IEEE International Conference Intelligent Security Informatics. IEEE Press, Richardson, Texas, USA, pp 266–268
20. Miller GA (1995) WordNet: a lexical database for English. Commun ACM 38:39–41. doi:10. 1145/219717.219748
21. Tamma V (2010) Semantic web support for intelligent search and retrieval of business knowledge. IEEE Intell Syst 25:84–88
22. Horringan JA (2008) Online shopping—Internet users like the convenience but worry about the security of their financial information. Pew Internet and American Life Project Report
23. Bansal M, Cardie C, Lee L (2008) The power of negative thinking: Exploiting label disagreement in the min-cut classification framework. In 22nd International Conference on Computational Linguistics (COLING) (pp. 15–18). 18–22 August 2008, Manchester, UK
24. Kim S-M, Hovy E (2007) Crystal: analyzing predictive opinions on the web. In The Joint Conference on Empirical Methods in Natural Language Processing and Computational Natural Language Learning (EMNLP-CoNLL) (pp. 1056–1064). Prague, June 2007
25. Thomas M, Pang B, Lee L (2006) Get out the vote: Determining support or opposition from congressional floor-debate transcripts. In the 2006 Conference on Empirical Methods in Natural Language Processing (EMNLP 2006) (pp 327–335). Sydney, July 2006
26. Niu Y, Zhu X, Li J, Hirst G (2005) Analysis of polarity information in medical text. In the American Medical Informatics Association (AMIA) Annual Symposium 2005 (pp 570–574). American Medical Informatics Association
27. Jindal N, Liu B (2006) Mining comparative sentences and relations. In the 21st national conference on Artificial intelligence (AAAI2006) Volume 2 (pp 1331–1336). AAAI Press
28. Yu H, Hatzivassiloglou V (2003) Towards answering opinion questions: separating facts from opinions and identifying the polarity of opinion sentences. In the 2003 conference on

Empirical methods in natural language processing (EMNLP) (pp 129–136). Association for Computational Linguistics

29. Baeza-Yates R (2013) Big Data or Right Data? In: Proceedings 7th Alberto Mendelzon International Work Foundation Data Management Puebla/Cholula, Mex May 21–23
30. Jones R, Kumar R, Pang B, Tomkins A (2007) I know what you did last summer: query logs and user privacy. In: Proceedings Sixth ACM Conference Information Knowledge Management ACM, New York, pp 909–914
31. Jones R, Kumar R, Pang B, Tomkins A (2008) Vanity fair: privacy in querylog bundles. In: Proceedings 17th ACM Conference Information Knowledge Management ACM, New York, pp 853–862
32. Lu H-M, Chen H, Chen T-J, Hung M-W, Li S-H (2010) Financial text mining: supporting decision making using web 2.0 content. IEEE Intell Syst 26:78–82
33. Jindal N, Liu B (2008) Opinion spam and analysis. In: Proceedings 2008 International Conference Web Search Data Min ACM, New York, pp 219–230
34. Schuster D, Rosi A, Mamei M, Springer T, Endler M, Zambonelli F (2013) Pervasive social context: taxonomy and survey. ACM Trans Intell Syst Technol 4:46:1–46:22. doi: 10.1145/2483669.2483679
35. Rosi A, Mamei M, Zambonelli F, Dobson S, Stevenson G, Ye J (2011) Social sensors and pervasive services: Approaches and perspectives. In: IEEE International Conference Pervasive Computer Communication Work PERCOM Work, pp 525–530
36. Aggarwal C, Abdelzaher T (2013) Social Sensing. In: Aggarwal CC (ed) Manag Min Sens Data, Springer, US, pp 237–297
37. Aggarwal C, Yu P (2007) A survey of synopsis construction in data streams. In: Aggarwal C (ed) Data streams SE—9. Springer, US, pp 169–207
38. Antoniou G, van Harmelen F (2008) A semantic web primer, 2nd edn. MIT Press, Cambridge
39. GIA (2010) Delivering Maximum Strategic Value with Market Monitoring GIA Best Practices White Paper (vol 2)
40. GIA (2010) How Social Media is Redefining Benchmarking GIA Services White Paper (vol 1)
41. Normann R, Ramìrez R (1994) Designing interactive strategy: from value chain to value constellation. Wiley, Chichester
42. Gibilisco S, Rouse M (2013) Hyperscale storage. In: WhatIs.com, TechTarget. http://whatis.techtarget.com/definition/hyperscale-storage. Accessed 13 Oct 2013

Chapter 5
IT Consumerization

Abstract The changes that materialized in the field of information technology (IT) during the last decade have produced important effects in the strategies of the companies that produce new technologies. Consumerization is one of the new trends that have forced firms to be more flexible. In the twenty-first century, many of the great technological innovations are developed commercially first for the consumer sector, and then find their way into business applications. Consequently, popular commercial innovations have had important effects on the way how the businesses operate. Industries are now learning to follow the consumers' behaviors not only in their markets but also in the Web. This Chapter aims to provide a better understanding of the advantages, the challenges, and the implications of the IT Consumerization on businesses. Also, it discusses enterprises' drivers and strategies that concern this trend as well as to understand its implications on the businesses.

5.1 Introduction

It is very common nowadays to see workers from different levels in different companies bring their own laptops to the work environment to use them to do their jobs. Also, it is normal to see employees using their own technological devices at work, and blurring the lines between personal machines and work-focused ones. Moreover, they are using social media to reach and communicate with companies' customers. As a result, and as the technology becomes more central in people's lives, consumer technologies have been steadily entering the workplace and increasingly deleting the barriers between home and work technologies [1]. This trend, known as the consumerization of IT, has the potential to play a significant role in improving business productivity and agility for enterprises. The consumerization of IT helps organizations to realize increased efficiency, productivity and enhance workforce capabilities while maximizing IT investments [1]. Now, with the concept of Consumerization, the pattern of using technologies and

V. Morabito, *Trends and Challenges in Digital Business Innovation*, 89
DOI: 10.1007/978-3-319-04307-4_5, © Springer International Publishing Switzerland 2014

innovations from business world by the consumers has been reversed [2]. One big and important example of this phenomenon is the use of the personal smartphones or tablet devices, since employees can take them anywhere and access any variety of content, e.g., from the "cloud" they subscribe to.[1]

Based on the previous examples and explanations, Consumerization can be defined as the trend for new technology innovations to begin first in the consumer market then to enter business environments. Historically, businesses organizations determined and controlled the kind and type of information technology used within their firms. However, increasing numbers of employees have become more self-sufficient and creative in meeting their IT needs. Therefore, the strategies associated with the term BYOD which stands for 'Bring Your Own Device', where individual employees can choose their own type of device to do their work, are beginning to flourish in the business world [3]. Now, organizations in general and IT departments in particular have to adjust and support the type of device their employee wants to use, not what they want to provide.

A major driver of mobile device usage in the work environments has been the emergence of cloud computing. As mentioned before, both personal and business data can reside in the cloud on large servers run by giant technology firms such as Amazon and Google, where staggering amounts of data are stored for retrieval from almost anywhere in the world. Combine this with the cloud-based social networks like Facebook (over 1 billion users), Twitter (over 500 million) and a host of smaller firms and the use of portable, mobile devices usage increases exponentially. In fact, a Gartner group prediction, reported by the Economist [4], states 1 billion smartphones will be sold in 2015, up from 468 million in 2012.

Consumerization is an unstoppable force. It has added the element of freedom to the IT sector. The best IT experiences are no longer in the office; instead, they are out in the consumer market place, which is driving consumer spending and shaping the IT department of the future (see Fig. 5.1).

5.2 Advantages and Risks Associated with IT Consumerization

Consumerization of IT represents both a challenge for the business, and an opportunity to improve best practice around systems management. Instead of IT being seen as a roadblock on how users want to work, it can provide a more subtle level of service. As a consequence, this approach can get the best return out of users' growing understanding and familiarity with IT.

---

[1] Cloud computing and mobile services issues have been discussed in Chaps. 2 and 3 respectively.

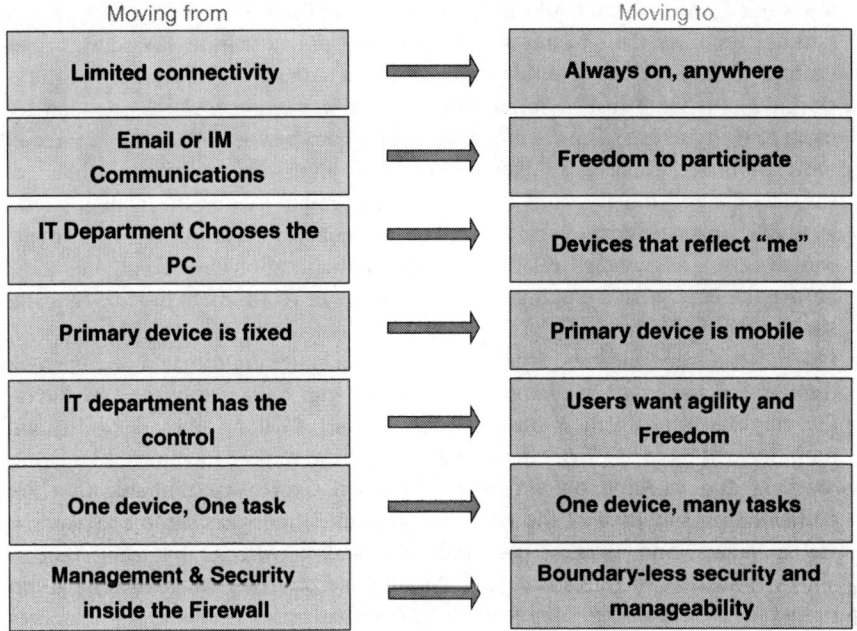

Moving from		Moving to
Limited connectivity	⇒	Always on, anywhere
Email or IM Communications	⇒	Freedom to participate
IT Department Chooses the PC	⇒	Devices that reflect "me"
Primary device is fixed	⇒	Primary device is mobile
IT department has the control	⇒	Users want agility and Freedom
One device, One task	⇒	One device, many tasks
Management & Security inside the Firewall	⇒	Boundary-less security and manageability

Fig. 5.1 IT Consumerization transformation. Adapted from [5]

5.2.1 Advantages and Opportunities of IT Consumerization

The continuous trend of IT consumerization at organizations promises with many opportunities and advantages that would help companies to achieve the required objectives. The possible opportunities show the various areas of the organization where benefits can be implemented by a proper introduction and utilization of IT consumerization. These opportunities were studied and presented by [6] and the [7] and they are as follows:

- *Financial opportunities*: consumerization of IT can result in saving time and money by increasing productivity, reducing spending and increasing user/customer satisfaction. Employees can be more productive due to permanent access to business data and transactions, and communication facilities. Cost cuts can be achieved by lower spending in hardware and other types of infrastructures, as employees will be more mobile and will use own devices and services. This can lead to a better customer satisfaction as well as its corresponding financial benefits [8]. Organizations that see IT consumerization as an opportunity to create a comprehensive strategy and clear governance model will be more likely to capitalize on the financial benefits of this trend [7].
- *Human Resources benefits*: since that consumerization of IT has been originally started by having employees bringing their own devices to the business, thus, it

has gained an important role in increasing workforce creativity and ability to find/use tools for their business tasks and continuous learning. Modern organisations should try to seize this opportunity in order to increase motivation of staff, support them in becoming more literate in current technologies and use them also in business life. This approach can help businesses to attract talented individuals and achieve a better retention of employees by offering them job satisfaction and the freedom to unfold their creativity for the benefit of the business and their customers. Moreover, Human Resources (HR) departments can discover advantages related to better collaboration and communications among the enterprise's employees as well as better recruitment process by using social media platforms [9].

- *Operational opportunities*: urgent issues can be better coordinated and resolved through the increased availability of staff that can be accomplished by having the employees using their own devices. Adding to that, more flexibility and mobility will have positive effect on working from remote locations, like home-working and working on the move. This will increase communication and collaboration initiative at the staff, enhance the employees ability to work in virtual teams, and increase peer influence and knowledge by using modern channels such as social networking, chatting and blogging websites. The ability to mobilize cross-disciplinary teams on the virtual space is essential for success. Moreover, IT consumerization is a good way to simplify and decentralize security policy and security governance, a trend that is irreversible and will lead in the middle term to the falling of traditional security models.[2]
- *Data Management opportunities*: successful implementation of the IT consumerization requires strong architecture that could result in better data management practices and results. For example, Cloud Storage can enhance the availability of data, which would help employees to increase online interaction and online data access, while using approved applications deployed via the company's own app server. Frequent data interactions can increase data accuracy, and at the same time the degree of data sharing will be increased [8]. Moreover, such storage architectures can allow for a better control of data flow within the organization [7].

5.2.2 Challenges and Risks of the Consumerization of IT

The increasing number of employees' private devices used in workplace is presenting a challenge for the managers [10]. This problem is among the other issues related to the consumerization of technology devices [11]. Also, the Information Security Forum (ISF), [12], has analyzed the challenges, trends and solutions for IT consumerization: according to this analysis, many of the issues that are related

---

[2] Chapter 7 discusses these issues as challenges to digital business identity.

to this topic are based on the fact that the devices that the employees are using are not suitable to be used at the work environment; hence, it is difficult to apply the same security standards and policies on those personal devices. Also, besides the misuse of the personal device legal matters that concern the ownership of device and the data on it are under question.

Nevertheless, the ISF's report [12] offers guidance that is related to organization's security response planning, that addresses how the people use the devices and what protection software they have as well as the provisioning and support they will need. It also provides the legal requirements to govern this trend. These advices are categorized into four key areas as follows:

- First section is about IT consumerization governance and looks at achieving appropriate visibility of the devices in the organization and defining policies around ownership.
- Second part is about users and employees' awareness and acceptable use policies.
- Third section is about the technical issues concerned with mobile devices and security issues related to them.
- Fourth segment is about the issues related to software and apps used on the consumerized devices.

Moreover, McAfee Inc. corporation, which is an information security specialist, has cooperated with Carnegie Mellon University, in a report entitled 'Mobility and Security' that addresses the consumerization related problems [12]. This report argues that enterprise policies and practices are well behind the arrival of new advancements. It shows that despite the results of a survey of 1,500 mobile device users and IT decision-makers that have found that 95 % of the corporations already have policies that govern the use of mobile devices such as smartphones and tablets, only one third of the employees at those companies were aware of such rules. Moreover, the guidelines that are currently in use within those businesses are inadequate to deal with situations when the employees tend to keep passwords, PINs and credit card details on their personal devices.

Furthermore, other survey results show that 63 % of mobile devices that connect to enterprise networks regularly are used for both work and private purposes which results in a blurring of the distinction between work and personal life of the worker. Although, there are concerns raised about the possibility of harmful software being introduced into the enterprise network by poorly protected smartphones, the McAfee study concludes that theft or loss of the devices is considered as a bigger security threat, since the lost smartphone can contain significant amounts of sensitive corporate data. According to McAfee, a third of such devices losses resulted in a financial impact on the organization. Additionally, European Network and Information Security Agency (ENISA), has provided a categorization for the risks associated with the consumerization of IT. These categories and the risks assessed under each one of them are summarized as follows:

Category 1: Risks Related to Costs

The risks under this category are:

1. Increased risk of loss of value in cases when employees bring bad reputation to the organization's name or brand by uncontrolled use of consumerized services/devices such as, e.g., Dropbox.
2. The increased variety and complexity of personal and mobile devices as well as different operating systems and applications that all requiring management will lead to increased costs.
3. The possibility of losing mobile devices would likely increase when the organization uses more of these equipment, which means more costs.
4. Additional spending might happen to ensure that the security requirements do not prevent appropriate consumerization or encourage inappropriate use of consumer devices.

Category 2: Risks Related to Legal and Regularity Issues

The risks under this category are:

1. Corporate governance and compliance control over employee-owned devices will not be optimal.
2. Since the consumerized personal devices may be owned and operated entirely by the end users, it will be difficult for enterprises to enforce their own policies that are related to HR, legal scope and context, and claims of ownership on intellectual property.
3. It is hard to discriminate between user and company data on the employee-owned devices, which may result in risks related to the intervention of businesses in the private life and property of employees.

Category 3: Risks Affecting Data (Confidentiality, Integrity and Privacy)

The risks under this category are:

1. the possibility of losing corporate data because of unauthorized sharing and usage of information on employees' devices by the services running on them;
2. the possibility of losing corporate data as a result of access by unknown users and unmanaged devices to enterprise networks;
3. the risk of losing corporate data as a result of difficulty in applying security measures and policies on application-rich mobile devices, especially when the device is owned by the employee;
4. increased risk of the corporate data being hacked due to external attack.

The following table (Table 5.1) summarizes and classifies the previous mentioned risks into primary and secondary categories. It provides cross-functional information for those interested primarily in one kind of risk who may need to consider the relationship between certain type of risk and others. For example, it is expected that businesses dealing with privacy issues, might also be interested in risks related to data loss.

Table 5.1 Primary and secondary classification/dependencies of identified risks

Category (cat) & risk (R)	Category			Comment
	Costs	Legal and regularity	Data	
Cat(1)\R(1)	X	(X)	(X)	Secondary categories due to effects on compliance and data loss
Cat(1)\R(2)	X	(X)	(X)	Secondary categories due to effects on compliance and data loss
Cat(1)\R(3)	X	(X)	(X)	Secondary categories due to effects on compliance and data loss
Cat(1)\R(4)	X		(X)	Secondary categories due to effects on compliance and data loss
Cat(2)\R(1)	(X)	X	(X)	Secondary categories costs from possible fines and costs caused by loss of reputation due to compliance violations
Cat(2)\R(2)	(X)	X		Secondary category as costs from possible fines due to compliance violation
Cat(2)\R(3)	(X)	X		Secondary categories as costs from possible fines and costs caused by loss of reputation due to compliance violations
Cat(3)\R(1)	(X)	(X)	X	Secondary category legal/regulatory from possible privacy violations
				Secondary category as costs caused by loss of reputation
Cat(3)\R(2)	(X)	(X)	X	Secondary category legal/regulatory from possible privacy violations
				Secondary category costs caused by loss of reputation
Cat(3)\R(3)		(X)	X	Secondary category legal/regulatory from possible privacy violations
Cat(3)\R(4)		(X)	X	Secondary category as legal/regulatory from possible privacy violations

Adapted from [7]

Moreover, more cost oriented businesses might also be interested in legal-related risks. In the table, the X symbol represents the primary category and the (X) symbol represents the secondary category. Additionally, the table provides explanations on why some risks are falling into one or more secondary categories.

5.3 Steps for IT Consumerization

Companies have to rethink their strategies to seize the opportunities associated with the consumerization of the IT devices rather than facing the consequences of this trend. Thus, it is safe to say that empowering users can help organizations to be more flexible and help employees do their jobs better. Therefore, many authors have provided their perspectives about how to take the advantage of IT consumerization in order to see it as an opportunity rather than a problem. One example is provided by [13] in which it is argued that companies will not be able to fulfill every business user need internally since budgets, skills and the time factors are very different from one department to another. Therefore, [13] proposed five ways to stay ahead of consumerization of the IT. Another example is provided by Intel IT center in a form of white paper [14] in which another five steps have been suggested as ways for companies to take the control of the this growing trend and to take the full advantages of it. The following part provides a summary of the previous mentioned sources for how the companies can cope with IT consumerization.

5.3.1 Step 1: Understand the Powerful Sources and Adopt the User Perspective

Today's employees are more technically capable to find their own ways to use their own devices in order for them to be more productive at work environment such as downloading, using a personal cloud storage service, or engaging with social media so that they can have better communication and work more efficiently. However, such procedures can conflict with the enterprise's IT security policies [13].

As mentioned before, cloud computing is the IT service that makes this even easier, with information and services accessible from anywhere and anytime by using any device. For example, if an employee knows he\she may later need access to a file created on his\her work computer, he\she can easily store the document using his personal cloud service. Although he\she may be relying on that service primarily for personal use, he\she can upload his\her work documents and then access them from any device [14].

5.3.2 Step 2: Rethink User Computing—Change Focus from Platform to User

The traditional approaches and practices of users' profiles management are not suitable any more in nowadays work environments because of today's complex computing landscape and the countless number of employees using consumerized devices. These devices form IT challenges for the IT departments because they run different operating systems that may occasionally connect to the corporate network, but are always connected to the Internet. The devices also typically have no management framework and are accessing applications and cloud services that may or may not be provided by or qualified for use by the existing IT infrastructure at the enterprise [14].

Organizations have to reconsider how they manage user computing in order for them to effectively meet the previously mentioned challenges of dynamic landscape and truly embrace consumerization. They need to develop a user-centered strategy designed to optimize the computing experience and keep the user as productive as possible on any platform, whether connected to the corporate network or not. A centralized management approach could be the one that can provide the flexibility and visibility that the company needs to securely deliver the right computing resources for users [14].

5.3.3   Step 3: Shorten the Time Frame for New Computing Approach Adoption

Many of the consumer technologies that are already in use by enterprises are advancing very fast. Businesses must be flexible enough to embrace rapid prototyping and iterative approaches aligned with methodologies such as agile or scrum. They should also prioritize use cases with a clear business value, and create a plan for addressing them, starting with the easiest. The various use cases that can happen may require different architectures or experimentation and may uncover the best solution that can become the standard that is followed by the company [13].

5.3.4   Step 4: Support Employee Owned Devices

In its report about IT consumerization [14], Intel has provided a set of best practices (see Fig. 5.2) for supporting employee-owned devices in the enterprise.

They may help organization to develop a stronger user-centered strategy and address some of the inherent security issues associated with the Bring You Own Device BYOD strategy, in particular:

1. *To identify and engage stakeholders*: companies need to consider creating a master vision of the BYOD program by engaging and collaborating with all key stakeholders early in the IT consumerization process. This covers employees from human resources and legal to IT, corporate services, and most importantly, end users. This is an ideal opportunity to define all the components of the BYOD program [14].
2. *To update security model*: the decision makers in the business need to develop a security model for employee-owned devices. This means shifting focus into a broader vision. In other words, instead of focusing solely on securing hardware devices, firms have to concentrate on protecting the corporate data that will be accessed by a range of devices [14].
3. *To decide which operating systems and devices to support*: this is an important procedure in order not to ensure that the technology choices wouldn't

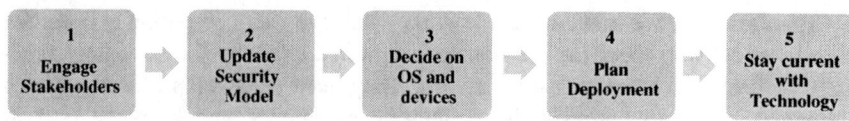

Fig. 5.2 Best practices for supporting employees' owned devices. Adapted from [14]

overwhelm the IT staff; this process included a holistic assessment of the
following components such as: associated costs of supporting the new devices
and the available services such as email and calendar.

4. *To enable the technology and plan deployment*: this step is about building the
infrastructure that will work best for the organization to support devices. This
includes considerations related to software requirements, bandwidth options,
management needs, and investment parameters [14].

5. *To stay up-to-date with changing and new technologies*: by staying aware of
technology trends, it is possible for decision makers to forecast what is coming
next and think about how it might fit within the existing infrastructure. One way
to do this is by creating a turnkey evaluation process to assess new technologies
and devices in order to efficiently identify those that can be added to the
program. This step can be achieved by focusing and assessing on the following
five elements: security, manageability, productivity, performance and ease of
use [14].

5.4 Business Scenarios for IT Consumerization

During the consumerization of IT, strategy planning, business requirements, policies, and scenarios provide ways to focus on and analyze the requirements of
different segments of users and the ways in which applications, devices, and
connectivity support users' work styles. Planning teams involve users categorization into segments and the identification of the various scenarios of IT consumerization that correspond to those sectors, which can result in a better
understanding of the different needs of users in the enterprise. This section
describes users segmentation and work styles according to [15] as well as some
typical scenarios for the different segments of users who belong to those segments
and types, adapted from [16].

According to [15], Microsoft has used qualitative and quantitative research in
several countries to understand the different types of information workers, which
can be segmented according to three factors: the degree of technology engagement, the degree of collaboration, and work location flexibility. Figure 5.3 illustrates users' segmentation along these three dimensions.

The three dimensions described previously help identify and describe work
style segments, such as those listed in Table 5.2.

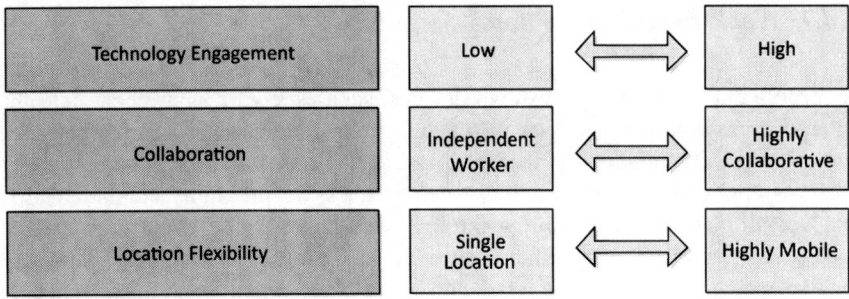

Fig. 5.3 Users segmented along three dimensions. Adapted from [15]

Table 5.2 Consumerization of IT work styles and attributes

	Non-PC worker	Generalist	Road warrior	Deskbound contributor	Techrealist	All star
Technology engagement	Low	Low	Medium	Medium	Medium	High
Need for collaboration	Low	Low	Low	Medium	Medium	High
Working location flexibility	Low	Low	High	Low	Medium	High

Adapted from [15]

Table 5.3 Consumerization of IT personas and work styles

Business scenario	Role	Work style
Work from your phone	Corporate attorney	Tech realist
Bring your own media tablet	Business manager	All star
Bring your own device for contractors	Contractor	Road warrior
The boardroom	Executive	All star
High-end sales	High-end salesperson	Tech realist
Retail sales	Retail sales person	Deskbound contributor

Adapted from [15]

According to [15] the All-star, Road warrior, and Tech realist work styles are the most applicable scenarios because of the average high level of technology engagement and requirement for location flexibility.

The personas that represent these work styles in the scenarios in this section are corporate attorney, business manager, contractor, executive, high-end salesperson, and retail sales person (see Table 5.3) [15].

5.4.1 Work from Your Phone

A corporate attorney brings his own devices, such as, e.g., a smartphone into the enterprise environment and uses it to obtain immediate access to corporate email and calendar, communication facilities, and in some cases, the access to some of business applications that can allow such contact. By providing communication and social platforms capabilities through web-based apps, employees can be productive regardless of whether they work at the office or remotely. They use their personal smartphone to read and write work email messages, schedule appointments, and send and receive instant messages. However, only some of them are able to access work files from their phone while in their offices because of security restrictions.

5.4.2 Bring Your Own Media Tablet

A business manager handles hectic schedules and endless lists of tasks and responsibilities. However, with the media tablet it is possible for that manager to accomplish a lot while being out of the office. For example, the media tablet can connect to the corporate data center and can be used to answer all the emails that are related to work and to solve the bending issues by conducting Instant messaging IM discussions while sharing documents on the screen with other employees at the company.

5.4.3 Bring Your Own Device for Vendors

An independent contractor for several construction companies can controls his\her own schedule while working for different customers from different locations. He\she can use mobile broadband and wireless hotspots to access the Internet from the worksites. These technologies can be used by the contractor to read email, to check work progress and status, to connect to the corporate network through smartphone to review the latest construction documents, to conduct conference calls with others as needed, and to display, explain and discusses proposed changes by sharing the screen of his\her laptop. Moreover, additional colleagues can join the conference calls from their own devices.

Furthermore, he\she also spends a few minutes browsing the latest news from friends on Facebook. Additionally, throughout each day, he\she can use Facebook on the laptop to communicate with friends and family [16].

5.4.4 The Boardroom

Executive decision makers are more and more adopting tablet computers for decision support. These roles are extremely time-constrained and are often reluctant to the use of computers in general. Tablet devices are replacing paper in fast-paced boardrooms and can enable executives to attend meetings or conference calls with all the supporting documents they need, which can be considered as a very large enabling factor for these roles. In general, information is pre-prepared by the executive assistant, so he\she can focus on preparing more effectively on making decisions [16].

5.4.5 High-Performance Sales

The tablet is extremely well-suited for sales conversations because it does not provide a physical barrier like opening a notebook to display the screen. Also, because media tablets and tablet PCs are thinner, lighter, and have longer battery life, they are very convenient for these ultra-mobile roles. A tablet is highly supportive when talking to a client because it can provide interactive, visual information that supports the conversation. Examples of new opportunities enabled by tablets include making an immediate competitive analysis between businesses, or providing highly personalized information during the conversation, such as personalized mortgage information [16].

5.4.6 Retail Sales

Tablets can provide local retailers with the opportunity to compete effectively with online stores. The types of devices that are used for retail applications vary, because the experience of shopping may involve using one or both hands and tablets can interfere with that experience. In addition, shoppers may spend too much time looking at the screen of a tablet or phone, rather than interacting with products in the store [16].

While kiosks remain popular if the customer needs to look for more information such as finding an out-of-stock item online at another store, some shoppers prefer to obtain recommendations from other consumers by using their tablets. Moreover, cash registers are increasingly being replaced by tablets and other handheld devices, which provide an opportunity to reduce costs [16].

5.5 Strategies for IT Consumerization

The previously explained business scenarios can be associated with one of the following strategies: going mobile, modernize the desktop, virtualize, and bring your own device. The key concerns about these strategies as well as the technologies that address the raised issues are explained in the following sub-sections.

5.5.1 Going Mobile Strategy

Many of the nowadays employees are exploring this strategy. They are interested in achieving productivity gains by using their own mobile devices, such as smartphones and media tablets. However, some key concerns about this strategy have to be addressed. These include: managing a diverse mobile platform, protecting information that flows across mobile devices, adopting applications for mobile consumption, and defining data ownership.[3]

Implementing mobile strategy includes enabling mobile device management infrastructure such as, for example, System Center Configuration Manager 2012 and Windows Intune, which is a cloud-based management solution that can provide a rich platform to manage Android, iPhone, and Windows Phone devices. Also, it includes information protection by using Active Directory Rights Management Services, which provide the infrastructure that is needed to protect office content and other Information Rights Management. Moreover, Windows Server 8 and Dynamic Access will provide an even more compelling solution [16].

5.5.2 Modernize the Desktop Strategy

This strategy is needed since that one size no longer fits all. This approach brings in popular user choices in scenario-driven ways to provide employees with the fashionable devices they seek that also enhance their productivity. However, the key concerns about this strategy include: supporting multiple device platforms, meeting user expectations for richer device experiences, and taking back previously realized discounts achieved by buying in bulk [16]. The Recommended initiatives that address these concerns include:

- migration to up-to-date Linux, IOS and Windows versions to reduce cost;
- reducing application portfolio and application migration;
- using virtualization to reduce application deployment costs by reducing testing efforts and decreasing the time that is needed to deploy apps.

---

[3] Chapter 3 on mobile services provide further insights and details about these issues.

This strategy leads us to the next technology which is desktop virtualization that separates the desktop environment and associated application software from the physical client device that is used to access it

5.5.3 Virtualization Strategy

This strategy enables enterprises to quickly achieve business benefits gained from IT consumerization by moving the desktop and/or applications into a data center. This strategy makes it easier to provide new desktops, but it requires investment in the infrastructure that supports it. The key concerns with this strategy include: roaming user experience across devices and locations, protecting user information, using virtualization technologies that include desktop virtualization and application streaming, and finally, delivering the required applications to privately owned devices by using application gateways or by transforming to cloud computing. Nevertheless, enabling such strategy includes new technologies such as server-based virtualization for application streaming and user state virtualization for a great cross-device experience [16]. Companies that provide desktop virtualization solutions include information technology giants. One example of these companies is Cisco, which provides Desktop Virtualization with collaboration with Citrix XenDesktop solution and desktop virtualization with cooperation with VMware View solution. Another example of those information technology pioneers is Dell, which provided Virtual desktop infrastructure (VDI) solution that provides new capabilities for its users such as high-performance 3D graphics, unified collaboration and VoIP with other products such as Microsoft Lync 2013. The users of this solution can access enhanced media and graphic software from virtually any place and on any device. Also, it provides IT departments with the ability to centrally host, manage and configure sensitive user's data and resources [16].

5.5.4 Bring Your Own Device BYOD Strategy

This strategy encourages talented employees and contractors, especially those in creative roles to stay at the organization. The key concerns with this strategy include: supporting rich experiences with native apps for multiple platforms, delivering applications and information in multiple ways, managing a diverse platform, protecting information. Nonetheless, enabling this strategy includes the utilization of new technologies. Examples of these include productivity apps from the cloud, such as Office 365, IT management services from the cloud, such as Windows Intune, virtualized desktops or apps, application gateways to publish apps to devices, and cloud services to deliver apps to devices [16].

5.6 Enterprise Drivers Behind the Consumerization of IT

The drivers that motivate enterprises to adopt IT consumerization strategy include increasing productivity, refocusing IT on strategic initiatives rather than device management, attracting and retaining valuable employees [16]. These motivational reasons are explained in the following points, according to [16]:

Increasing productivity. When employees are away from their desks, devices that provide access to information related to work can increase their collaboration and productivity [9], since that mobile devices can access email and provide instant messaging service, calendar, voice, and other capabilities at any time and place [8].

Refocusing IT on strategic initiatives. IT employees will be relieved when the retail channels and users become responsible for obtaining and supporting their own mobile devices. Thus, IT department is relieved of some time-consuming aspects of supporting an enterprise infrastructure, which would enable IT staff to focus on strategic initiatives and projects [16].

Attracting and retaining valuable employees. Providing employees with a controlled freedom of information access would encourage best employees to stay at the firm and would attract and retain valuable employees as important assets of the enterprise. As a result, enterprise human resources departments are moving toward rich consumerization of IT environments to improve workplace satisfaction [16].

5.7 Considerations Related to IT Consumerization

The consumerization of IT is not an unrestricted strategy, nor appropriate in all environments, because many devices are not secure enough. Also, legal considerations with regard to licensing, security, and privacy exist. Moreover, the ability of the users for being self-supporting and tech-savvy is under question. The organization that wants to adopt a consumerization of IT in a cost-effective manner has to evaluate the benefits and risks of such a strategy, before applying it [16]. Therefore, there are some important considerations to investigate for an effective IT consumerization strategy and according to [16] they can be categorized into: business and other considerations, technology considerations, and user support considerations. As for *business and other considerations* for consumerization of IT strategies, according to [16] they include:

Business value. The business value and the Return on Investment (ROI) of a consumerization of IT solution should be investigated, explained and emphasized to potential customers instead of only specific details about technology or infrastructure.

Level of consumerization of IT within an enterprise. Organizations need to have clear view about the degree of IT consumerization that is already existed, in order to take full advantage of the productivity potential and mitigate the risks involved

Table 5.4 Desktop delivery option

On your own	Bring your own	Choose your own	Here is your own
Consumer desktop		*Enterprise desktop*	
Consumer OS	Consumer OS	Enterprise OS	Enterprise OS
Local workspace	Local workspace	Local workspace	Local workspace
		Session roaming	Session roaming
Virtual desktop			
Virtual workspace (server or local)	Virtual workspace (server or local)	Access to hosted desktop	Access to hosted desktop
Public access apps	Remote desktop	Session roaming	Session roaming
	Remote apps	Apps virtualization	Apps virtualization
	VDI	Roaming environment	Roaming environment
		Data synchronization	Data synchronization
		VDI	VDI

Adapted from [16]

with the adoption of this strategy; indeed IT departments frequently underestimate the number of workers who already use their own devices.

Organizational policies and acceptable device use. Appropriate practice of privately owned devices usage in the workplace must be defined and communicated to all staff within organization. That is because people are often unaware of the privacy and security risks involved in using certain software applications.

Legal considerations. It is crucial to consider the different legal and privacy legislation that differs globally among countries when planning consumerization of IT strategies. Therefore, enterprises must address a number of legal issues, including: the owner of the data on a privately owned device, accessing the corporate data remotely from a personal device, and legal issues related to privacy laws and contracts permits.

Financial and tax considerations. This category includes licensing costs, data plans, and support. Enterprises have to establish baseline needs at the beginning of consumerization of IT strategy planning in order for them to be able to determine the financial impact and allow tracking of benefits and investments.

As for *technology considerations*, common infrastructure-related issues that enterprises are concerned with include: the optimum choice of a consumerization of IT strategy in order for the enterprise to realize business benefits, the needed changes in the infrastructure to be able to support a consumerization of IT strategy and the support of different mobile devices.

Moreover, additional delivery options are associated with device options, as shown in Table 5.4.

Finally, considering *user support considerations*, there are direct effects for IT consumerization on the existing IT policies and procedures regarding hardware and software failure. Also, different support strategies can be utilized to control the support efforts as well as the costs while providing support to the organization.

Table 5.5 Sample IT support policy

	Devices	Operating systems	Files & settings	Apps
On your own	You	You	You	You
			Corp	Corp
Bring your own	You	You	You	You
		Corp	Corp	Corp
Choose your own	Corp	Corp	You	You
			Corp	Corp
Here is your own	Corp	Corp	You	You

Adapted from [16]

Therefore, it is important to establish a communication strategy or policy that clearly defines personal and IT responsibilities and expectations from all parties. The support matrix, adapted from [16], shown in Table 5.5 is an example of who is responsible for specific types of issues with different categories.

5.8 Social Platforms

Social media has a huge impact on not only the work environment, but also on the society in general, therefore it is hard to underestimate such implication. For example, by the beginning of 2011, the average user of Facebook website spent 1,400 min, which equals to 23.3 h, on this social platform each month [5]. With the vast growth of social media as a way of communication and interaction between people, it's not only the technology that is changing; however, it is the people and the society themself that are developing accordingly with the new online or virtual world and opportunities. This situation can be better demonstrated by examining the fact that one-in-six United States (US) couples who got married in the last 3 years have met online, which proves the importance of such platforms. Moreover, around the world, social media and new and smart mobile devices are becoming very important in personal relationships among people in a way that makes it challenging to make separation between the technology and personal social networks.

Nowadays, as a consequence, employees expect and demand more freedom at work environment. They want to have instant access to the types of applications that would help them to be more communicative in their personal life. Also, on the work side, they consider that having the ability to access consumer social networks through their personal devices, would allow them to build conductive work relationships that would result in better business performance. However, at work places, 56 % of employers do not allow access to non-work related resources or websites and 63 % ban their employees from saving personal data and files on company's computers. Moreover, a recent research claim that nearly half of all the workers (46 %) surveyed have graded their employers with extremely low marks for applying IT consumerization strategy [5].

This situation should not be the norm, since after the success of customer directed services such as Facebook and Twitter, social networking platforms are finding their way into businesses' environments. Such circumstances can be particularly applied to the case of young employees since this category of workers expects to have access to the same technologies at work that they are familiar with in their life as consumers. For example, Microsoft's $1.2bn acquisition of Yammer has positioned the software giant to introduce enterprise social networking capabilities to its existing business collaboration systems such as SharePoint, Exchange, Lync and Office 365 [17]. This acquisition by Microsoft is a clear example of the importance of social networking within work environments.

Yammer can enable companies to offer their employees functionalities that are similar to Facebook and Twitter and at the same time to work in accordance to the security standards of the enterprise firewall and can be integrated with other systems at the enterprise that are managed by a company's own IT department. It is well accepted and regarded by the experts who follow the enterprise social networking market. The employees who use Yammer can set up user profiles, send and receive "tweets" like messages, participate in discussion forums and receive information about what their colleagues are doing. Yammer will accompany Skype software, which is a communication product that Microsoft acquired last year for $8.5bn and it is expected to integrate with its mainstream business applications [17].

5.9 Case Studies

In this section we investigate some IT consumerization at work environments related case studies and we provide explanation about its role for the business success.[4]

The first case study is about a business communications solutions provider called Avaya. This company brings social, multimedia experience to enterprise telephony [18]. Avaya is exploring the social dimension of unified communication by using the Avaya Flare, which is a drag-and-drop and touch-screen user interface that a person can use to arrange calls, conference conversations, videoconferences, and instant messaging communications by browsing through on-screen contact profiles that are represented by profile pictures and "existence" indicators, which show the available people in the system. Moreover, it is possible to add personal Facebook profiles to the system, in addition to those that can be added from the corporate directory. Flare is based on the idea of utilizing a directory of social profile pictures, which enables the user to quickly create a group of people that he\she wants to communicate with, without facing the complexities associated with traditional videoconferencing

---

[4] The case studies introduce some of the topics further discussed in Chap. 6 on Digital Work and Collaboration.

systems. This means that the person, who is calling for the conference, does not have to spend time at the beginning to assemble the right group of people and the required supporting documents. Flare is branded an "experience" because even though its first incarnation was a tablet-sized desktop device, the value of it is in the software or app that can also be used on desktop computers and other devices such as iPad. Avaya's strategy for mobility within the enterprise is to take advantage of the consumer gadgets that executives and employees are already bringing to work such as tablets and smartphones. Moreover, with its one-X software for smart phones, Avaya also allows its employees to make the mobile phone acts as an extension of the corporate network. That means employees can transfer calls from their desk to their mobile phones as they are leaving their offices, or take a call on their mobile while they are on their way into the office and transfer it to their desks when they get there [18].

POINT OF ATTENTION: Companies have already realized the potential advantages of IT consumer related products that are being brought to the offices, starting to act in ways that allow them to seize the opportunities coming with them rather than blocking their usage at work environments.

The second case study discusses how Royal Dutch Shell started with the BYOD strategy, since the company has realized that the employees will use their own devices at the workplace, whether authorized or not [19]. The hoped potential benefits of this strategy include increased flexibility, choice and a more engaged workforce. Shell has started a period of six months rollout of a Mobile Device Management (MDM) software-as-a-service (SaaS) platform from AirWatch. After that, it has made BYOD available to users across the company, including its contractors and employees in joint ventures, likewise. Shell's AirWatch MDM platform supports around 6,000 individual devices. It provides support to any employee-owned Apple and Android phones, and tablets that meet its minimum operating system requirements.

POINT OF ATTENTION: It is necessary to realize the importance of engaging people from all departments at the company in order to comply with all needs and to be able to have a successful consumerization of the IT.

The introduction of BYOD represented the first manifestation of consumerization at Shell; however, beyond the need to introduce an MDM platform, the project required significant non-technical collaborated work with other stakeholders in the business to ensure the company was ready for a new way of working. These included representatives from the HR, legal and tax departments, among others [19].

5.10 Summary

In this Chapter, detailed explanations about the concepts and definitions related to IT consumerization and its advantages for the IT department in particular and for the whole organization in general have been provided. Also, it delivered a summary for steps that can be followed to ensure best IT consumerization. Moreover, enterprise drivers and recommended strategies as well as different business scenarios for IT consumerization have been explained. Consumerization is not a fleeting concept; it represents a fundamental shift in the way business solutions will be delivered by IT. Its implications on the future of the enterprise require IT innovation that goes beyond simply supporting BYOD strategy. It is safe to say that IT has an opportunity and a responsibility to evolve its role and culture to one that focuses first on the business and users. In an ever changing business environment that brings new security and compliance challenges, IT must balance flexible user choice with secure, cost-effective management standards across the organization. IT can prepare for the future by understanding and anticipating what users will need next.

However, despite its potential benefits, the challenges associated with the consumerization of IT need to be well addressed in order to know how to seize the opportunities associated with this trend. Many issues that are related to the business, technology, and user support have to be considered thoroughly in order not to face situations that the company has no control over devices that access important corporate data.

Finally, the Chapter has discussed case studies, confirming the importance, benefits and issues associated with the consumerization of the IT. These case studies show many considerations that have to be well-thought-out before transforming to new strategies to accept and support employees own devices.

References

1. Nunziata S (2011) The consumerization of IT. CIO Insight, p 8
2. Strategies G (2007) Consumerization. Growth strategy pp 1–2
3. Taylor P (2013) Personal device use is challenge for IT bosses. In: Financial times. http://www.ft.com/cms/s/0/20b8886e-a3e4-11e2-ac00-00144feabdc0.html#axzz2lMz9OnWl. Accessed 21 Nov 2013
4. The economist (2011) consumerisation—the power of many. economist pp 1–4
5. D'Arcy P (2011) CIO strategies for consumerization: the future of enterprise mobile computing. White Pap Dell, Dell Headquarter Round Rock, pp 3–14
6. Docherty J (2009) Consumerisation of IT: a growing headache for the future. In: Financial times. http://www.ft.com/intl/cms/s/0/96910f70-915f-11de-879d-00144feabdc0.html. Accessed 21 Nov 2013
7. ENISA (2012) Consumerization of IT: top risks and opportunities responding to the evolving threat environment. ENISA, Heraklion, pp 1–18

8. Copeland R, Crespi N (2012) Analyzing consumerization—should enterprise business context determine session policy?. In: 16th international conference on intelligence in next generation networks pp 187–193
9. Tufts H (2012) Let consumerization work for you. Strateg HR Rev 11:289
10. Gibbs M (2011) IT consumerization: it is biblical. Netw World 28:1
11. Niehaves B, Köffer S, Ortbach K (2013) IT consumerization under more difficult conditions—insights from german local governments. In: Proceedings of the 14th annual international conference on digital government research, pp 205–213
12. Security CF & ISF (2011). Advises on consumerisation. Comput Fraud Secur 20(3):20–23. doi: 10.1016/S1361-3723(11)70058-6
13. White M, Openshaw E (2012) Five ways to stay ahead of consumerization of IT. In: Information week. http://www.informationweek.com/it-leadership/5-ways-to-stay-ahead-of-consumerization-of-it/d/d-id/1107906?. Accessed 21 Nov 2013
14. Intel (2012) Five steps to consumerization of IT in the Enterprise. White Pap from Intel
15. Harteveld A (2012) How the consumerization of IT affects your business—microsoft recommendations for a consumerization of IT strategy. Microsoft Services Enterprise Architecture, Microsoft Corporation, Redmond, pp 1–22
16. Harteveld A (2012) Microsoft recommendations for a consumerization of IT strategy. Microsoft Services Enterprise Architecture, Microsoft Corporation, Redmond, pp 1–16
17. Taylor P (2012) Consumerization of corporate IT accelerate. In: Financial Times. http://www.ft.com/cms/s/0/a2fb5172-c077-11e1-982d-00144feabdc0.html#axzz2lGryjslF. Accessed 21 Nov 2013
18. Carr DF (2011) How Avaya Is Embracing Social, Consumerization Trends. In: Information week. http://www.informationweek.com/how-avaya-is-embracing-social-consumerization-trends/d/d-id/1101720? Accessed 21 Nov 2013
19. Twentyman J (2012) Shell: "Consumerisation will force more change than any other trend." In: Financial Times

Part II
Digital Management Trends

Chapter 6
Digital Work and Collaboration

Abstract The fast evolution of the Information Systems (IS) during the last decade makes it able to cover more areas in business and other fields. One example of these areas is the way that people communicate and collaborate in business environments. In business, the digital or IT collaboration is divided into electronic communication tools, electronic conferencing tools, and collaborative management tools. The previous mentioned systems have evolved tremendously in the last few years in order to improve the way a group of people from the same organization work together in a productive way. Also, Computer-Supported cooperative work (CSCW) is centrally concerned with teamwork, learning, problem solving, knowledge building, task accomplishment and other cognitive achievements by small groups of people. There are many theories useful for framing the cognitive work that groups undertake in CSCW settings, and they may in principle not be reducible to a single theory. This Chapter will look in details into the origin of the digital collaboration, its importance for work environments and its types. Also it will explain the different digital collaboration tools.

6.1 Introduction

Collaboration can be defined as the experience that integrates people, processes and technology. The continuous development in the field of information systems aims to find new methods to improve the interactions between people and the information they need to communicate, which represents the center of enhancing productivity at business environment. The objective of the continuous improvements of the collaboration technology is to allow people to share information as naturally as possible, by empowering people to work and share without limits and by engaging them in the process of collaboration. These goals have to be met through providing people with best tools that allow them to connect with peers and organizations. Another term that can be considered as the synonym for digital work collaboration is Computer-Supported Cooperative Work (CSCW) [1], which

V. Morabito, *Trends and Challenges in Digital Business Innovation*,
DOI: 10.1007/978-3-319-04307-4_6, © Springer International Publishing Switzerland 2014

started as an effort by technologists to learn from different kinds of scientists and specialists such as economists, social psychologists, anthropologists, organizational theorists, educators, and others who could explain and provide information about group activity. It also became a place for system developers to share experiences about technical opportunities and limitations. Examples of the collaboration systems include desktop and video conferencing systems, collaborative authorship applications, electronic mail as well as refinements and extensions, and electronic meeting rooms or group support systems [2].

The development of the previous mentioned ISs aims to enhance collaboration at work environments and is categorized by Kay [3] into three categories. The first one is the *electronic communication tools*, in which, the purpose of these instruments is to facilitate information sharing by giving the people the ability to send messages, files, data or documents to each other. This category includes e-mail, instant messaging, fax machines, voice mail and web publishing tools. The second class is the *electronic conferencing tools*, in which, they provide more interactive methods of sharing data and information. This type typically includes teleconferencing and videoconferencing tools. However, new technologies have emerged in order to have more interactive techniques for conferencing and data sharing. Examples of these technologies comprise data conferencing which lets a set of PCs that are connected together to share and view a common whiteboard which users can add to its content or modify it. Another example is the electronic meeting systems which include conferencing rooms that are enhanced with large-screen digital projectors that are connected to several PCs.

The third category of digital collaboration is the *collaborative management tools*, which simplify and enhance the management and organization of group activities. This category includes four technologies. The first one is the electronic group calendars which facilitate events scheduling and meetings with multiple members. Also, they have the ability to automate reminders and alarms for all group participants. The second technology is workflow systems that help in managing tasks, due dates and documents. The third on is the project management systems which help schedule, track and chart the steps in a project and have the capacity to help plan, organize, and manage resource pools and develop resource estimates. The fourth and last one is the *knowledge management systems* that make it possible to collect, organize, manage, and share information in a variety of formats. Thus, they can identify, create, represent, distribute, and enable the adoption of insights and experiences [3]. There are many benefits of implementing collaboration systems at any business; for example, they allow the organizations to:

- Have more flatten organizational hierarchy which can be reflected in a better and easier communication among the different levels within the organization.
- Provide the ability to personalize communications to enhance the quality and speed of decisions.
- Save time by reducing delivery times, simplify workflows by having already configured workflows routes, and increase workforce interaction and productivity.

- Have people who are not in the same geographical location to work together on a project. This is very beneficial for companies with offices in multiple cities and countries.
- Establish trust and understanding across time zones within teams from different functional departments by having frequent video discussions.
- Customers would have faster access to information and personal experiences which would improve their responsiveness.
- Complying with environmental concerns by reducing travel and greenhouse gas emissions by meeting virtually and supporting telecommuting.

6.2 Collaboration Types

Salopek [4] has divided or conceptualized collaboration into four types. These types depend on two variables, the time and place. These categories are:

- *Same Time (synchronous) and Different Place (remote)*, which represents the remote interaction, and it is supported by technologies such as electronic meeting systems, videoconferencing systems and instant messaging software applications like email and chat programs.
- *Same Time (synchronous) and Same Place (collocated)*, which characterizes the face to face interaction, and it can happen using meeting rooms, shared tables and whiteboards.
- *Different time (asynchronous) and Different Place (remote)*, which is accomplished by continuous communication and coordination, and it uses systems like electronic meeting system, blogs and workflow management system to have the work done.
- *Different Time (asynchronous) and Same Place (collocated)*, which represents the continuous work on the same task, and it can occur in meeting rooms and by using large displays and whiteboards.

The previous explained collaboration categories can be illustrated in a form of matrix, in which the X axis represents the time and the Y axis illustrates the place (see Fig. 6.1). This matrix is first presented by [5].

6.3 Cross-Organizational and Cross-Border IS/IT Collaboration

Globalization has an important effect on the way that IS or IT develops. As a result, many investments in the field of IS or IT have deployed and being implemented cross organizations that are located in different countries and world regions. Cross-system integration and collaboration technologies play essential

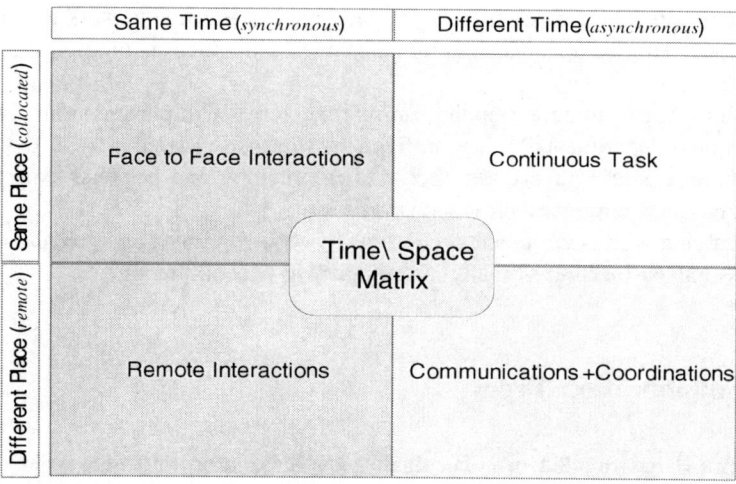

Fig. 6.1 The CSCW matrix. Adapted from [5]

roles, however, economic, social and other external factors are also important to be considered for large IS and IT projects to be successful and productive. IS productivity is the focal point for many academic literatures, unlike the links between international and multinational collaboration processes and its benefits and contributions in the digital markets, which have been studied rarely [6].

There is a big difference of the influence of the digital collaboration in the global economy in comparison to a single country or region. For example, there is a difference in the infrastructures from the development level and maturity points of view. There are also external factors such as regulatory, legal, social, and cultural environments, which may also vary substantially. Another reason is about the different or even conflicting goals that the various stakeholders in global IS projects often have. Managing teams that are globally distributed requires a more demanding standard of management and collaboration to those needed for more typical virtual groups within the same economy or region. Researchers and practitioners need to investigate the previously mentioned causes and other issues that affect the collaboration between people either in a positive or negative way, in order for information systems to be more successful and productive in the global economy [6].

However, confusion can happen because of the lack of common understanding of the Cross Organizational Collaboration (COC), since, a thorough examination of examples of COC reveals that there are many opportunities associated with this term. For example, businesses could implement cross-organizational knowledge management to unite their abilities for product development, but they might also collaborate to increase the efficiency of products replacement in their supply chain processes. Thus, it can be observed that there are many varieties of different contexts in which COC can happen. Such cases result in various conceptualizations that can be overlapping and contradicting [7].

It is safe to say that most COC approaches aim to use IT as an enabler. However, in contrast to electronic collaboration which is broadly defined as collaboration between individuals by using the new advancement in electronic technologies, the topic of our investigation is the integration and collaboration of people, information systems, and processes across different organizations to accomplish a pre-defined task or objective by using digital and electronic means. Therefore, it can be referred to digital cross-organizational collaboration (digital COC) as the subject of interest [7].

Digital collaboration covers many fields such as learning, design, process management and e-commerce. This capability of digital collaboration is empowered by the wide spread use of internet by people. Today, many technologies exist to support long-distance teamwork on any aspect of a group project by only using the internet as a way of information sharing. In the past, these technologies could be so expensive, which prohibits communities from having such means of knowledge sharing, or they had steep learning curves, especially for elderly communities who are uncomfortable with the advanced technologies.

Today many of the best electronic tools for information sharing are not only easy to use, but also almost free. Such tools provides possibilities to work on group related tasks in a collaborative style which allow participants to write and edit shared files, track versions and provide them with other videoconferencing capabilities, which all occur via the Internet [8]. The new development in the field of digital collaboration tools has opened the opportunity to solve problems such as:

- sharing large digital files among team members that are located in different geographical locations;
- keeping databases that are being used by different users in different locations synchronized and up to date;
- reducing the costs of transportation, phone calls, or mailing physical media.

Digital collaboration will only prove its importance if companies are able to utilize the new technologies and advancements in this arena to carry out processes such as sales, marketing and development from distance and over the network [8].

However, the increasing importance and demand for technology support services combined with the decreasing budgets and staff resources create several challenges for information technology (IT) departments. One way to tackle such an issue is the collaboration. This can happen by developing, e.g., what is known as a *Community of Practice* (CoP) [9]. The aim of this community is to develop relationships and create more collaboration opportunities among institutions [10]. The key concepts behind this idea are the communities of practice, the community coordinator and the technology steward. Next section will discuss these concepts in details.

6.3.1 Communities of Practice

Community of practice (CoP) is a term that is widely used in several disciplines such as knowledge management, organizational learning and education. CoP can be used to serve one or more distinct purposes within an organization, and is considered as a resources sharing platform that supports digital collaborative networks for those who have the same interest [10].

The term *Community Coordinator* (CC) refers to a member of the community who is responsible about the leadership role within this community and has the task of planning, coordinating and facilitating personal interactions, meetings and other activities, and has the purpose of consistently advance the general organization of the CoP. This role is considered as the most important factor for the success of the community. The key functions of this role can be summarized as follow according to Koan [10]:

- identify the important and new developments in the domain of interest;
- plan, organize and facilitate the community's events;
- informally link community members, across organizational units' boundaries;
- foster the development of community members' skills and abilities;
- help to build community's practices including the knowledge base, best practices, tools and methods, lessons learned and learning events;
- assess the situation of the community and evaluate its contribution to the members' knowledge and the organization's productivity.

Moreover, the way to support continued interactions among members of a community is to utilize technologies for facilitating on-going electronic communication and ways for storing and accessing the artifacts produced by the community. The person who is responsible about doing that for the community is called *technology steward* (TS) and the role function can be described as a person who helps a community to choose, configure, and use technologies and tools to best suit its needs. This position is different from the IT support one as he or she stays engaged with the changing goals and needs of the community and is typically also a member. However, this role can be distinct from that of the community coordinator and can be performed by a different member [10].

Taking these issues into account, the potential benefits of developing such a community can be evaluated from different perceptions. For example, in a contribution by Koan [10], a group of data collection methods that include interviews, short questionnaires and online survey were used to evaluate the value of such communities from two points of view. The first one is from the participants' perspectives, which data showed that they valued the knowledge sharing and collaboration and they believe that the time and effort involved was worthwhile. The second one is from the leaders of the organizations that the participants are coming from. They all strongly agreed that the collaboration could expose their staff members to new ideas, help them improve existing skills and develop new ones, solve common and unusual problems, and all except one respondent (who disagreed), agreed or strongly agreed with the idea that increased collaboration could help their staff improvement processes [10].

Thus, technology is an essential part of the educational experience. Nevertheless, because of shrinking resources and increasing demand for services, the IT specialists who support that kind of technology experience constant pressure to do more activities and perform services with fewer resources. However, fortunately, those specialists don't have to be alone while facing such a challenge. Inter-organizational communities of practice can transform and improve the way IT departments do business. IT leaders can address those challenges by encouraging and supporting employees who work for them to move beyond institutional boundaries, they can find new resources and solutions to their problems. Collaborating with colleagues from other organizations is a strategy for success, that can be achieved by implementing healthy communities of practice [10].

6.4 Digital Collaboration Systems and Ideas

This section will provide investigation about the technologies and systems that are used to play the roles of digital collaboration tools. This examination will look at the usage of the tool as well as its limitations.

6.4.1 Electronic Messaging Systems

Electronic messaging systems refer to the systems that provide one to one communication tools with messaging infrastructure such as email and instant messenger functionalities. Messaging systems use the available networks and computing assets that are shared by the company in addition to the services shared by the other parties in the world [4]. Thus, the individual services, which together referred to as electronic messaging, are developed to address a specific need and are designed to make effective utilization of resources in a given situation.

Therefore, different technologies can be used to develop messages exchanging systems in order to keep with the company's policies regarding appropriate use. Some typical guidelines for various services include:

- email and instant messaging, which enables person-to-person communication;
- email list which provide the space for small group discussions;
- forum and chat services, which give the opportunity for large group discussions.

Despite its benefits for the organization, electronic messaging systems cannot be fully secure and reliable, since messages are using store and forward technology that involve many systems in the process of exchanging messages. These systems could not be fully secured [4].

6.4.2 Electronic Meeting Systems

Electronic meeting systems (EMS) provide real time conferencing functionalities that may be managed by either local or remote resources. They are the computer applications that support creative and collaborative way of finding solutions for the emerging problem and for decision-making of people inside a single organization or across several ones [4]. The term is synonymous with *Group Support Systems (GSS)* and essentially synonymous with *Group Decision Support Systems (GDSS)*. Electronic meeting systems form a class of applications for computer supported cooperative work. Based on their features, they can help to find solutions for many harmful and inhibitive features while working as group [11].

This software system is a suite of tools that provide configurable features of collaborative working methods; the latter can be used to produce predictable and repeatable ways of collaboration among people working together for the same goal or outcome. In these systems, typically users have their own computers, and each one of them can participate in the current running session simultaneously. This way of sharing and participation can eliminate the waiting time for users to speak and contribute to the content of the session. It provides the opportunity for the appropriate people to contribute, allowing the group to focus on the creative ideas, instead of their available resources [11].

Most EMS systems provide the standard functionalities such as brainstorming, categorization, discussion, voting, agenda and automatic minutes. However, these systems differ in many aspects such as handling the communicated information and the ways they are administrated and integrated within the IT environment of the business. Moreover, modern EMS support both synchronous conferences, where participants meet at the same time and asynchronous meetings, where participants participate at different periods of times [12].

However, electronic meeting systems need to be distinguished from classic groupware and from web conferencing systems. The main difference from groupware is the degree of collaboration. Groupware provides support for collaboration within groups of participants where their contributions are recognizable. In contrast, EMS enables the group to produce an artifact in a cooperative way, in which the whole group is responsible about it and can take credit for it. Also, during the execution of a business process, both groupware applications and EMS support and complement each other: the groupware provides teams with capabilities related to researching and documents creation during the preparation stage for an EMS session or throughout the implementation of the results of such a conference. Moreover, web conferencing systems and electronic meeting systems complement each other's capabilities during the online conference or workshop. EMS systems extend the web conferencing system by providing tools that enable interactive production and documentation of group results. In contrast, web conferencing software complement EMS with screen-sharing as well as the ability for the voice interaction functionality that is necessary in synchronous online conferences and does not exist in EMS [12]. The idea behind the electronic meeting systems is to improve group efficiency, and satisfaction. EMS supported meetings overcome traditional face-to-face conferences and workshops in the following ways, according to [11] and [12]:

- achieving increased openness and less personal bias through anonymity;
- the advantage of 'Any-place' or online capability which overcomes the barriers that are related to the time and travel cost;
- increased interactivity and participation by having the ability of parallelization;
- the ability of conducting more complicated analysis that require voting and analysis in real time;
- the possibility of decreasing preparation efforts by using meeting templates;
- the ability to have automatic, comprehensive and neutral documentation of the discussions and outcomes.

However, on other hand, those systems used to have some disadvantages that have been overcome by the technological progress. Examples of these drawbacks and how the new technological advancements solve them are explained in the following points:

- The ability of the internet to provide easy access to remote materials.
- The previously high demands for specialists have been cut greatly by utilizing systems that can be supported by its regular users.
- Users became more familiar with web conferencing tools which helped in overcoming the traditional cultural barriers that hindered the use of such systems.
- The cost of such systems before using the web has been reduced, likewise.
- The number of people who can work on systems simultaneously and efficiently is actually grown.

6.4.3 Asynchronous Conferencing Systems

In this category of digital collaboration tools, the exchange of the content can occur instantly or over the time using tools such as bulletin board systems [4]. The formal term used in computer-facilitated communication, collaboration and learning is *asynchronous conferencing* and is used to define technologies that are associated with interaction delay among the contributors in such conferences. The concept behind its usage is in contrast to *synchronous conferencing*, which indicates 'chat' applications that provide its users to communicate in a simultaneous manner in real time. The communication in such systems does not require face-to-face conversation and it can last for undefined and long time. It is most useful in situations that involve online discussions and idea sharing which are suitable for learning scenarios or for circumstances when work forces, who are involved in problems solving tasks, are located over separated geographical locations [13]. Examples of such systems include bulletin board, email, online forums or polls, blogs, wiki pages, newsgroup, social networking sites and shared calendars [14]. Nonsynchronous conferencing offers its members the flexibility and control over the time dimension they need to produce an artifact. It offers anonymous participation and can encourage reluctant members/learners to share their points of view and lets the participants to contribute and interact simultaneously on different topics [14]. Due to the time constraint, however, the delay between the message exchanges usually leads to situations where people loss their interest which in turn may affect the coherence of the conversation. This can happen when too many entries are made in very little time, which makes it hard to have a useful outcome of the discussion.

This method of collaboration provides more suitable way for the participant, since that the worker can contribute from anywhere, as long as there is access to the conference or the forum through the internet. This feature may be considered as an advantage for those who work from home or other geographical locations. It also provides the advantage that the subject under investigation can be reached at any time, which provides the people who are involved in the discussion with the possibility to think and reply. However, there is an absence of physical and social "existence" in these types of systems, which can affect the progress and outcome of the discussion. Also, the emotions are missed from such virtual discussions, which can lead to misinterpretation of the contributed entries [14].

On the disadvantages side of such systems, the discussion thread might get deleted because of either a technical failure or due to the fact that people might lose their interest in the topic under investigation. Threads with older access time might also be replaced by ones with new entries.

6.4.4 Document Handling Systems

Document handling systems or document management systems (DMS) provide tools for management, storage and editing functionalities that can be used on a group of documents [4]. These systems are used to track the different versions, store and archive electronic documents. It is often referred to as a component of *Enterprise Content Management* (*ECM*) systems and related to digital asset management, document imaging, workflow systems and records management systems. DMSs commonly provide storage, versioning, metadata, security, as well as indexing and retrieval capabilities.

The issues that accompany the use of such systems are the security, data integrity and quality, standards that govern the way these systems work, user compatibility, and the way the workflow is pre-configured in such software applications. Several associations in industry issue their own standards of document control criteria that are used in their particular field [4]. Moreover, government regulations instruct the companies that are working in certain industries to control their documents in a specified way and certain format. Examples of such industries include accounting, food safety, medical device manufacturing, Healthcare, and Information technology [4].

6.4.5 Social Software and Collaborative Systems and Tools

Nowadays, people are using social networking massively. This is happening because of the increasing role of the internet in enabling communication between people. Traditional forms of communications, such as telephones, mail and even face-to-face meetings, are slowly being replaced by computer based systems where different kinds of socialization are enhanced through media sharing, reflection on past experiences and a bundle of additional services, supporting socialization among people [15]. Based on the previous facts, organizations are trying to integrate social collaboration capabilities into their strategies, operations, and processes. Whether it is with customers, partners, or employees, these organizations use social collaboration tools to improve efficiency, solve problems, create opportunities, boost productivity, and drive innovation that makes them more competitive and successful.

The term *social software* is general and it applies to systems used outside the work environment or workplace. Software products such as email, calendaring, text chatting, wiki, and bookmarking belong to social software category. However, when these applications are used at work to facilitate the accomplishment of business tasks, processes and objectives, then they are called *collaborative software*.

Collaborative software is an application designed to assist people involved in a common task in order to achieve their predetermined goals. These applications aim to transform the way the documents and media files are shared to enable more effective team collaboration. Therefore it is important to understand the differences in human relations and communications, because it is necessary to ensure that appropriate technologies are employed to meet the interaction's needs [15]. Collaboration means individuals working together in a coordinated manner, to achieve a pre-defined goal. The use of such software at the work place stimulates a *Collaborative Working Environment* (*CWE*) that supports individuals as well as those who work as a team regardless of their geographical locations by providing them with the necessary equipment that aids communication, collaboration and the process of problem solving. Moreover, collaborative software can support project management related tasks, such as jobs allocation, deadlines management, and shared calendars [16].

Examples of such collaboration software in the market include: Microsoft SharePoint, IBM Lotus notes and Google apps for business. The latter one contains many useful applications such as Google Doc for file sharing among team members, Google Calendar for scheduling meeting at times that works for everyone with features such as reminders, Google Drive for storing, sharing and accessing files from everywhere, Google Sheets that enable spreadsheet management with easy charts and discussion style comments, and finally, Google Slides that allow users to create presentations together.

Also, Siglin [17] has provided examples of other video collaboration software. The first one is provided by Accordent Inc., which its history is based on rich-media capture. This company produced the Capture Station and PresenterPRO products which have gained the ability to capture live content that synchronizes with PowerPoint, webpages, and live video streams. Moreover, beyond just the live streaming capabilities, the company has polling, chat, and other real-time feedback applications that help in the delivery process to a diverse audience within the enterprise. Another example is produced by Adobe Systems Incorporation that introduced a collaborative tool called Adobe Story that provides the creative and enterprise customers with the ability to jointly create a video script.

Taking the above issues into account, collaboration tool refers to any tool that helps people collaborates. These tools have the ability to promote collaboration among people in general and within work team members in particular. The ideal criteria that the collaboration tools have to meet are to foster collaboration, to be easy to learn and use, and to have built-in or easy to use backup. In what follows, we are going to list and explain some of the most adopted collaborative tools in the market such as Skype, Dropbox, and others. Moreover, it is worth noting that these technologies can be considered as a representative "type" of the main common features available at present. However, in the near future further evolution of the information and communication technologies may reconfigure and in some case substitute some of them.

Skype

This application is a free voice over Internet Protocol (VOIP) service and instant messaging that is developed by the recently acquired company by the software giant, Microsoft. Skype can be used to meet the following goals:

- calling and video conferencing over the internet;
- train team members on using software using screen sharing ability with others;
- cheap calls on landlines and mobile devices;
- instant text messaging from computer to computer;
- conduct meetings and conferences.

Dropbox

Dropbox is a file hosting service that offers many capabilities such as cloud storage and file synchronization. It allows users to share contents through folders, which they can create on their computers. Dropbox synchronizes those folders in order to appear the same folder (with the same contents) despite the media or the device that is used to view them. This product can be used to meet the following goals:

- storing and backing up any kind of file;
- immediate synchronization and sharing of files across computers and among users who are located in different geographical locations;
- sending and sharing files that are large to email.

Google Drive and Google Docs

Google Drive is a file storage and synchronization service provided by Google and it provides users with features related to cloud storage, file sharing and documents editing in a collaborative manner. In this service, the files shared publicly on Google Drive can be searched with web search engines. Google Docs is a freeware web-based office suite offered by Google within its Google Drive service. It allows users to create and edit documents, spreadsheets and presentations online while collaborating with other users live. With Google Docs, users and companies can do the following:

- create, collaborate on, share and edit documents online;
- collaborate in a real time, which means that the users can see the changes instantly;
- manage different revisions of a document;
- create online forms for conducting community surveys.

Microsoft SkyDrive

SkyDrive is a file hosting service from Microsoft that allows users to upload and sync files to cloud storage and then access them from a Web browser or their local device. It allows users to keep the files private, share them with contacts, or make the files public, which means that users do not require a Microsoft account to access them. The features of the Microsoft SkyDrive service include:

- It allows users to upload, create, edit, and share Microsoft Office documents directly within a Web browser.
- It provides the ability to integrate with Microsoft office and outlook.
- Users can share the documents on social networks.
- It supports geo-location data for photos uploaded onto the service.

Microsoft OneNote

OneNote is a software from Microsoft that enables a free-form information gathering and provides capabilities for multi-user teamwork. It can accept entries such as users' handwritten or typed notes, sketches and audio explanations. Notes can be shared with other OneNote users over the Internet or a network, and it is available for different operating systems. Also, Microsoft offers a web-based version of OneNote as part of SkyDrive or Office Web Apps, providing users with ability to modify notes via a Web browser. This software allows companies and users to:

- create notes, outlines, clippings of websites, and collections of images;
- share and collaborate the created notes;
- access the notes from mobiles, Web or desktop devices;
- outlines collaborative presentations;
- maintain a shared repository for research and project notes;
- maintain a digital field journal.

6.4.6 Online Communities

Online community represents a virtual community that exits on the internet and the participants in this body are interacting with each other remotely. They are websites that are organized by their own members who can access interactive discussions and share documents and media files [4]. These communities can be represented by information systems that allow members to post content or to let a limited number of members to start posts or new subjects, such as Weblogs. Online communities have also become a way for work collaboration among team members at the work environments, especially when they are located in different geographical places in the global organizations. However, noteworthy socio-technical change may have arisen from the fast spread of such Internet-based social platforms [18].

It is essential in such virtual presence to have the necessary technologies to keep members interested, manage assets, and support community relations during the development of the online community. Everything needs to be well managed in order for the virtual community to be effective and useful to its participants. Therefore, the developers have to consider members' ability to use and manage such technology in order to avoid the loss of interest that can arise by some participants. Also, the developers need to keep the community updated with what attracts its members to participate in regular bases. Moreover, it is important to have specified sections for members' feedbacks because their needs can change all the times. Additionally, due to the fact that there are barely any face-to-face communications in the virtual community environment, developers need to make sure that the community members don't have any problems with interacting with other participants.

The intention behind developing the online communities is to encourage people to exchange knowledge in a collaborative manner since it focuses basically on information sharing. Finally, these virtual societies encourage self-learners to discuss and solve real-world problems/situations as well as focus on collaborative patterns of teamwork and thinking.

6.4.7 Crowdsourcing

Hammon and Hippner [19] define Crowdsourcing as *"the act of outsourcing tasks originally performed inside an organization, or assigned externally in form of a business relationship, to an undefinably large, heterogeneous mass of potential actors"* [19]. This process combines the efforts of numerous self-identified participants, where each contributor of their own initiative adds a small portion to the greater result. In crowdsourcing, a community or "crowd" that is often coordinated over the internet is invited to participate in tasks normally accomplished by companies or group of specialists. An invitation to a crowd might have the goal of generating a large amount of artifacts, or to distribute the required job among many participants. Those using crowdsourcing techniques expect that having many participants to solve a problem increases the possibility of generating a significant innovative solution [20]. The incentive to participate can have a monetary and/or non-monetary nature.

Crowdsourcing is considered as an innovative way of re-structuring certain tasks in a way that the power of several participants can be combined to achieve multiple possible ends. The big benefit of such an approach for organizations and researchers is that it decreases the costs by taking the advantages of talent and time of others. Also, contributors can also achieve some benefits for themselves by interacting with experts, since they can practice their unprofessional skills while practicing their hobby [20].

Examples of Crowdsourcing include the Amazon Mechanical Turk, in which the users can complete variety of tasks such as labeling images with keywords, which provides opportunities to judge the relevance of search results, transcribing podcasts, finding contact information or labeling data to prepare it for the use in machine learning [21]. However, Crowdsourcing has been innovatively used for big projects as well. For example, computer scientists at Carnegie Mellon University have created a project called reCAPTCHA, which uses humans' abilities and intelligence to identify distorted words on websites. Moreover, many other websites such as Google Books and the New York Times, use this kind of service for text digitization [22].

Nevertheless, despite its powerful features, many research areas related to Crowdsourcing need to be covered. It is important to study the possibilities and limitations of crowdsourcing. One important area of research is to understand the motivations and rewards that attract participants and how these prizes can be different depending on the different markets. However, motivation may not be only based on external benefits. For example, intrinsic incentives such as fun and friendship could be powerful methods for motivation, and may have positive effects on the quality of the results. Kittur [22] argues that more research is needed to understand the influences involved in the different stages of crowdsourcing such as tasks' reception, acceptance and completion [22]. Also, it is necessary to create plans for incentive mechanisms and frameworks that suit existing business models and real world systems such as workflow, human-provided services, as well as crowdsourcing. These plans should have the ability to monitor crowds actions and, on the one hand, to adapt at runtime incentive mechanisms to prevent various negative effects such as free riding, multitasking, biasing, anchoring, and preferential attachment; on the other hand, to be able to switch when it is needed between different evaluation methods, rewarding actions, and incentive situations at runtime, while considering the overall costs cut [23].

Moreover, it is important to understand how to structure jobs to meet the requirements of the various markets. Kittur [22] offers the following example: in Mechanical Turk, tasks that take a long time or have unclear payment mechanisms or description tends to be less appealing for participants than short, simple jobs that have a high certainty of the prize, even if it is lower that long and difficult tasks. Dividing work into short and simple subtasks may be more suitable for some areas, while chunking work to avoid the switching costs of people choosing another task to do could be more appropriate to some other markets. Therefore, it can be concluded that matching the format of the work to the characteristics of the market could possibly lead to a faster outcome with better quality [22].

In conclusion, Crowdsourcing is a powerful method to solve a variety of problems in faster and less expensive ways in comparison with traditional ones; however, more research is needed for not only to treat crowd workers as simple sensors or processors, but also to join their human intelligence and creativity. As a result, instead of focusing on simple and independent tasks, it would be possible to work on more complex jobs where people need to work together in a collaborative manner [22].

6.5 Case Studies

In this section we investigate some digital collaboration at work environments related case studies, providing explanation about their role for the business success.

The first case study is about a project called reCAPTCHA and it is about using humans' abilities to detect the meaning of distorted words on websites. This project is initiated by computer scientists from Carnegie Mellon University, in which people are collaboratively using their humans' thinking, processing and understanding abilities to identify two unclear words on websites they use. The distorted words were chosen from scanned books and digital archives, which computers cannot read using Optical Character Recognition (OCR) technology. Consequently, as the people read and enter the two words into specified fields at the websites, in order to identify themselves as humans and not automated services or programs, they contribute to digitizing books and media that are not recognizable by computers. The creators of this project hope that reCAPTCHA continues to have a positive impact on modern society by helping to digitize human knowledge [24].

POINT OF ATTENTION: There are tasks that cannot be accomplished by machines regardless how smart and fast they are. In such cases, there are no alternatives for humans' brains. Moreover, despite the size of the work that needs to be accomplished, crowdsourcing provides an effective way of humans' collaboration that can participate positively in the project success.

The second case study discusses the digital collaboration in educational webinars. This word is combination of 'web' and 'seminar' which refers to a seminar that is conducted over the web. This technology provides a platform for people to communicate and collaborate over separated geographical locations by using the internet as a two-way of information and data sharing, which would lead to higher effectiveness and involvement by the participants. The Webinar platform is entering the education field after it proved its effectiveness in the business arena. This technology is investigated by [25], in which the authors studied the impact of using webinar in the field of education. In their research, they explained Campus Connect Initiative as a project that was launched in 2004 by Infosys Technologies Ltd as a partnership between industry and academia, aiming to enhance the quality and quantity of the talented and skilled people in India. The target of Campus Connect team was to reach more than 500 academic partners in a professional and cost effective manner for sharing many related aspects such as technology, skills, and domain knowledge. This required reaching the academic institutions across many cities and deliver lectures which required about 5 hours of travel. However, travelling for that time wasn't an efficient approach. Hence, the team decided to use WebEx, which is a globally acclaimed online meeting and collaboration applications and software services provider. The introduced technology has succeeded to achieve high satisfaction rates from both the members of the faculties and the students.

POINT OF ATTENTION: Despite the benefits that can be gained through utilizing digital communication and collaboration platforms, it is important as well to consider the challenges that accompany this usage such as the need for high end infrastructure, online helpdesk and support, cost of hosting and licensing, restricted audience involvement, and the limitations regarding the usage of the multimedia materials.

Furthermore, the benefits that the Infosys team has achieved include effective collaboration and information sharing among the presenters and the participants, great target access, no location dependency, and interactive platform.

6.6 Summary

In this Chapter, detailed explanations about the concepts related to digital collaboration definition, characteristics, types and its advantages for long distance teamwork have been provided. Also, it explained the importance of digital collaboration across institutions as well as the systems and tools that are available to play the roles of collaboration applications at work environments or educational institutions. Moreover, it provided a description for the crowdsourcing concept as well as the incentives and rewards in social computing. Digital work and collaboration is basically about using digital devices, open source data and cloud technology to share knowledge, manage information and to have the user generated work shared and contributed by communities of people regardless of time or place. Furthermore, it allows a broader network of participants to collaborate and work together on projects. However, despite its potential benefits, the challenges associated with the adoption of the digital work and collaboration systems need to be well addressed in order to know how to utilize these systems in an optimal way and to get the best out of them. Examples of these limitations include the storage capacity, the speed of the internet and issues related to security.

Finally, the Chapter has discussed case studies, confirming the importance, benefits and issues associated with digital work and collaboration. These case studies show many considerations that have to be well-thought-out before introducing the tools that represent this new technological enhancement.

References

1. Schmidt K, Bannon L (2013) Constructing CSCW: the first quarter century. Comput Support Coop Work 22:345–372. doi:10.1007/s10606-013-9193-7
2. Grudin J (1994) Computer-supported cooperative work: history and focus (Long Beach Calif) 27:19–26
3. Kay R (2004) Roots of digital collaboration. Computerworld 38:41
4. Salopek JJ (2000) Digital collaboration. Train Dev 54:38–43
5. Baecker RM, Grudin J, Buxton WAS, Greenberg S (1995) Readings in human-computer interaction: toward the year 2000 (2nd ed). System, p 595
6. Romano NC, Pick JB (2012) Cross-organizational and cross-border IS/IT collaboration. Electron Mark 22:5–7. doi:10.1007/s12525-012-0084-4
7. Madlberger M, Roztocki N (2010) Digital cross-organizational collaboration: a metatriangulation review. In: Proceedings of 43rd Hawaii international conference on system sciences, pp 1–10
8. Masie E (1999) Digital collaboration enables long-distance teamwork. Comput Resell News 44
9. Wenger E (1998) Communities of practice: learning, meaning, and identity. Syst Thinker 9:2–3. doi:10.2277/0521663636
10. Koan RM (2011) IT collaboration across institutions. In: Proceedings of 39th annual ACM SIGUCCS conference, pp 87–94
11. Martz WB, Vogel DR, Nunamaker JF (1992) Electronic meeting systems. Decis Support Syst 8:141–158

12. Nunamaker JF, Dennis AR, Valacich J, Vogel DR, George J (1991) Electronic meeting systems to support group work. Commun ACM 34:40–61
13. Schrire S (2004) Interaction and cognition in asynchronous computer conferencing. Instr Sci 32:475–502. doi:10.1007/s11251-004-2518-7
14. King K, Ellis TJ (2009) Comparison of social presence in voice-based and text-based asynchronous computer conferences. In: Proceedings of 42nd Hawaii international conference on system sciences, pp 1–10
15. Bhana I, Johnson D (2006) Developing collaborative social software. Comput Sci ICCS 3992:581–586
16. Software C (2013) Collaborative software. In: Wikipedia. http://en.wikipedia.org/wiki/Collaborative_software
17. Siglin T (2011) Video collaboration tools. Streaming Media, pp 60–64
18. Stewart T (2010) Online communities. Behav Inf Technol 29:555–556. doi:10.1080/0144929X.2010.523615
19. Hammon L, Hippner H (2012) Crowdsourcing. Bus Inf Syst Eng 4:163–166. doi:10.1007/s12599-012-0215-7
20. Shepherd H (2012) Crowdsourcing. Contexts 11:10–11. doi:10.1177/1536504212446453
21. Doan A, Ramakrishnan R, Halevy AY (2011) Crowdsourcing systems on the World-Wide Web. Commun ACM 54:86. doi:10.1145/1924421.1924442
22. Kittur A (2010) Crowdsourcing, collaboration and creativity. XRDS Crossroads ACM Mag Students 17:22–26. doi:10.1145/1869086.1869096
23. Scekic O, Truong H-L, Dustdar S (2013) Incentives and rewarding in social computing. Commun ACM 56:72–82. doi:10.1145/2461256.2461275
24. Ahn L Von, Maurer B, Mcmillen C, Abraham D, Blum M (2008) reCAPTCHA: human-based character recognition via web security measures. Science (80-) 321:1465–1468
25. Verma A, Singh A (2010) Webinar—education through digital collaboration. J Emerg Technol Web Intell 2:131–136. doi:10.4304/jetwi.2.2.131-136

Chapter 7
Digital Business Identity

Abstract This Chapter explores the identity challenges for businesses both as security and privacy issues. Furthermore, digital identity will be discussed also with regard to brand management in current digital ecosystems, and the consequent constant revision of value propositions and business models for re-branding a company digital business, due to strict time-to market. Case studies conclude the Chapter providing insights and points of attention suitable to support IT executive as well as other CxO managers in facing one of current main challenges of digital business.

7.1 Introduction

The digital trends discussed in the first Part of this volume contribute to an inedited blurring and openness of companies' boundaries, by changing the infrastructure at the basis of digital business, increasing the volume of data stored, information production as well as the flexibility and capacity of sourcing activities (often involving costumers and final users, likewise). Furthermore, the advent and the actual leadership consolidation of companies such as Facebook, Twitter, or Google, allow creating digital business as a platform exploiting the above infrastructure.

In a sense, the shift from value chains to value constellations, outlined by Normann and Ramìrez [1] in the last decade of last century, has been followed by a consequent shift from a concept of market as related to more or less stable industries, to a digital market vision based on multi-sided platforms [2, 3]. As a consequence of the digitalization discussed in the Chap. 3 of this book, companies from different industries actually move their business or part of it on digital platforms where they compete often through "encounters" with co-opetitors[1] and

---

[1] When in co-opetitition companies can be competitors and partners due to a partial common set of interests, depending on the specific goals of a given business at hand [4, 5].

customers, in a continuous reconfiguration of traditional industries and the rapid creation of new bundled sectors and market based on new digital products and services.

Taking these issues into account, companies see their identity as represented by their brands, constantly challenged by new digital business scenarios, rapidly changing market roles, with constantly new entrants and new customers' needs; thus, digital business identity is often characterized by very short life-span due to the velocity of new digital products and services design and distribution. The consequence is a continual revision of value propositions and business models for re-branding a company digital business. Besides these strategy and marketing facets of digital business identity, the technical and social challenges to privacy and security related to this openness and "instability" [6] of digital competition are worth mentioning. As pointed out by Aral et al. [7] social media platforms raise significant management questions such as, e.g., how to right balance the business needs for growth with privacy concerns. In what follows, we will discuss the two issues, starting from the latter, trying to elicit the key issues for the management companies that need to effective design and control their digital business identity. As for privacy and security factors, we are going to consider the technological perspectives that often prevail in their discussion, while abstracting from it the main management drivers and challenges.

7.2 Privacy and Security Drivers and Challenges

Chapter 5 on IT consumerization has shown some of the main risks associated to the BYOD emerging trend in organization. In particular, the Chapter has shown that the decision makers need to develop security models for employee-owned devices, addressing key concerns such as, e.g., managing diverse mobile platforms, protecting information across different and heterogeneous mobile devices, and defining data ownership. However, this is only a part of the current challenges that a company has to face in order to protect its identity at internal level, in terms of privacy of data and security of its own information infrastructure. Apart from IT consumerization, other phenomena such as the diffusion and pervasivity of social networks and mobile services (discussed in Chaps. 3 and 4, respectively) create major concerns for a business digital identity as well as for citizens at global level.

Considering cybercrime, as reported by Paul Hyman on the Communications of the ACM (CACM) [8] on March 2013, security companies evaluations about the costs of the cybercrime worldwide were $110 billion every year according to Symantec Corp.; while approximately $1 trillion according to Mc Afee Inc. However, apart from the presence of no standard mechanism for accounting for losses or the failure to detect losses, Hyman pointed out also that the following identity-related motivations security experts see as constraints and causes for a limited accuracy of costs estimations [8]:

- *Failure to report*, for example, due to the unwillingness of organizations victims to report the issue, perceiving it as a damage for their public image or, as we call it in this Chapter, digital identity [8].
- *Self-selection bias*, due to the type of population considered in the surveys; for example, bias can come from the contrary of the above mentioned failure to report issue (i.e. mostly organizations having not detected damages may be available to respond) or from a consequence of great public losses by respondents, leading to an underrepresentation of companies with moderate unreported losses [8].

As a consequence, scholars are actually considering most of the available survey, such as, e.g., the one presented above as being to be carefully evaluated as for reliability due to the fact that many of them may present under- or overinflated estimates of the scale of the risk of cybercrime [8]. According to a report titled *'Measuring the cost of cybercrime'* [9], presented in 2012 by an international team of scientists led by the University of Cambridge, the cost of protection against cybercrime often exceed the cost of the threat itself [10]. The analyses and the consequent evaluation presented in the report have followed the framework shown in Fig. 7.1, considering all the main types of cybercrime, such as, e.g., online payment and banking fraud, fake antivirus, patent-infringing pharmaceuticals.

As for the main constructs of the framework, apart from the above cited cybercrimes and their supporting infrastructures, the others were defined by [9] as follows:

- **Criminal revenue** is "*the monetary equivalent of the gross receipts from a Crime*" [9, p. 4]. For example, the revenue of a phishing advertised by email spam is the sum of the money withdrawn from the accounts of the subject that is victim of the phishing activity.
- **Direct losses** are "*the monetary equivalent of losses, damage, or other suffering felt by the victim as a consequence of a cybercrime*" [9, pp. 4–5]. Example of such kind of losses are, among others, money withdrawn from victim accounts; time and effort needed to reset account credentials (for both the company, such as, e.g., a bank and the customer); pain suffered by the subject target of the cybercrime action; deferred purchases or not having access to money [9].
- **Indirect losses** are "*the monetary equivalent of the losses and opportunity costs imposed on society by the fact that a certain cybercrime is carried out, no matter whether successful or not and independent of a specific instance of that cybercrime*" [9, p. 6]. They include, among others, important issues related to digital business identity, such as the loss of trust in electronic transaction (e.g., online banking).
- **Defense costs** are "*the monetary equivalent of prevention efforts*" [9, p. 6], including security products, security services, such as, e.g., training, regulations and/or law enforcement, etc.
- **Cost to society** is "*the sum of direct losses, indirect losses, and defense costs*" [9, p. 6].

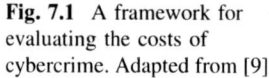

Fig. 7.1 A framework for
evaluating the costs of
cybercrime. Adapted from [9]

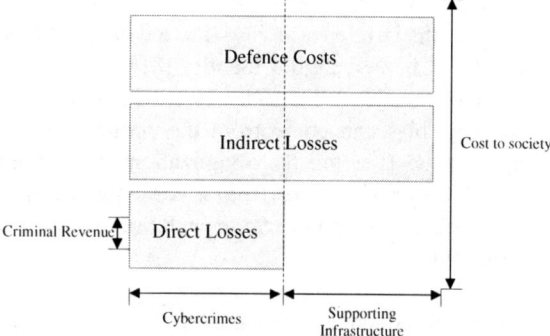

As for the report findings, one of the main suggestions concerned the fact that indirect costs of cybercrimes on business are several times higher than the direct costs. Furthermore, as pointed out by Ross Anderson, one the researchers of the report, *"A small number of gangs lie behind many incidents and locking them up would be far more effective than telling the public to fit an anti-phishing toolbar or purchase antivirus software"* [10, p. 1]. Thus, a conclusion from the study is that public and private spending should be focused less on defense of computer crime (i.e. antivirus, firewalls etc.) and more on policies and methods for finding and punishing the criminals.

However, another relevant point resulting from studies such as the one presented above [9], is the need for policy and methods for augmenting the awareness in the users and code of conducts, leading to habits suitable to preserve an organization as well as individuals digital identity. As a consequence, apart from the focus on technical aspects related, e.g., to authentication and authorization digital identifiers (such as strings or tokens) these policies and methods should encompass social implications and what can be called an ethical perspective focused on trust and privacy oriented practices, in particular, for having a comprehensive and effective digital business identity management [11, 12]. Taking these issues into account digital identity (in general as well as for a business perspective) is a complex topic, which requires multidisciplinary competencies for its investigation, including the ones grounded on legal literature, but also other perspectives in order to really understand the connection between, e.g., privacy and identity [13]. Furthermore, digital business identity can be considered a specific case of personal identity, referred to an organization instead than to an individual. Thus, according to, e.g., Paul Beynon-Davies personal identity can be regarded *"as a phenomenon which is enacted at the intersection between signs, patterns and systems"* further *"conceived of as a continual, enacted accomplishment"* [14, p. 4] from the data stored about us and the information flows we are involved in.

Taking these issues into account, digital business identity management may benefit from comprehensive frameworks adopting a multidisciplinary as well as systemic perspective on the inner and outer context challenges to it. Considering

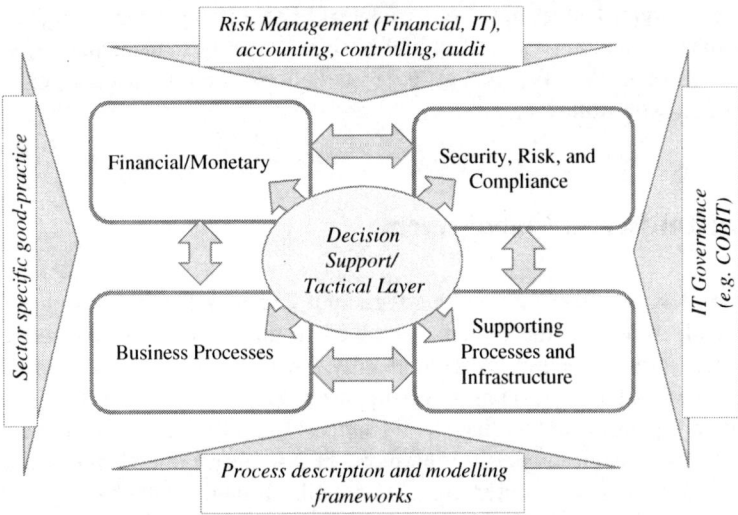

Fig. 7.2 An enterprise identity management framework. Adapted from [15]

the state of art on business information systems, an interesting solution for *Enterprise Identity Management* has been proposed by Royer and Meints [15].

The framework, resulting from a comprehensive literature review and findings from a qualitative expert interview study, uses Balanced Scorecard (BSC) [16, 17] concept as a basis for a decision support approach, resulting in an *Enterprise Identity Management (EIdM) Decision Matrix* [15]. As shown in Fig. 7.2, the framework comprises four perspectives and corresponding indicators: financial/ monetary, security/risk/and compliance, business processes, and supporting processes and infrastructure. Coherently with the BSC concept, the perspectives should be translated into metrics, which echo the goals of the introduction of an Enterprise Identity Management solution. For example, according to [15] metrics for the *financial monetary perspective* can be the estimated costs for security incidents (e.g., on the basis of historic or benchmark data); while for the *security/ risk/and compliance perspective* they can be the mapping of users and accounts in the different systems (for having an "account density" representation), or the achievable quality of audit logs (content, time frame covered, revision process, evaluation support) versus required quality of audit logs.

It is worth noting that metrics may derive by standards and other good-practice adopted externally as well internally to the organization, shown in Fig. 7.2 as the four external blocks "bounding" the considered perspectives (for example, IT Governance frameworks such as, e.g., COBIT in the right hand side of Fig. 7.2).

Solutions such as the one discussed above, are suitable to provide companies ways to manage digital business identity focusing primarily on their inner context and enterprise architecture and information infrastructure. However, a digital business identity is built also through interaction and exposure to users and societal as well as cultural factors in the outer context. These issues concern digital brand management as another facet of digital business identity management, involving departments other than IT, such as, e.g., marketing. These topics are going to be discussed in what follows.

7.3 Digital Brand Management

This book has discussed in previous Parts and Chapters the technological trends that actually represent the digital market environment where businesses create, maintain, and revise their own digital identity. This is what in the previous Chapter has been called the outer context of organization compared with the inner one focused on the infrastructure that should support the preservation and defence of a digital business environment. Furthermore, it has been pointed out how digital business identity in the outer context is built through and challenged by its exposure to users through a company image or brand. However, has argued by Topalian [18] the literature on corporate identity and on corporate branding, in many cases superimpose the two perspectives, extending branding from products to organizations and corporate identity, likewise. Thus, as a first step, in this Section some definitions are provided in order to better understand the challenges of the evolution of corporate identity and branding towards a comprehensive digital business identity.

As for corporate identity, Topalian [18] points out the importance of providing a definition, such as, e.g., the one by the British Standards Institution [19], stating that corporate identity is *"the articulation of what an organisation is, what it stands for, what it does and how it goes about its business (especially the way it relates to its stakeholders and the environment)"* [18, p. 1119]. As a consequence, according to Topalian [18] the actual identity of a business is made up of three key factors: *what is* (for example its operational and human features); *a vision of the future*; and *how the former are experienced* by the selected target audience of users and consumers, once recombined in an offering and a *corporate image*. The latter can be defined as the sum of perceptions and expectations of the stakeholders and the public of a given business [18, 19]. Thus, a corporate identity is designed and somewhat controlled by the organization; whereas corporate image is dependent on the target audience perspective and the different information sources contributing to it, with a certain if not higher degree of volatility.

However, as argued by Abdullah et al. [20] it is important to guarantee a consistency between the identity and the image the company is portraying. To this end, considering a vast literature on brand personality as *"the set of human characteristics associated with a brand"* [21, p. 347], are worth to be mentioned the dimensions often referred as the "Big Five", including *sincerity, excitement, competence, sophistication* and *ruggedness* [20].

Combining corporate identity and image to the concept of brand, it can make easier the understanding of the challenges that businesses have to face due to higher flexibility, reduced time-to-market, and industry boundaries instability as well as the unpredictability introduced by the aforementioned digital trends. Indeed, businesses cannot rely anymore on years for creating their own digital identity or brand; whereas, due to the above factors, they may have to revise it according to new business models every 2 years or even less.[2] Furthermore, it is worth to be considered that as argued by Topalian [18] and shown also in the Chapters dedicated to *Social listening* and *IT Consumerization* of this book, the constant change is related also to the fact that "personalisation" has substituted what "mass customisation" has been in manufacturing [18].

Considering, for example, a study by Brynjolfsson et al. [22] digital business identity seems to be a relevant factor in an omnichannels retail competition. As for this issue, their research focuses on medium-sized retailing company selling women's clothing, in order to investigate online and offline markets for understanding the role of IT for competitive advantage in the two kind of channels [22]. The results have shown that the competition has variability across products, with a relevance to Internet retailers of selling niche products. Accordingly, the study by Brynjolfsson et al. [22] provides a set of recommendations that can be connected to the definition of a clear and recognizable brand as digital business identity. Indeed, the suggestion of having a connection between attractive pricing strategies and curated content, may require a focus on brand to avoid direct price comparisons [22]. However, they also pointed out that differentiation through selling niche products, as a way to competitive advantage, should be based on user experience rather than price [22]. As a consequence, it can be enabled by a focus, on the one hand, on *distinctive features* (providing retailers less price competition when the changes add value without annoying customers [22]), giving emphasis to product knowledge for consumers, having access to inedited volume of information on products and services actually available on the market; on the other hand, *exclusivity*, relying on offering products and services not provided by competitors, can allow an improved differentiation when coupled with switching costs creation strategies (through, e.g., loyalty programs) [22].

In recent years, the diffusion of social networks and 2.0 applications have raised their relevance to companies aiming to carry out differentiation strategies, with a consequent effect, in particular, on brands and marketing activities (as also seen in Chap. 4, when analyzing social listening perspectives and methods for marketing intelligence). As a consequence, as argued by Barwise and Meehan [23], the above mentioned digital trends ask companies "get the basics right". Companies need today than ever to develop and deliver services and products fitting captivating brand promises. Accordingly, Barwise and Meehan [23] point out that businesses have to integrate digital trends, such as, e.g., social media, into their "marketing playbooks", in order to design and deliver effective brands strategies, considering the four key qualities shown in Fig. 7.3. It is worth noting that, in order to build *trust* by delivering the established customer promise (the second block-related

---

[2] Business model innovation is going to be discussed in Chap. 9.

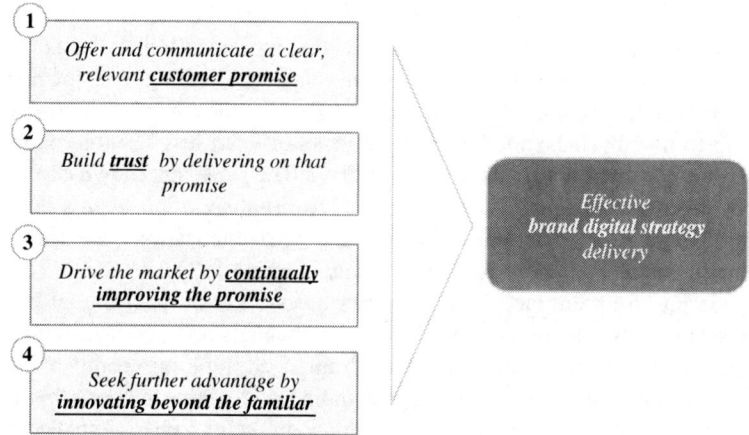

Fig. 7.3 Key qualities for effective brands strategies, incorporating social media in marketing playbooks. Elaborated from [23]

quality in Fig. 7.3), organizations should consider digital business identity management from an inner context perspective; as discussed in the previous section, the latter is essential to guarantee a suitable infrastructure preserving privacy of data and reliable transactions for the target customers.

As for the above mentioned inner perspective, it is important to note that, as argued by [18], a successful corporate identity as well as a brand strategy should be "lived" and understood by employees in order to be effectively transmitted to people in the outer context of the organization, either in customer relationship activities, when employees are in charge of a given touch point, or as indirect "testimonial" of the brand in their everyday life, reinforcing its reputation, likewise. Indeed, in recent years, we have assisted to a specific interest by researchers in investigating the role of employees about the management of reputation by businesses in social media [24].

7.4 Case Studies

In this Section we discuss case studies illustrating issues related to digital business identity management in the inner as well as the outer context of an organization.

The first case study is based on [25] and discusses a specific technical issue related to the inner context of organizations, having a business impact on digital business identity in the outer context as well. The topic concerns a narrower perspective on digital business identity as related to phone numbers, web and email addresses. As for this issue, according to an independent study commissioned by TalkTalk Business, a United Kingdom (UK)'s leading provider of B2B data networking and telephony solutions,[3] even small changes to a company's phone numbers, email and web addresses may lead to an increase number of business prospects, e.g., for Small and medium enterprises (SMEs) [26].

Considering the case study, it concerns DHL, a world market leader in sea and air mail, founded in the United States then becoming DHL Express, a division of the German logistics company Deutsche Post DHL. The case focuses on migration and switch issues for DHL in the UK, due to compliance to new regulations. Indeed, starting in April 2006 the Ofcom (an independent regulator and competition authority for the UK communications industries) decided to implement a package of measures to address consumers and industry concerns about Number Translation Services (NTS) calls, that are calls to 08 numbers ('NTS numbers') [27]; among the effects of the Ofcom initiatives, 0870 numbers would no longer offer companies revenue from rebates. Considering that DHL was using around five hundred 0870 numbers across many of its brands, the company had to find a new inbound solution in order to ensure income and maintain highest customer service. Otherwise, the effects of the new regulation might have resulted in loss of revenues, while still paying to use the numbers. Thus, DHL decided to involve TalkTalk Business, which managed an inbound migration project, aiming to move the nearly five hundred 0870 numbers towards 0844 numbers (compliant with the new regulations) rates, in a short timeframe of 4 weeks. Once completed, the migration solution by TalkTalk Business allows DHL, on the one hand, to keep inbound revenue stream while complying Ofcom regulations thanks to a volume dependent pricing model; on the other hand, the migration and the consequent switch to 0844 numbers had no impact on customers [25].

> **POINT OF ATTENTION**: Digital business identity management asks organizations to consider carefully the implications of changes due to, e.g., new regulations, impacting on narrower aspects such as telephone numbers, email and web address, in order to avoid loss in revenue and "contacts" with customers.

The second case study is based on [28] and considers Vibram,[4] an Italian based company among the world leader in high performance rubber soles, manufacturing and licensing the production of Vibram-branded rubber outsoles for footwear. Notwithstanding the Vibram soles are a widespread component of top running shoe brands (e.g., Patagonia), the company name requires more awareness by the consumers in order to be recognized for itself apart from its distinct technology. To this end, in 2009, Vibram worked with AMP Agency's integrated media unit to a digital campaign, aiming to engage core customers online and creating a direct dialog

---

[3] TalkTalk Business: http://www.talktalkbusiness.co.uk/.

[4] Vibram: http://www.vibram.com.

with passionate runners [28]. The company invested its full media budget online. The 5 months campaign, beginning in February 2009, used a combination of digital tactics, surrounding dedicated trail runners with messages on their digital networks, advertising on top running sites (e.g., Runnersworld.com), rich media banner including 60 custom videos, and social listening (see Chap. 4) for identifying opinion leaders and influencers, e.g., among trail-running bloggers, giving them Vibram-soled trail running shoes for trial and review, engaging them through access to company representatives for more-detailed product information, etc. [28].

According to [28], the campaign gathered 3.1 million paid media impressions and 100,000 social media impressions, thus obtaining a *return on engagement* as well as a *return on relationship* (for example, moving from 57 % surveyed having limited brand awareness prior to campaign to 100 % surveyed said Vibram components will play a determining role in future purchase decision).

> **POINT OF ATTENTION**: Digital business identity management asks organizations to invest in mixed digital media strategies as well as to adopt social listening methods and techniques to have significant return on engagement and return on relationship.

Finally, we discuss a case study based on a research by Cova and Pace [29] on a digital brand community, that is the web community "my Nutella The Community" promoted in Italy in early 2004 by the firm Ferrero, an Italian based worldwide manufacturer of chocolate and other confectionery products[5]. Allowing to fans of the famous Nutella chocolate cream to create their own pages, as argued by Cova and Pace [29], the idea behind this brand community was based on "*an inversion between marketing the producer and its brand and marketing the consumer*" [29, p. 1102], where the focus is on providing a virtual space that facilitates the fans self-exposure. Furthermore, the company role was of non-intrusive enabler ("*taking a step backwards*"), leaving the customers being the protagonists and leaders of the brand-related initiative; thus, the company reduced its control over the brand as digital business identity to answer the challenges of consumer empowerment by the information technology and digital channels [29].

> **POINT OF ATTENTION**: Digital business identity management asks organizations to enable self-exposure of customers through digital initiatives, "taking a step backwards" about the control on them, in order to have positive and value added effects from both the public and the target audience in the company outer context.

---

[5] Ferrero: http://www.ferrero.com.

Considering the time when "my Nutella The Community" has been carried out, it can be considered a kind of pioneer experience and a sort of "template" to digital business identity in the current outer context of organizations, where social networks such as, e.g., Facebook, enable in an inedited way the self-exposure of 2.0 empowered consumers. As for these issues, echoes of these arguments coming from an early 2.0 experience can be found, e.g., in some of the recommendations resulting from a research by Malhotra et al. [30] on how to create brand engagement on Facebook. In particular, among the eight ways that according to them brand managers have for increasing the number of "likes" received by a post it is worth to be mentioned the self-exposure related *"Express yourself through photos"*, and among the constraints that prevent having "likes" *"Enter Our Contests"* and *"Deal (or No Deal)"*, which mean that exposed control is not a source of effective digital business identity management.

7.5 Summary

This Chapter has explored the digital business identity challenges considering the inner and the outer context of an organization. The former is focused on the infrastructure that should support the preservation and defense of a digital business environment. To this end the Chapter has discussed the main challenges related to the inner context, providing also examples of frameworks for evaluating the costs of, e.g., cybercrime and for Enterprise Identity Management. Besides the inner context of an organization, the Chapter has pointed out how digital business identity in the outer context is built through and challenged by its exposure to users through a company image or brand. Accordingly, digital business identity has been discussed also with regard to brand management in the current digital ecosystems. Finally, case studies have concluded the Chapter, providing insights on how IT executives as well as other CxOs can manage digital business identity initiatives through a focus also on narrower aspects of the inner context, such as telephone numbers, email and web addresses, etc. and savvy investments on digital media in the outer context of organizations; the latter enable a return on digital identity through the self-exposure of customers and the companies "taking a step backwards" about the control of their digital brand initiatives.

References

1. Normann R, Ramìrez R (1994) Designing interactive strategy: from value chain to value constellation. Wiley, Chichester
2. Eisenmann TR, Parker G, Van Alstyne MW (2006) Strategies for two-sided markets. Harv Bus Rev 84(10):92–101. doi: 10.1007/s00199-006-0114-6
3. Sambamurthy V, Zmud R (2012) Competing in digital markets. In guiding the digital transformation of organizations. Legerity Digital Press
4. Levy M, Loebbecke C, Powell P (2003) SMEs, co-opetition and knowledge sharing: the role of information systems. Eur J Inf Syst 12:3–17 (ST–SMEs, co-opetition and knowledge sharin)

5. Brandenburger A, Nalebuff B (1997) Co-opetition: a revolution mindset that combines competition and cooperation, 1st edn. Currency Doubleday, New York
6. Greenwood P-E (2012) The new instability: how globalisation, cloud computing and social media enable you to create an unfair advantage. Egxacting
7. Aral S, Dellarocas C, Godes D (2013) Introduction to the special issue—social media and business transformation: a framework for research. Inf Syst Res 24:3–13. doi: 10.1287/isre. 1120.0470
8. Hyman P (2013) Cybercrime: it's serious, but exactly how serious? Commun ACM 56:18–20. doi:10.1145/2428556.2428563
9. Anderson R, Barton C, Boehme R, Clayton R, Eeten MJG van, Levi M, Moore T, Savage S (2012) Measuring the cost of cybercrime. Elev. Annu Work Econ Inf Secur (WEIS12), Berlin, DE, June 25–26
10. Anderson R How much does cybercrime cost? http://www.cam.ac.uk/research/news/ how-much-does-cybercrime-cost
11. Birch D (2007) Digital identity management technological, business and social implications. Gower Publishing, Aldershot
12. Birch D (2007) The identity vision. Digit. Identity Manag. Technol. Bus. Soc. Implic. pp 1–8
13. Sullivan C (2011) Digital identity. University of Adelaide Press, Adelaide
14. Beynon-Davies P (2011) The enactment of personal identity. In: ECIS 2011
15. Royer D, Meints M (2009) Enterprise identity management—towards a decision support framework based on the balanced scorecard approach. Bus Inf Syst Eng 3:245–253
16. Kaplan RS, Norton DP (1992) The balanced scorecard: measures that drive performance. Harv Bus Rev 70(1):71–79
17. Martinsons M, Davison R, Tse D (1999) The balanced scorecard: a foundation for the strategic management of information systems. Decis Support Syst 25:71–88
18. Topalian A (2003) Executive perspective: 1—The development of corporate identity in the digital era. Eur J Mark 37:1119–1132
19. BSI (1995) BS7000 Part 10, Glossary of Terms Used in Design Management. British Standards Institution, London
20. Abdullah Z, Nordin SM, Aziz YA (2013) Building a unique online corporate identity. Mark Intell Plan 31:451–471
21. Aaker, Jennifer L (1997) Dimensions of brand personality. J Mark Res 347–356
22. Brynjolfsson E, Hu YJ, Rahman MS (2013) Competing in the age of omnichannel retailing. MIT Sloan Manag Rev 54(4):23–29
23. Barwise P, Meehan S (2010) The one thing you must get right now when building a brand. Harv Bus Rev 88:80–84
24. Rokka J, Karlsson K, Tienari J (2013) Balancing acts: managing employees and reputation in social media. J Mark Manag 1–26. doi:10.1080/0267257X.2013.813577
25. TalkTalk Business (2012) DHL Case Study—Transport and Distriubution Inbound. Retrieved from http://www.talktalkbusiness.co.uk/Global/Final-Assets/Collateral/Case-Studies/case_ study_dhl.pdf. Accessed 16 January 2014
26. TalkTalk Business (2013) SME digital identity has major impact on perception. http:// www.talktalkbusiness.co.uk/news-events/news-ttb-listing/video-news/sme-digital-identity-has-major-impact-on-perception/%23. Accessed 18 Nov 2013
27. Ofcom (2008) Changes to 0870 calls and modifications to the supporting regulations. Retrieved from http://stakeholders.ofcom.org.uk/binaries/consultations/0870calls/summary/ 0870condoc.pdf. Accessed 16 January 2014
28. Macumber K (2010) Case study: the brand that went 100 % digital. In: iMedia Communication Inc. http://www.imediaconnection.com/printpage/printpage.aspx?id=25759. Accessed 25 Nov 2013
29. Cova B, Pace S (2006) Brand community of convenience products: new forms of customer empowerment–the case my nutella the community. Eur J Mark 40:1087–1105
30. Malhotra A, Kubowicz Malhotra C, See A (2013) How to create brand engagement on facebook. MIT Sloan Manag Rev 54:18–20

Chapter 8
Digital Governance

Abstract The growing use of information and communication technologies (ICT) is fostering the formation of "knowledge societies", thus providing greater avenues for people to participate on their own development process, revolutionizing the way they live, communicate, and work, likewise. The developing of these technologies is rapid, thus mechanisms that can help to manage and measure this growth is imperative. As a result, a new research area concerned with the governance of these new developments has arisen: information technology (IT) governance is a subset discipline of corporate governance focused on information systems and their performance and risk management. This Chapter aims to offer an overview of digital governance as a comprehensive perspective on IT governance, by taking a look at the opportunities and challenges in this field. Furthermore, the Chapter provides examples of digital governance models that have arisen from the state-of-the-art research in this domain.

8.1 Introduction

The new technological advances in the information and communication technology (ICT) field have resulted in the digital revolution and the emergence of the Information and communication age. This development has created an enormous impact on social, political, and cultural livelihood of the people, which resulted in transforming the whole world to a different and new era that many firms are still struggling to implement and apply frameworks to their work environment [1]. Also, the increasing use of ICT in different facets of human life is leading to multidimensional and often unpredictable changes. Moreover, ICT diffusion is changing the way individuals interact with each other and with the society as a whole, and the way the society provides space for its inhabitants to interact with each other. New modes of communications have become available which are faster, efficient and have the ability to reach every individual in the society. For

V. Morabito, *Trends and Challenges in Digital Business Innovation*,
DOI: 10.1007/978-3-319-04307-4_8, © Springer International Publishing Switzerland 2014

instance, the internet and other communication systems have developed and spread sharply in many countries around the globe including poor societies [2].

However, many scientists argued that the development of ICT is likely to have more drawbacks rather than benefits in the future life. Therefore, it is imperative to have rules to control the way the ICT is evolving, and this is how the domain of digital governance has emerged, first as *IT governance*. The latter can be considered as a branch of the overall corporate governance that focuses on IT infrastructure, organization, and systems, providing methods and framework for evaluating their performance and managing decisions for value generation as well as the risks that are associated with its practices. The interest in IT governance is related to the need for compliance and greater accountability of IT investments and use, as well as to a strategy need for superior business results for all stakeholders [3].

Notwithstanding IT performance is directly linked to the long term consequences of the decisions made by top management, top-level executives traditionally relegate important IT related resolutions to the IT professionals in the company, which cannot always guarantee the best results for all stakeholders. As a consequence, IT governance should involve everyone: board members, top management, staff and customers. It establishes a set of policies and practices used by the organization to enhance a transparent accountability of individual decisions. Also, from the governmental sector point of view, for example, *digital governance* is the use of information and communication technologies by the public sector with the intention to improve information and service delivery, to encourage citizens' participation in the decision-making process and to make government practices more accountable, transparent and effective [1].

However, this definition can be generalized to private sector, introducing revenue oriented and market share goals, instead of a public value orientation [4]. Furthermore, according to, e.g., Macintosh [2] the advent of more complicated and advanced digital technologies has produced a growing community that is interested in the research in this field. Its aim is to make IT related decision making more transparent and inclusive. Therefore, it is important to understand the advantages, the challenges, and the success factors to have good governance of the IT. Also, it is important to discuss digital governance practice and implementation as well as its impact on business\IT alignment. Social networking software and argumentation systems are just two examples of the ongoing research in this important area of digital governance. Other areas are concerned with collective intelligence methods and open innovation, which enable aggregation of distributed information and individuals'preferences to generate a solution to a problem, which can be more optimal than an individual could have provided alone.[1] In this context, several collective intelligence mechanisms have emerged. One of the most famous examples is the *Information Aggregation Markets (IAMs)*. The concept that the IAM is based upon is to bring a group of participants together via

---

[1] See also the discussion about Crowdsourcing in Chap. 6.

invitations over the internet and to allow this disparate pool of human individuals to make predictions or to propose solutions about the likely outcome of future uncertain events or complicated problems. The efficient markets' hypothesis states that when such a market reaches equilibrium, it encompasses all the available information that is good enough to provide a solution for a proposed problem. Research has shown that IAMs can increase user participation in innovation management processes in corporate environments [2].

Taking the above issues into account, digital governance can be considered as a more comprehensive concept than IT governance. However, it is worth noting that the latter is a key component and requirements for a company having effective digital governance. Thus, in what follows IT governance will be adopted when we discuss a firm based perspective; while digital governance will refer to current digital ecosystems and value constellations [5], blurring the boundaries between inner and outer context of a company.

8.2   Opportunities and Challenges Related to Digital Governance

Digital governance is different from IT management and IT controls. However, when this diversity is not recognized, the problem is related to the fact that also when considering IT governance, the latter is often confused with good management practices and IT control frameworks. While IT management is about good administration of assets and resources, IT governance adds a vision and leadership dimension. In other words, IT governance is about the good supervision of IT resources on behalf of the stakeholders who expect a return from their investment. The people who are responsible about this stewardship will look to the management to implement the necessary systems and IT controls [1].

However, as argued by Aoun et al. [6], many enterprises are still careworn to implement and apply IT governance frameworks to their work environment, despite the prefigured potential benefits for the performance and profitability aspects. The motivations for this resistance to adopt IT governance standards is often related to the high costs of implementation and that they often are too normative or abstract, failing to reflect reality.

Nevertheless, as we are going to see in what follows, IT governance actually may provide opportunities and benefits in terms of strategic value and return on investments that the above perceived drawbacks may prevent a company to obtain. In particular, implementing a good IT governance is the basis for an effective digital governance, which helps people in organizations to make fast, informed and reliable decisions; thus, enabling good decision making process.

Table 8.1 shows the decision making areas that can be addressed by having good governance to solve key drawbacks and risks, likewise. Thus, good digital governance enables groups to make effective decisions, allowing them to do this in

Table 8.1 Governance benefits for risks associated to key decision making areas

Key decision making areas	Risks	Governance benefits
Identifying the relevant decisions	Misdirected effort	Good governance allows to identify the decisions that have a real impact on organizational goals, ensuring policies' focus and the commitment of the organization on them
Involving the right people	Wasted effort (lack of recognized decision rights)	Good governance reduces transaction costs through clear and accountable lines of authority and competencies, establishing *who* has to be consulted
Accounting for process followed and the outcomes of decisions	Decisions are poor, without feedbacks and not implemented	Good governance allows to ensure legitimacy to decision making resulting choices, through a transparent agreed process that people monitor to see whether has been followed or not

Adapted from [1, 7, 8]

an efficient way, likewise. Also, it ensures they track the results of those decisions and hence to direct them towards the desired goals. However, many factors affect the implementation of the IT governance within organizations. Accountability, transparency, decentralization, and administrative reform are examples of these problems. What follows will shed light on the most important challenges that were observed in several research concerned with this topic [1, 9], in particular the discussion will focus on decentralization within organizations, digital ownership, and managing expectations.

Considering the first challenge, *decentralization* in large organizations is not a single case, but the normal situation and without it, probably, the required objectives will not be accomplished. Therefore, it might be contributing to the challenges that hinder the digital development. In addition, decentralized decision-making and the culture are other factors that can hinder well-established IT governance. In such situations, there are no definite regulations about who is responsible about the different jobs. As a result, everyone ends up making decisions about everything, all the time, all over the place, and then they execute on those diverse decisions. The result is an ongoing battle within the organization about whose fault it is. IT governance, at its core, clarifies accountability, roles, and decision-making. It addresses concerns related to building a responsive development environment whose output is effective content, applications, and interaction.

The second challenge concerns *digital ownership*, which is related, e.g., to web existence of firm, since sometimes, web teams and business divisions within organizations tend all to claim the ownership of the organizational web presence. Indeed, the web teams feel they should take the control over the websites and social channels because they feel they have the skills and knowledge to maintain the quality of web presence. Similarly, business managers and employees think that they should own this ability over their parts of the website because they think they know better about their contents and how to interact with customers. However, the organizational digital presence is an extension to the organization's physical and human existence, and together, they should represent the brand and support the complex needs of the business at large. This is important because it cannot be expected for the global business to run solely from the decisions and efforts that are coming from one small team.

In response, organizations need to develop a mature operational model, one which includes not only the core web team and business stakeholders but also the web managers within the organization and deep and rich support infrastructure that can include legal department, business experts and ICT specialists as well as external vendors. Most importantly, those team members need to realize that they are stewards of the digital presence and not the owners of service.

Finally, *managing expectations*, often "unreasonable", is one of the main challenges to an effective IT governance implementation. During the investigation of any problem, business analysts suggest or demand a particular solution. These resolutions will be considered as the expectations they demand from the concerned stakeholders. However, if these potential answers for the investigated problem were not met, a cycle of discussions about the suggested solutions, responsibilities and other issues will happen, while the problem is not solved yet. As a result, managing these expectations will take a long time while they remain unaddressed.

8.3 Digital Governance Mechanisms

Digital governance has been also defined by [10] as the leadership and organizational structures, processes and relational mechanisms, ensuring that an organization's IT sustains and extends its strategy and objectives. From this description, it can be seen that it is beneficial to study the relational mechanisms required for the deployment of the digital governance while designing IT governance for an organization, since it is important to recognize that it depends on a variety of sometimes conflicting internal and external influences.

Determining the right combination of mechanisms is therefore a complex endeavour because what works for one case does not necessarily work for another. This means that different organizations may need a combination of different structures, processes and relational mechanisms. To this end, De Haes and Van Grembergen [10] proposed a framework to place IT governance structures, processes and relational mechanisms in a comprehensible relationship to each other (see Table 8.2). Structures involve the existence of responsible functions such as IT executives and a diversity of IT committees. Also, processes refer to strategic decision-making and monitoring practices, and finally, the relational mechanisms

Table 8.2 Structures, processes and relational mechanisms

	Structures	Processes	Relational mechanisms
Tactics	IT executives and accounts	Strategic IT decision-making	Stakeholder participation
	Committees and councils	Strategic IT monitoring	Business/IT partnerships
			Strategic dialog and learning
Mechanisms	*Roles and responsibilities Definition*	*Strategic information systems planning*	*Active participation by key stakeholders*
			Shared understanding of business/IT goals
	IT organization Structure	Balanced scorecards and strategy maps	Collaboration between key stakeholders
			Active conflict resolution
	CIO commitment	Service level agreements	Partnership rewards and incentives
	IT strategy committee	COBIT and ITIL	Business/IT colocation
			Cross functional business/IT training
	IT steering committee(s)	IT alignment/ governance maturity models	Cross functional business/IT job rotation

Adapted from [10]

include business/IT participation, strategic dialogue, shared learning and proper communication.

Furthermore, De Haes and Van Grembergen [10] have proposed a maturity model for IT or digital governance, providing a method of scoring so that an organisation can grade itself from (0) *nonexistent* to (5) *optimized* in controlling IT processes. The basic principle of such a maturity measurement is that an organisation can move to a higher maturity only when all conditions described in the higher maturity level are fulfilled. Management can use this tool to obtain a quick self-assessment or reference in conjunction with an independent review. This defines the "as-is" position of the enterprise relative to IT control and governance maturity, and allows the enterprise to select an appropriate "to-be" level and, after an accurate analysis of the gaps, develop a strategy for improvement [10].

According to De Haes and Van Grembergen [10] the six levels that construct this model are explained as follows:

0. ***Non-existent***: the organization is not aware of the relevance of IT governance practices; as a consequence no action is implemented. IT budgets and decisions are made centrally at the IT department, while business units inputs are informal and on a project basis.
1. ***Initial/Ad Hoc***: at this level, the organization has realized that IT related issues exist and need to be addressed. Nevertheless, the top management considers and manage them on an individual basis (for example, once problems emerge or a project is proposed), without a clear or structured strategy for IT governance. Furthermore, there is inconsistent communication between different departments.
2. ***Repeatable, but Intuitive***: at this level, the awareness of IT governance objectives and practices are developed and implemented by individual managers. However, IT governance activities are becoming established within the organization, with active senior management involvement and support. At this level of maturity implemented, the IT steering committee has already started to formalize its roles and duties. Finally, there is a draft governance charter such as roles, responsibilities, delegated retained and powers, shared resources, and policies.
3. ***Defined Process***: at this level, IT governance is understood and accepted. Also, the IT governance Key Performance Indicators (KPIs) are developed, documented and incorporated with the strategic and operational planning and monitoring processes, supported by the adoption of standard tools. Finally, the IT steering committee is operative, with governance agreement, participation, and formalized policies.
4. ***Managed and Measurable***: at this maturity level, there is a full understanding of the IT governance issues throughout the enterprise, supported by official training, likewise. IT governance is evolving into an enterprise wide process, being its activities integrated with the overall enterprise governance process. At

this level, IT decisions are shared between IT department and other business units.

5. *Optimized*: There is an advanced understanding of IT governance, with a reinforced training and communication as well as processes developed through a comparison with external best practices. At this level of maturity, enterprise governance and IT governance are strategically linked to increase the company business value and competitive advantage. Finally, it is worth noting that at this stage, IT governance can enable the organization to evolve towards the design of comprehensive a digital governance.

8.4 Digital Governance Success Factors

The Critical Success Factors (CSFs) are the areas in which achieving satisfactory results will ensure a successful competitive performance for the parties involved in the project or process. These parties could be individual, department or organization related elements. They are the areas of activity that should receive constant attention from the management. CSFs are used by organisations to be able to focus on a number of aspects that help to define and ensure the success of the business, and consequently help the organisation and its personnel to understand the key areas in which to invest their resources and time [11].

In the area of digital governance, few studies have been undertaken to cover the CSFs related to this field. For example, Guldentops [12] identifies five key success factors mainly related to structures and processes for control and governance of IT. As for these issues, it is worth to be considered, for example, the study by Nfuka and Rusu [11], focused on forming IT strategy and IT steering committees, aligning IT and the business in strategy and operations, cascading of IT goals and strategy, applying emerging management best practices and implementing a governance and control framework for IT [11]. Furthermore, Nfuka and Rusu [11], investigated ten studies concerned with CSFs related to IT governance. Also they took into account that IT value to be realized by effective IT governance is due to an efficient and cost effective IT delivery, innovation and business impact [11]. This way it was possible to broadly and multi-dimensionally identify CSFs across the entire IT governance objective/life cycle such as *direct, create, protect, execute* and *monitor*. Thus, they started with seventeen CSFs that they discovered from those studies; then, they filtered and categorised them to finally end with four main classes that contain eleven CSFs [11]. These categories and the CSFs under each one are listed in Table 8.3.

The result of this analysis [11], as mentioned before, has revealed eleven Critical Success Factors (CSFs) that should be considered for effective IT governance in this environment. It was done using IT governance related areas such as strategic alignment, value delivery, risk management, resource management and

Table 8.3 Categories of CSFs for IT Governance implementation

Strategic Alignment Related Critical Success Factors
1.   IT Leadership to understand business goals and IT contribution and bring it to executives attention
2.   Involve and get support of senior management
3.   Encourage and support IT/Business communication and partnership
4.   Engage key stakeholders
5.   Define and align IT strategies to corporate strategies and cascading them down in an organization
6.   Consolidate IT structures that ensure responsiveness and accountability

Value Delivery and Risk Management Related Critical Success Factors
7.   Consolidate, communicate and enforce policies and guidelines for cost-effective acquisition and use of IT across the organization

Resource Management Related Critical Success Factors
8.   Consolidate, standardize and manage IT Infrastructure and applications to optimize costs, responsiveness and information flow across the organization
9.   Provide IT governance awareness and training for optimal use of IT
10. Attract, develop and retain competitive IT professionals

Performance Management Related Critical Success Factors
11. Consolidate performance measures and benchmarks to track and demonstrate success

Adapted from [11]

performance management. Another example is the one produced by the IT Governance Institute (ITGI), in which they also established several CSFs emphasising IT as an integral part of the enterprise and the importance of awareness, communication, stakeholders' involvement, accountability and monitoring across the organization.

In a more commercial arena, PricewaterhouseCoopers (PWC) proposed a set of Critical Success Factors (CSFs) that reflect its best practices for IT governance implementation [13]. Some of these CSFs intersect with the ones mentioned in other studies such as [14] and [15]. The CSFs that were proposed by PWC are shown in Table 8.4.

Apart from CSFs, creating a digital governance structure could be a difficult job especially when so many stakeholders and processes are involved. However, by breaking this task into small, strategic steps, the organization would be able to achieve the required results and would transform this obligation into a manageable effort. Therefore, a set of recommended steps for digital governance implementation was created and proposed in the United States (US) of America by the digital services advisory group, federal chief information officers council, and federal web managers council [16]. Although these recommendations were created to be applied in US government offices, we believe that the proposed six steps (*1- Gather a Core Team; 2- Assess What You Have; 3- Determine What You Want; 4- Build or Validate Your Governance Structure; 5- Share, Review, and Upgrade; 6- Establish and Implement*) they provide a light perspective to complement and

Table 8.4 PWC critical success factors for IT Governance

Critical success factors	Description
Senior Management commitment and vision	The commitment of senior management through continuous support, regular follow-up, provides adequate resources and sustenance for IT governance during conflicts, and consequent better chances for success
Communication and change management	Enabling diffused and cross units conversations and communications may reduce resistance to change
Focus, execute and enforce	Planning an exception management process for relevant deviations from standards are key issues for IT governance. This can be a mechanism for stakeholders to request controlled changes as exceptions
Define a benefit management system and set achievable targets/expectations	IT governance may be enabled and enforced by a clear definition and communication of expected benefits and how to measure them
Evolution, as opposed to revolution	IT governance requires a sustainable plan, considering and allocating an adequate time for the organisation to absorb the change having cultural impacts
Don't over-engineer IT governance	IT governance measures are key factors to its success. However, organizations do not have to amplify the effort with "byzantine" processes, templates, metrics and too many monitoring committees

Adapted from [13]

"filter" the adoption of other standards such as, e.g., COBIT, CMMI, or TOGAF, actually diffused also in private organizations.

8.5 Digital Governance Impact on Business\IT Alignment

Nowadays, digital governance is very important for organisations who are implementing its practices during the day-to-day operations. In particular, in order to reach appropriate digital governance, its core component at firm level should be first developed. Indeed, when a specific IT governance model is chosen and implemented, then IT should support and even improve the business goals, or in other words, proves that IT is aligned to the business needs, which is called business/IT alignment [17–20]. Business\IT alignment can be defined as a dynamic state in which a business organization is able to use information technology (IT) effectively to achieve business objectives.

However, the previously described alignment is not what is often experienced in organizations, since IT and business professionals are usually unable to bridge the gap between the two parties because of the differences in objectives, culture,

Table 8.5 Key minimum baseline of seven IT governance practices

Best practice #	Best practice description
1.	IT steering committee (IT investment evaluation/prioritisation at executive/senior management level)
2.	Portfolio management (incl. business cases, information economics, ROI, payback)
3.	IT budget control and reporting
4.	IT leadership
5.	IT project steering committee
6.	CIO (Chief Information Officer) reporting to CEO (Chief Executive Officer) and/or COO (Chief Operational Officer)
7.	Project governance/management methodologies

Adapted from [17]

and incentives and a mutual ignorance for the other group's experiences and knowledge. Consequently, the outcome of such situation can result in expensive IT systems that do not provide the required results and adequate return on investment. For this reason, the search for Business/IT Alignment attempts usually concentrated on improving the business value that is a result of the IT investments.

Since that the goal of IT governance is to achieve a better alignment between the business and IT domains, an important question in this research field needs to be answered, which is whether the implemented IT governance's processes, structures, and relational mechanisms participate in the achievement of business/IT alignment or not.

The study presented by [17] have analysed the impact of IT governance on the alignment of business and IT. The results of this study suggest that IT governance is indeed high on the agenda. Also, it suggests that there is a clear relationship between the use of IT governance practices and business/IT alignment. It revealed that the highly aligned organisations do get more advantages from mature IT governance compared to poorly aligned organisations.

Moreover, it also provides a key minimum baseline of seven IT governance practices (see Table 8.5) that each organisation should at least have and supplement with policies that are highly effective and easy to implement. In order for organisations to implement these practices successfully, they have to make sure that at least a maturity level of two is obtained, to ensure that it positively impacts business/IT alignment.

8.5.1 The effect of IT Governance Maturity on Performance

IT governance exists in every organization that implement IT practices. However, IT policies at organizations may differ between enterprises; depending on issues such as if rights and responsibilities are well distributed among the appropriate people, if the formalized processes and policies for important tasks are implemented, and if suitable documentation exists. In a study prepared by [21], the authors defined the internal IT organization efficiency as the IT governance maturity. However, one might argue, that internal efficiency measurements of the IT organization are of moderate importance only; and what matters the most is the external efficiency of the services that the IT department delivers to the business, therefore, Simonsson et al. [21] refer to the external efficiency as IT governance performance. In their study, they look at the correlation between IT governance maturity and IT governance performance, and created a framework to analyse them.

The research data collection was made through 35 case studies and the hypothesis was tested for the IT governance of the 34 IT processes of the COBIT framework, which is the most well-known framework for IT governance maturity assessment, and stands for Control Objectives for Information and related Technology. According to Cohen's correlation, statistically significant medium positive and small positive correlations were identified for most processes. The processes that are related to definition of the organization, roles and responsibilities, quality management, and cost allocation had the strongest correlations to IT governance performance. Other processes such as the problem management have demonstrated no correlation with the performance of IT. The results from the research presented in this study have implications for both practitioners and academia [21].

From a practitioner's point of view, the results of the study infer that stakeholders who are concerned with IT management can concentrate their IT governance improvements efforts to the IT processes that showed strong correlation with IT governance performance. According to those results, improved activities, documentation, monitoring and role assignment of the quality management process would have positive effects on the business stakeholder satisfaction while, on the other hand, improvements of the problem management process would not have the same influence [21].

From an academic point of view, the outcomes can be used to improve the frameworks that are currently used for IT governance. For instance, COBIT's representation of project and program management could be improved based on the analysis of the causes behind the weak correlation to IT governance performance. Finding a way of linking business performance to IT governance performance and IT governance maturity would allow new methods to improve business performance by using IT [21].

8.6 Case Studies

The first case study is about the implementing of IT governance in a public sector organization [22]. In this case study, the authors have identified the critical success factors and then proposed a novel framework for achieving the required IT governance level. The case study discussed an identified enterprise in Oman aiming to provide quality services to its citizens and consequently to align itself to the e-government strategy to increase delivery, integration and quality of electronic government services, thus, leading its adoption by citizens, residents and businesses. That is, because all government agencies need to integrate seamlessly to provide electronic services to its stakeholders, thus, increasing their interaction. For example, the system integration of Ministry of Education with Ministry of Manpower and Public Authority for Social Insurance is necessary for e-government system to verify employment history and social security status seamlessly [22].

However, after completing preliminary interviews, it became clear that the selected enterprise had significant gaps in its security policies and programs, exemplified by the lack of consistency across technologies, systems, and processes relied on. It was also identified a lack of alignment between strategic plans and the actual frameworks in place to support its services, which have caused significant level of misunderstanding over just who own which role in the enterprise, and a serious security issue as various consultants and subcontractors were working with highly confidential citizens' data. This has also produced confusion with regard to data access, accounting, auditing and usage statistics over a multiyear period, further complicating the integration process. Consequently, the vulnerability assessment considered the four major security issues mentioned below:

1. protection of sensitive personal data;
2. the division responsible about application services lacks with regard to consistency to audit data analysis history;
3. integration issues between the legacy and 3rd party information systems the enterprise already used, as well as other different systems from other various government agencies;
4. the lack of monitoring mechanisms, providing top management with the ability to validate that their security programs and initiatives were working well.

In summary, there was lack of analytics and reporting systems on the use of data and its implications across the enterprise. The above mentioned problems called for a robust IT governance framework, delivering measurable value to the business while improving the productivity. Enterprises needed to have a strategic IT governance structure and practices with a focus on security and compliance over the long-term (since security variables are actually challenging and are continually changing). The use of COBIT framework in this case study has proved that it can effectively solve these challenges, providing quality outcomes, likewise [22]. However, research studies show that IT governance implementation that covers the all 210 control objectives of COBIT is time and resources consuming. Therefore, the authors selected the most critical control objectives based on the goals of the enterprise, implementing IT governance as suitable as possible to this case study, within a shorter time and with limited resources. As a result, the data collected by analytics could be used to monitor the IT performance and revisit the control objectives, making the adoption of COBIT controls more consistent and rewarding [22].

POINT OF ATTENTION: Security is a focal point and challenge of any digital and IT governance implementation; therefore, companies have to put more efforts to address it. Also, it is important to notice that not all elements of the available IT governance frameworks can be applied to all case study, hence, stakeholders should consider the components that suit their case studies.

The second case study discusses the implementation of IT governance to support e-commerce technology that radically influenced and affected the airline industry and its customers [23]. In this study, Iskandar et al. [23] explained that the effects of e-commerce on that sector are great, especially with regard to the move to online airline e-ticketing. For example, on the 1st of June 2008, the industry moved to 100 % e-ticketing as a requirement by the International Air Transport Association (IATA). Therefore it can be considered that the e-commerce transformation presents gigantic, significant and risky investments in IT. That is due, in particular, to the exposure of business's data and systems to external environment. The risk of an enterprise not knowing the identity of its business partners is increased by e-commerce transactions and that requires a mutual effort of both IT and business management. As a consequence, e-business and e-commerce are more concerned with IT governance due to their inherent risks. These threats require the adoption of strong controls, policies, and management practices. Therefore, each and every organization should have a thorough measure that reflects the risks, as well as the benefits of a project. Organizations can achieve the best out of such situations by implementing effective IT governance practices [23].

Taking the above issues into account, Iskandar et al. [23] argued that each airline company has started its own way for IT governance implementation. However, despite the fact that these corporations are beginning to experience success with implementing IT governance mechanisms to better manage their IT resources, individual governance mechanisms cannot alone promise the successful implementation and execution of IT governance policies and procedures.

> **POINT OF ATTENTION**: The implementation of the digital and IT governance is no longer an option. Organizations have to understand that in order for them to stay in the competition; they have to act fast regarding understanding digital governance structures, processes and mechanisms. Also, implementing IT governance requires the engagement from all parties within the organizations, and especially from the senior executives.

Thus, companies must be able to better understand the complex playing field of their competitive environment as well as to put together a reliable set of governance techniques that are simple, easily shared and implemented, and that engage managers who make key decisions for the company.

8.7 Summary

The digitalization[2] of business has blurred and to some extent opened the boundaries of private and public companies. This change requires organizations to see traditional IT governance as a first relevant step towards a comprehensive perspective, defined as *digital governance* in this Chapter. However, organizations are increasingly dependent upon IT to sustain and improve their operations and gain competitive advantage. Accordingly, it is critical that IT departments deliver operational excellence by simultaneously demonstrating added value. IT must manage costs, guarantee security and integrity of business information, ensure availability and continuity of business operations, protect assets and reduce IT-related business risks. There is also an increasing pressure on IT to automate and sustain compliance with regulations. Taking these issues into account, IT governance is still the proposed way to meet the previous demands. It is an important element in any organization and has a great effect on its efficiency and effectiveness. Furthermore, it is considered to be an integral part of enterprise governance and has the ability to provide mechanisms for leadership and organizational structures and processes. However, IT governance requires the commitment and involvement of an organization's IT professionals as well as its security professionals. Finally, to be truly effective, IT governance also requires the commitment and involvement of additional groups such as the board of directors, executives, and IT management.

In conclusion, this Chapter has offered some insights into digital governance and, in particular, into the IT governance domain as its core component at firm level, covering the advantages and challenges when implementing it in the

---

[2] Digitalization is discussed in Chap. 3.

organization. Thus, the Chapter has described a summary for steps that can be followed to ensure best IT governance implementation in order to seize its opportunities, to face its challenges and to understand the mechanisms of the digital governance. To this end, this Chapter has provided an IT governance maturity model, also looking at the impact of IT governance on business\IT alignment as well as the effect of IT governance maturity on IT governance performance.

References

1. Alam M, Ahmed K (2008) E-Governance: challenges and opportunities. In: Proceedings of the 2nd International Conference on theory and Practice of Electronic Governance, pp 264–267
2. Macintosh A (2008) The emergence of digital governance. Significance 5:176–178
3. Weill P, Ross JW (2004) IT governance: how top performers manage IT decision rights for superior results. Harvard Business School Press, Boston
4. Benington J, Moore MH (2011) Public value—theory and practice. Palgrave Macmillan, Basingstoke
5. Normann R, Ramìrez R (1994) Designing interactive strategy: from value chain to value constellation. Wiley, Chichester
6. Aoun C, Vatanasakdakul S, Chen Y (2011) IT governance framework adoption: establishing success factors. In: Nüttgens M, Gadatsch A, Kautz K, Schirmer I, Blinn N (eds) Government and sustainability in information systems. managing transfer and diffusionof IT SE—15. Springer, Heidelberg, pp 239–248
7. Accenture (2012) Digital Governance: Good for Citizens, Good for Government. White Paper from Accent
8. Oakes G (2011) Why should i care about governance? In: digitalgovernance.com. http://digitalgovernance.com/articles/why-should-i-care-about-governance-0. Accessed 15 Nov 2013
9. Rana VS (2011) E-Governance challenges for Nepal. In: Proceedings of the 5th International Conference on Theory and Practice of Electronic Governance, pp 333–336
10. De Haes S, Van Grembergen W (2004) IT governance and its mechanisms. Inf Syst Control J 1:27–33
11. Nfuka EN, Rusu L (2010) Critical success factors for effective IT governance in the public sector organisations in a developing country: the case of Tanzania. In: 18th European Conference on Information Systems, pp 1–15
12. Guldentops E (2004) Key success factors for implementing IT governance. Inf Syst Control J 2:22–23
13. PWC (2006) IT governance in practice. White Paper from PWC, pp 5–27
14. Huang R, Zmud RW, Price RL (2010) Influencing the effectiveness of IT governance practices through steering committees and communication policies. Eur J Inf Syst 19:288–302. doi:10.1057/ejis.2010.16

15. Bowen PL, Cheung M-YD, Rohde FH (2007) Enhancing IT governance practices: a model and case study of an organization's efforts. Int J Account Inf Syst 8:191–221. doi:10.1016/j. accinf.2007.07.002
16. Whitehouse (2012) Digital services governance recommendations. In: Whitehouse. http://www.whitehouse.gov/digitalgov/digital-services-governance-recommendations. Accessed 28 Nov 2013
17. De Haes S, Van Grembergen W (2009) An exploratory study into IT governance implementations and its impact on business/IT alignment. Inf Syst Manag 26:123–137. doi:10.1080/10580530902794786
18. Luftman JN (1996) Competing in the information age : strategic alignment in practice. Oxford University Press, New York
19. Henderson JC, Venkatraman N (1993) Strategic alignment: leveraging information technology for transforming organizations. IBM Syst J 32:4–16
20. Broadbent M, Weill P (1993) Improving business and information strategy alignment: learning from the banking industry. IBM Syst J 32:162–179
21. Simonsson M, Johnson P, Ekstedt M (2010) The effect of IT governance maturity on IT governance performance. Inf Syst Manag 27:10–24. doi:10.1080/10580530903455106
22. Shivashankarappa AN, Dharmalingam R, Smalov L, Anbazhagan N (2012) Implementing it governance using cobit: a case study focusing on critical success factors. In: World Congress on Internet Security, pp 144–149
23. Iskandar M, Akma N, Salleh M (2010) IT governance in airline industry : a multiple case study. Int J Digit Soc 1:308–313

Part III
Digital Innovation Trends

Chapter 9
Reinventing Business Models: The Third Way of Digital Innovation

Abstract This Part of the book explores digital innovation in practice presenting in the Chap. 10 some of the most interesting innovative ideas of 2013, based on observation and continuous scouting of research projects. However, digital business innovation is a multi-facets concept, which has received different interpretations over the years. As a consequence, in this Chapter we discuss the underlying issues and the most relevant concepts for understanding Business Model Innovation (BMI), providing general insights on the state of the art and basic constructs of this research stream, suitable to support an understanding of its evolution in current digital business innovation experiences and practices.

9.1 Introduction

The concept of a Business Model (BM) is not completely new in the field of economics, as the term appears for the first time in the literature in an article dated 1957 [1] and, subsequently, in 1960 [2]. Moreover, we can argue that this concept is, implicitly or explicitly, an integral part of the behavior of any economic entity in any historical period [3]. At the same time, within the fold of standard economic theory, the problem of setting up a business model that makes the creation and appropriation of value by production companies possible does not arise since it is assumed that consumers buy goods and services when the price is lower than the utility achieved, while the companies will provide these goods and services if the price is equal to or higher than cost of production automatically appropriating the value associated with them. In summary, any matter is resolved by the price system, which is, however, only a simplified model of the real economic system in which entrepreneurs and managers need to consider the crucial points such as:

- the creation of solutions that meet the perceived needs of customers;
- the structure of costs and revenues;

V. Morabito, *Trends and Challenges in Digital Business Innovation*, DOI: 10.1007/978-3-319-04307-4_9, © Springer International Publishing Switzerland 2014

- the mechanisms for appropriating the value of the product and making a profit on existing markets or that have yet to be created;
- the consequences of technological innovation.

The first studies in the field of strategic management [4] identify organizational design as the key element behind new types of emerging business models, emphasizing its central role in enabling companies to successfully manage the complexity of a new competitive environment [5, 6]. However, it is only in recent years, which were characterized by the economic changes created by the advent of the Internet, new post-industrial technologies and the opening of markets [7] with the gradual spread of dynamics such as outsourcing and the offshoring of many business activities, that the term business model has become a much discussed topic of research that underwent a very wide spread among academics, consultants and managers [8]. In fact, the business model was established as the independent unit of analysis of business and economic dynamics [9]. Providing a definition of the concept of business model is a useful starting point for discussing its implications and relevance in the context of economic and managerial studies. In addition, the concept of business model is emerging as one of the main levers of change and strategic innovation for organizations operating in all sectors. In particular, two complementary visions of the business model arise from the literature in the field of technological innovation management: the first one conceptualizes the business model as a fundamental tool through which companies can commercialize innovative ideas and technologies [10], while the second identifies the business model as a new layer of innovation added to product innovation and process innovation [11].

A significant example of the growing awareness by top management of the business model as a crucial tool to acquire and consolidate a sustainable competitive advantage and improve their ability to create and capture value can be seen, for example, in the results of the Global CEO Study 2009 produced by the IBM Institute for Business Value [12], interviewing 1,130 entrepreneurs, CEOs and general managers working in different industries. The study, in fact, reports that 7 out of 10 companies claim to pursue business model innovation as a strategic priority and 98 % are still, to some extent, re-adapting their business model. The tumultuous development and the spread of information and communication technologies have certainly contributed in a decisive way to the interests of the business and the academic world towards the business model as a fundamental enabler of the ability to compete and innovate. However, other determining factors such as globalization and deregulation have not only made the emergence of new types of business models possible, making this notion even more significant [13], but also introduced new competitive pressures that have reshaped entire industries by redistributing profits. These factors are forcing companies to rethink from the bottom up the way in which all of their business operations are organized and managed and to increasingly pursue innovation in the adapting of their business model to the new economic environment rather than in innovating a product or a single process [14].

Despite the growing attention to the theme of the business model as a fundamental management tool for the development of strategic innovation on which the competitive performance of organizations rest, at this moment in time, scientific literature does not provide a unified and homogeneous definition, but it is characterized by a marked fragmentation also from a conceptual point of view [11]. In fact, the concept of business model is used to analyze diverse dynamics and aspects, such as e-business [15], issues of strategy as a competitive advantage, value creation and business performance [16] and the management of technology and innovation [11].

Another issue on which authors disagree is the positioning of the concept of a business model relatively to the traditional units of analysis such as the single company or its network. According to some researchers, the business model can be identified at a company level [16], while others argue that the business model sits at a network level [17], while a third approach conceives the business model as an intermediate entity between the company and the network [18]. In addition, while some authors try to identify an adequate definition of the concept [7], others focus on the analysis of the relationship between business model and other dimensions such as information systems [19] and business strategy [20] and others focus on the constituent elements that make up the business model [11]. In order to outline a complete picture of the thematic area of interest, it is helpful to trace the various contributions of the authors through the analysis of certain definitions that show the widest resonance throughout the literature.

Table 9.1 shows some of the definitions that have been proposed for the concept of business model highlighting the crucial concepts identified by various authors. It is possible to observe that all these definitions agree in considering the business model as an essential element of business performance. In fact, the business model establishes the fundamental logic according to which the company intends to create and deliver value to its customers and appropriate the returns from that value by the coherent and harmonic interaction of its elements. This is because the business model is the fundamental framework for the analysis and management of each strategic choice made by the company [7] as well as for the proper communication and dissemination of such strategic choices to the entire organization [15]. Therefore, the ability to build strong and sustainable business models is a prerequisite for the competitive success of any company [21].

This is true for any organization in any economic environment, but it has become particularly relevant for companies that today have to operate in the new digital economy, which is characterized by the rapid and continuous interaction of innovative applications and services. In fact, especially where the company's business is increasingly linked to innovation and technology, the real source of competitive advantage is to be identified in the ability to build a business model fitting to the current economic and technological environment, because that is what allows an enterprise to transform a technological innovation in sustainable economic value for the business itself [11].

Table 9.1 Definitions of business model

Authors	Definition	Key concepts
Magretta 2002 [21]	A story that explains how companies operate. A good business model is able to answer to the long-standing questions of Peter Drucker: Who is the customer? To what does the customer attribute a value? It also provides an answer to the question that every manager must ask: how do you earn money in this business? What is the fundamental economic logic that allows us to deliver value to customers at an appropriate cost?	Who is the customer; What is the customer's concept of value; In that way we can deliver value to the customer at an appropriate cost
Osterwalder, Pigneur, Tucci 2005 [7]	A description of the value a company offers to one or more customer segments, the architecture of the firm and its network of partners to create market and deliver that value	Customers of reference; partner network; the system of relations, the positioning in the value chain of the business
Christoph Zott and Raphael Amit 2010 [22]	A system of interdependent activities that transcends the focal firm and extends its boundaries	What are the activities of the organization
Chesbrough and Rosenbloom 2002 [11]	A coherent framework that takes technological characteristics and potential as input and, through customers and markets, converts them in economic output. The business model is conceived as a focusing device that mediates between technological development and the creation of economic value	Technology; structure of the value chain; mechanism that generates economic value
Venkatram and Henderson 1998 [23]	A strategy that reflects the architecture of a virtual organization along three primary vectors: interaction with clients, asset configuration and knowledge leverage	Organizational strategy, customer interaction, asset configuration; leverage of knowledge
Bouwman 2002 [24]	A description of the roles and relationships that exist in a company, its customers, partners and suppliers, as well as the flow of goods, information and money between these parties and the main benefits for the parties involved, in particular, but not exclusively, customers	Roles and relationships in the value chain; exchange modes between actors

(continued)

Table 9.1 (continued)

Authors	Definition	Key concepts
Torbay, Osterwalder and Pigneur 2002 [25]	The architecture of the organization, its network of partners for creating, marketing and delivering value and relational capital to one or more customer segments in order to generate profitable and sustainable revenue streams	Network of partners, value creation; relational capital; customer segmentation
Leem, Suh and Kim 2004 [26]	A set of strategies for business management that includes a revenue model, high complexity of business processes and alliances	Strategy; revenue model; business processes; alliances
Haaker, Faber and Bouwman 2006 [27]	A collaboration effort between several companies in order to provide a joint offer to their consumers	Network of companies, value proposition
Shafer, Smith and Linder 2005 [15]	A representation of the fundamental logic and strategic choices of a company to create and capture value within a value network	Creating and extracting value, network value

9.2 Fundamental Elements of a Business Model

An analysis of the literature shows that several authors have focused on the identification and study of the fundamental elements that make up a business model [7, 15] and, based on this analysis, it is possible to build a unified conceptual framework that will hold together the various components identified by various authors that can contribute to integrate and organize the research in this area, which is still very fragmented.

Table 9.2 shows a summary of the literature with the aim of providing a structured organization of the various research contributions pointing out the authors whose researches are the basis of the conceptualization here proposed. This approach identifies four fundamental dimensions of the concept of BM—offer to customers, value network, architecture and finance—which, in turn, are divided into a number of constituent elements. Within the context of an analysis of the concept of BM it is useful to briefly examine these dimensions and their components and discuss their role.

9.2.1 Offer to Customers

This dimension includes the value proposition that a firm intends to create for its target customers in order to meet their needs through a given combination of goods

Table 9.2 Business model conceptualization

Business model area	Constituent elements	Relevant literature
Offer to Customers	Customer value proposition Customers segments Customer relational models Distribution and sales channels	[3, 7, 11, 15, 18, 19, 21, 23, 24, 25, 27, 28, 29, 30].
Value Network	Supply relations Partnership relations	[7, 15, 18, 19, 22, 24, 25, 26, 27, 28].
Architecture	Key processes Key competences Strategic assets	[3, 7, 11, 18, 19, 22, 23, 25, 28, 29, 30].
Finance	Cost structure Revenue model	[3, 21, 25, 26, 28, 29, 30].

and services. Thus, the BM of a company must contain a description that summarizes how it intends to deliver value to current and prospective customers and, in particular, this value must be greater than the alternatives provided by competitors.

9.2.2 Value Network

According to this perspective, the business model of a company defines its position within the value chain in which it operates and its relations with the various stakeholders. This chain is a multi-actor network that includes suppliers, intermediaries and partners through which value is created and exchanged.

9.2.3 Architecture

This dimension refers to all resources (human, technological and financial) and skills as well as their organizational configuration which enables the company to align, manage and utilize its assets in order to create and render marketable competitive value propositions.

Businesses must be able to identify from the number of resources needed to manage their own affairs those few strategically crucial ones that enable them to successfully implement their own business model. In addition, the companies' focus has to be brought to those critical processes that ensure sustainability, reusability, and scalability in the customer value offer.

Table 9.3 BM dimension: the offer to customers

Constituent element	Description
Customer value proposition	A short and detailed summary of the overall experience the company promises to offer to its own customers
Customer segmentation	Specific groups of customers whom the company intends to offer value to
Customer relational model	The relationships the company establishes with its customers
Sales and distribution channels	The channels representing contact points with the customers

Table 9.4 BM dimension: value network

Constituent element	Description
Supply relations	The network of relations with suppliers
Partnership relations	The strategic alliances with competitors and non-competitors (for example, companies producing complementary products/services)

Table 9.5 BM dimension: architecture

Constituent element	Description
Key processes	The set of essential activities (planning, development, production, sales) which allow the execution of the BM
Key competences	The set of people and competences, by means of which the value created can be provided to customers in the most efficient and effective way
Strategic assets	The specific set of resources, technologies and facilities that make up the company's competitive advantage

Table 9.6 BM dimension: finance

Constituent element	Description
Cost structure	The factors that define the level and the trends of costs and the relation between production and costs themselves
Revenue model	The system through which the company's revenue is generated

9.2.4 Finance

The financial dimension of the BM explains how the company is able to generate sales and profits [15]. In particular, the profit formula defines a company's profitability, specifying how a company creates and captures value for itself in terms of profit and it is of the utmost importance, because it determines the feasibility of the proposed value for the customer, with a direct influence on revenues and margins [7], thus determining the company's financial capacity.

Tables 9.3, 9.4, 9.5 and 9.6 illustrate in detail the elements that make up the various dimensions of the Business Model and which, although distinct on an analytical level, in reality are strongly interrelated and interdependent.

9.3 Business Model and Strategic Innovation

In the current economic environment, which is defined by intense technological acceleration [31], as well as by increasing competitive pressures because of the growth of supply associated with the opening of markets, organizations and companies are required to provide a continuous focus on innovation in order to create and deliver value to their customers and then maintain or improve their market position. The drive for innovation, at the same time, typically induces a general increase of the competitive standards in many areas, thereby resulting in a greater difficulty in achieving a successful performance on the market. Traditionally, innovation has been conceived and pursued through two key dimensions: product innovation and process innovation [32]. Product innovations are incorporated in goods or services offered by a company to protect its margins through differentiation or the renewal of its offering; while process innovations relate to change in the manner in which the activities are carried out in order to improve the efficiency or effectiveness of manufacturing operations.

However, in recent years there has been a major change in the way companies define and seek innovation [10]. In fact, the focus of businesses is increasingly on innovation of the business model as an alternative or as an essential complement to product and/or process innovation. Rarely has a technological change (of a product or process) taken place without producing as a result a change in the business model and vice versa. In fact, the most successful organizations are those that combine technological and business model change to create innovation.

But what factors have prompted organizations to move the center of their strategic action from what they do to the way they conduct business and generate profits? Two different interrelated aspects seem to have originated this trend: the configuration of the business model in relation to existing products and the alignment between the innovations and the business model.

9.3.1 The Business Model Configuration

The proper structuring of the business model and its adaptability to variable market conditions and competitiveness are fundamental not only in the search for new sources of competitive advantage, but also for sustaining existing competitive advantage. The innovation of the business model can prove to be the crucial lever that allows the company to remain competitive in the race to product or process. In fact the products that are incorporated into an innovative and efficient business model are less likely to be rendered obsolete by the introduction of new products by competitors, as it is generally more difficult for competitors to replicate and replace a whole system of activities rather than a single product or process. The *Apple* case is illustrative of this point [7, 33, 34]. The production of highly innovative software and hardware products has always been the focus of Apple and, traditionally, most of its business operations were taking place in the field of personal computers. The launch of the iPod, the portable media player, in combination with the iTunes software, a system that allows users to access the Apple store to buy online music and other types of content and transfer them from an iPod to a computer, corresponds to a formidable innovation of Apple's business model. In summary, not only Apple has developed and brought to the market hardware and software products with a high degree of innovation, but it has radically transformed its business environment, adding music distribution to its activities. This transformation has resulted in the construction of new ongoing relations, on the one hand with customers, allowing them to access, acquire and store digital music, and on the other hand with business partners, namely all the major record labels, which have been integrated into Apple's business model through the creation of Apple's online music store. The interoperability between its products, which is the core of Apple's business model, allows the company to create and extract value on an ongoing basis and to effectively defend itself from competitors. In fact, also with the hypothetical introduction on the market by another company of a new, highly advanced mp3 player, offered at a lower price, only a small number of iPod customers connected to their iTunes account would be willing to change brands, because the value related to the purchase of an Apple product is perceived as exceeding the mere purchasing cost, as it gives access to a whole system of activities related to the distribution of music. Essentially, Apple has managed to shift the locus of competition in the fast-paced technology market from product innovation to the innovation of the business model of reference for an entire market, acquiring a formidable competitive advantage.

9.3.2 Offer and Business Model Alignment

The true value of innovative ideas and technologies for the most part depends on the business model through which they are brought to market [32]. In fact, even the most promising technologies are unprofitable or are destined to failure without a solid business model that allows a profitable commercialization [11]. As it is now widely recognized both in theory and in business practice, innovation is a fundamental activity for the growth of a business and its survival in the long term and therefore requires the design and implementation of a focused innovation strategy guided by the objectives of the company itself. An effective innovation strategy must understand and take into consideration two fundamental aspects: the technological dimension and the size of the market. Product (as well as process) innovation is therefore not enough to build a sustainable competitive advantage that ensures profits, but companies are also called, and are expected to excel, in formulating and implementing effective business models [3].

It can rightly be argued that the "original sin" of many of the so-called dot.com that collapsed at the outbreak of the new economy bubble during the years 2000 and 2001 can be identified precisely in the absence of an economically successful, grounded and sustainable business model. In reality, many companies with a registered domain on the Web were entirely aimed at attracting as many users as possible to their websites, which provided some service, and to pursue this end they faced huge advertising investments. However these companies lacked a business model that could convert the number of users who visited their sites in cash flows and profits. Therefore, once the available capital was quickly depleted, they were no longer able to continue operating. This is the case of Pets.com [35], a company specializing in the sale of pet products online, which, after collecting substantial funding through venture capital operations in the startup phase, went from IPO (Initial Public Offering: i.e. the first offer of securities to the public by a company on a regulated market) to bankruptcy in less than a year. At the base of the failure of this company (and many others) was the inability to build a business model that would allow translating the clicks of users who had been attracted into profits.

In summary, the crucial factor for the success of a company is not the value of an idea or technology itself. The most important element is the construction of an effective operating and strategic model, meaning a complex system of activities and relations through which the potential value of an idea or technology is actually transformed into economic value. The centrality of the business model can be defined through the two following core processes any company is necessarily called to deal with in order to operate on the market and survive:

- *Value creation*, meaning the value that is generated by the entire value chain made up of the company, its suppliers, distribution partners and customers. The maximization of the created value requires cooperative relationships among the various actors, who must protect their own interests and create value for their partners at the same time. In this sense, a proper business model involves the construction of a system of relations which enables effective coordination in the acquisition and use of resources beyond the individual company boundaries, taking also into account the fact that the various actors involved in the creation of value will also seek the appropriation of that value and therefore their interests will tend to diverge.
- *Value capture*, with the focus being the way in which the company is able to retain a part of the value created "at the expense" of customers, suppliers, partners and competitors.

This way, the business model must be understood and used as the primary tool through which companies can, on the one hand, operate to expand their target market (value creation); on the other hand, they can be able to grab a share of the profit resulting from this enlargement of the market.

The evolution of the economic and technological environment has resulted in a substantial change in what was the traditional relationship between customer and company [3]. The opening of markets, on the one hand, and the new information and communication technologies on the other have not only made the reduction of the production costs of many goods and services possible, but, even more significantly, have expanded the possibilities for consumer choice, made the comparison of alternatives more transparent in terms of quality and prices, enabling the emergence of new customer needs and new tools to deal with them, thus making consumers more aware and demanding. Companies are thus called to adopt an approach that is increasingly focused on the customer, keeping in mind that the advent of new technologies has resulted in the enhancement of the capacity of processing data associated with a significant reduction in costs, making it possible to manufacture and supply with competitive prices, products and services tailored to each type of user.

These developments require businesses to radically rethink and reconfigure the value proposition presented to customers moving from a *supply-driven logic*, according to which companies compete mainly in the field of execution of operations, to a *demand-driven logic*, where the commercial relationship is increasingly based on collaboration and interactivity criteria and the new competition dynamics are based on the ability to build and strengthen customer relationships through a highly personalized offer built on the specific needs of different customer segments.[1] This new context has not only changed the challenge of creating value with tools, methods and new interactions, but it also has companies facing the need to reconsider the process of economic value appropriation. A profitable and sustainable business model must articulate not only the operations and processes that underlie value creation and appropriation activities, but also the roles played by the various relevant stakeholders such as customers, suppliers, competitors and suppliers of complementary services, outlining the relationship between the parts that make up an enterprise's network. In the light of the great variability of markets and of increasingly accentuated competitive dynamics, it is the network of relationships created by a company which determines its competitiveness. So we can say that today the competition is not only among individual organizations, but also, and mainly, among value creation systems composed by networks of companies.

One of the major complexities of the digital economy also lies in the fact that the traditional value chain centered on the offer system has turned into a complex value network in which each actor can play multiple roles and also those activities that had always been limited to companies, for example, research and development, production, distribution and marketing can now be performed (at least partly) by actors external to the company.[2]

---

[1] As shown also in Chap. 4 on Social Listening.

[2] As shown by the Crowdsourcing practice discussed in Chap. 6.

9.4 Digital Business Model Innovation: Conceptualizations

The advent of the digital economy can be really conceived as a new industrial revolution both in terms of magnitude and extension of the economic transformations made possible by the Internet and new digital technologies. These changes are structural and have a fundamental strategic relevance [36] as they present completely new strategic challenges and opportunities such as the possibility of establishing a direct relationship with customers bypassing other actors in the value chain. No business entity, whether a startup or an established company with years of experience, can afford to ignore the changes that have already occurred and are still in place and that involve significant changes with respect to the so-called industrial economy and will therefore be called upon to design and implement a business model able to deal with and exploit such characteristics of the digital economy.

Table 9.7 compares the essential features of the processes of transformation of the traditional industrial economy on one side and that of the digital economy on the other. Companies operating in a competitive market environment must create value for their customers, specifically, this value must be perceived by customers as being superior to that offered by competitors. In the transition from a traditional industrial digital economy the whole process of value creation is entirely transformed. In the industrial economy a process of value creation starts from raw materials and from the physical inputs that are needed to produce finished products or services. The outputs are finished or intermediate goods used as input for another transformation or value creating process. Knowledge, such as engineering know-how or production methods and processes as well, is applied to facilitate the process of physical transformation. The industrial economy is driven by the offer side with a constant focus on cost containment, while, as already discussed, the digital economy is fundamentally driven by customer demand. In the digital economy, the essential input of the value creation process is information itself, for example, customer profiles and preferences that companies need to collect, organize, select, synthesize and distribute [37] in the transformation process to be able to provide customers with customized solutions. In summary, information, in the digital economy, is an essential source of value and every business is an information business [38]. In particular, the web offers unique and unprecedented meeting and exchange opportunities between companies and customers. Web servers can monitor and record the navigation of millions of users and produce in real-time pages with a highly personalized content based on the profile and preferences of the single user.

Information and knowledge play a crucial role both in the traditional and the digital economy. However, in the industrial economy knowledge generation and application processes are essentially aimed at making production more efficient through cost reductions, while in the digital economy they are mainly directed to intercepting the customer's preferences and expand his choice. The digital economy offers companies a variety of tools (e.g., web-based supply chain management

Table 9.7 Comparison between the industrial and the digital economy

	Industrial economy	Digital economy
Business process orientation	• Guided by offer	• Guided by demand
Economic focus	• Cost minimizing	• Value maximizing
Product policy	• Offer standardization	• Offer personalization
Value chain configuration	• Linear value chain	• Non-linear value network
Key inputs	• Raw materials, intermediate products	• Digital information
Output	• Intermediate or finished products or services	• Products or services with a high information/knowledge content
The role of information	• A supporting and connecting element during the phases of production	• A source of value

systems, online commerce, interactive customer service) that enable the creation of value not only through the reduction of costs, but also and above all making them more capable of responding to customer needs. In fact, in a world where access to information is permanent, immediate and almost ubiquitous, value creation depends on the ability to locate, select, filter and communicate the information which the consumer perceives as actually useful.

The Internet, however, proved to be a destructive force for many companies, completely transforming entire sectors, because the network is not only a tremendous source of access to data and information in a digital format, but it also constitutes a new channel of distribution and marketing. In fact, the advent of the Internet has challenged the traditional way of doing business, as it has, and still is, significantly transforming the traditional rules of competition, offer value propositions and business models [39]. First of all, the market is no longer just a physical place and geographically fragmented, but rather becomes a digital, open and transparent space. At the same time, the network has also intensified competition since the easier access to information and the reduction of variable costs stimulates competition on prices and therefore requires the maximization of operational efficiency. In addition, it is easier for potential entrants to access distribution channels and reach new customers.

A third factor that contributes to intensify the competitive pressure is the ability of the network to get the manufacturer and the end user closer and in direct communication, drastically reducing the need for intermediaries in the sale of goods and services. In this sense, the network can undoubtedly be counted among the most significant radical innovations, that is those innovations that have as a fundamental trait of a total discontinuity with previous technologies, whose technical skills they tend to displace (making them in some cases so obsolete to cause their withdrawal from the market), resulting in a drastic transformation of the productive processes of economic activities they touch and producing a different distribution of wealth compared to the situation before their introduction. A clear example of the overwhelming impact of the Internet is given by the recording industry, which had to completely reconfigure its value chain and its traditional business model in response to new distribution channels made available by the digital network, which were competing with the traditional sales channels, as well as the phenomenon of piracy and illegal downloading of music content which make it extremely difficult to capture the value originating from online transactions.

Another area that was particularly affected by the rapid evolution of the digital world is the newspaper publishing market, which faces major strategic challenges especially related to building a business model that allows providers of new information services to create and appropriate part of the value generated by the production and publication of content that users generally expect to have free access to. The formulation and implementation of an appropriate business model are vital to meet the challenges of the digital economy, which requires a paradigm shift. Companies are called to deal with the Internet and the opportunities of electronic commerce, but, to be able to acquire the benefits, they must be able to identify the disruptive nature of these innovations in order to effectively reconfigure their distribution strategies or the entire business model [3].

Taking the above issues into account, Table 9.8 identifies a number of attributes that make the Internet and electronic commerce disruptive innovations [40]. Organizations operating in the digital economy must identify and exploit economically these specific attributes of the Internet and of electronic commerce and their success depends mainly on the ability to build a business model that can capitalize on these particular characteristics. In the context of the digital economy, the innovation of the business model can be defined as the creation and utilization of new knowledge (which can be technological, organizational or market-related) that enables a company to benefit from the disruptive attributes of the Internet in order to design and implement an innovative system to provide customers with highly personalized products and services targeted to the needs of the customers themselves.

Among the successful examples of innovation of a business model that can profitably make use of some of the above features of the Internet as a disruptive innovation we can mention Dell's build-to-order and direct sales model, which redefined the value chain linked to the world of personal computers in the late nineties, eBay's and Priceline' reverse auction system, the Amazon affiliate network, and online virtual communities (e.g. Yahoo!) [41, 42].

9.5 The Business Model in the Information and Communication Economy

The consolidation of the information and communication economy is the culmination of the process of evolution that had the service economy gradually replaced the industrial economy, and its extraordinary success is mainly due to the strengthening of its main infrastructure, the network. In this context, information is

Table 9.8 Characteristics of the internet as a disruptive innovation

Elements of discontinutiy	Description
Open platform	The internet represents an open and public network which allows a constant flow of communication and collaboration in real time
Network externalitics	Network externalities exist when the value of a given product/service to any single user becomes greater as the number of users of the same product/service increases
Connectivity and interaction	E-commerce enables the company to establish new relations and ways of interacting with their customers, suppliers and partners
Information sharing and exchange	The Internet allows information to reach a large number of people without sacrificing the quality of the information content which it distributes
Production and consumption convergence	The involvement of the consumer-user in the early stages of design and production of highly customized goods and services
Digital resources	Information and data in a digital form, duly selected, organized and summarized, become a source of essential value that enables companies to formulate new value propositions
Cost transparency	Users are able to quickly and easily access a vast amount of information regarding prices and characteristics of the products and services offered by the various competitors
Industry extension	The value creation made possible by the Internet and new digital technologies allows companies to transcend the boundaries of traditional business
Speed and frequency of changes	In the digital economy companies need to continually adapt to changes, which are extremely fast and frequent
Virtual capacity	The recent progress in networking and storage technologies has led to the creation of an extensive market place available to users

Adapted and integrated from [41]

defined as any product that can be digitized, represented as a sequence of bits and thus distributed rapidly and at an irrelevant cost over the network.[3] Newspapers, books and music content and movies are just a few examples of digitized information products. Digitized information is costly to produce, but can be reproduced and distributed at a negligible cost; using the terminology of economic theory, these products are characterized by high fixed costs and low marginal costs. This type of cost structure implies that there is a minimum efficient scale of production and dissemination and that the declining average costs requires an increase in sales. In summary, there are significant economies of scale on the supply side. On the demand side, that is, from the point of view of consumers, it is possible to identify four key features of digitalized products [43]:

- *Experience goods.* An experience good can be defined as a product or service the value of which can only be judged through its actual consumption. Thus, the consumer is not able to judge its utility before purchasing it. The producers of

---

[3] The difference between *digitizing* and *digitalization* has been discussed in Chap. 3.

experience goods must devise strategies to persuade users to overcome their reluctance to buy information before knowing the characteristics. A possible tool to create or stimulate future demand, even at the cost of decreasing actual revenues, is the offer of free copies or of promotional prices. A second fundamental way is investing in reputation, for example through promotional campaigns, which help consumers to learn about the features of the new product and boost their trust in the company. Given these characteristics, the central problem of the information economy can be summed up in the contrast between the need for users to understand the characteristics of the main product/service that is being offered to them and the need to have them pay a price which is functional to generating a revenue at least sufficient to cover the costs of producing the information.

- *Informational overload.* In an environment where users have at their disposal an extreme amount and variety of information that can be accessed anywhere and at any time, there exists a problem of information overload. On the one hand, users are called on an expensive and complex selection of useful or productive information, while, on the other hand, this overabundance of information generates scarce attention. Consequently, information retrieval and filtering services have a high value for consumers. In fact, the search engines like Google and Yahoo! are some of the most visited websites and they make money thanks to sponsored links and paid advertising; what they sell is really just the attention of people who use them, so the larger their user base, the higher the revenue, while the product, that is the selected information, is offered free of charge to the consumer.

- *Transition costs.* These are the costs that a consumer incurs into when switching from one product to another or from one technology to another with different use features. These costs originate from past investments and influence the decisions of both consumers and producers and include several components: the costs related to the cognitive effort of processing new information and learn different features, emotional costs due to the uncertainty and operational risks associated with the products and technologies in use. The presence of transition costs is not exclusive to informational products, but their effects are particularly significant and pervasive in the digital economy. When the costs associated with the transition from one provider to another are so high as to reduce any benefit from switching and deter the consumer, this creates a *lock-in* situation where users are tied to existing products. So transition costs are a barrier to entry for new producers, while existing suppliers have an interest in stimulating the use of a given information product and create switching costs so as to achieve the *lock-in* effect constraining the customers, while having him perceive that as a component of the perceived value, a concrete advantage of not switching supplier.

- *Positive network externalities.* A product exhibits positive network externalities, or network effects, when the value of the product for the individual consumer positively depends on the total number of users who make use of that product. In other words, the access to the network created by the good or service in question of another user is beneficial for current users. Communication technologies, such as the telephone, the fax and internet access, are a clear example of products displaying network externalities. Therefore, the use of these technologies is not possible until a critical mass of users is not reached. The trend observed for technologies exhibiting significant network effects is a relatively long period of introduction followed by an explosive growth. In fact, when the number of users is small, the incentive to connecting is limited, but once it reaches the critical threshold, this incentive becomes high and, typically, the product takes over the market.

Innovating and exploring new business models can be equally profitable, if not more, from a strategic standpoint than innovating products [11]. It is therefore important to analyze emerging business models in order to understand the factors that lead to the success or failure of innovation processes. One of the economic models that are most popular among Web 2.0 companies, which exploits the peculiarities of the information economy, is the so-called "freemium" (combination of "free" and "premium"). This model involves two or more variants of a given product or service that are distributed at different prices. The basic version is made available to users for free, while the other versions providing additional features are sold for a fee [11].

9.5.1 The Strategic Variables

Companies, especially in the current economic context, look at innovation as the key driver for improving their performance and strengthening their competitive position [10]. The configuration (or reconfiguration) of a business model is often the direct result of technological innovation which makes it necessary to bring to the market the results of this innovation process, opening up the opportunity to intercept unmet or unexpressed needs [3]. However, this need for innovation is to some extent restrained by the impact of globalization and the convergence of different technologies over economic processes, mainly due to the drastic shortening of the product market cycle and the increasing costs of development. These factors have led to a significant reduction in the profitability of investments in innovation, and since the innovation process involves higher costs and risks, the incentive to innovate is, as a result, lower. The rationale of the global market, then, requires companies to maximize their ability to combine and hold together the sometimes conflicting goals of operational efficiency and technological innovation to improve the quality of products and services offered to customers.

Accelerating the acquisition of innovation and containing the costs of research and development have become inescapable imperatives for companies wishing to remain competitive in the current economic and technological environment. Another critical element is related to the fact that the fundamental characteristics of the market—globally integrated and hyper-competitive—have undermined the very architecture of innovation processes that were the basis for the growth of companies for many years, pushing towards a profound transformation of these processes. In 2003, Henry Chesbrough in his book "*Open Innovation: The new imperative for creating and profiting from technology*" [44] identifies and compares the old and the new paradigm of innovation: *closed innovation* and *open innovation*, addressing the subject of how the technologies needed for innovation originate, are developed and adopted.

9.5.2 From the Traditional Model of Innovation to Open Innovation

According to the traditional model of innovation, the creation of value in the form of innovation is based on the transformation of inputs (investments in research and development) into outputs (new products and opportunities), and this process takes place entirely inside the company. R&D departments are therefore a crucial strategic asset for companies, as they constitute the main lever for building and preserving a competitive advantage. The investments necessary for research laboratories and the protection of intellectual property correspond to barriers to entry for potential entrants, especially as the research and development are generally subject to significant economies of scale. At the base of the closed innovation paradigm is the idea that the company should take full control, both in terms of management and ownership, of the entire innovation process, from development to marketing, using only its own resources and internal networks in a self-sufficient manner. The acquisition and the maintaining of a competitive advantage is based on the first-mover position, which provides significant barriers to entry also and especially through a proactive management of intellectual property aimed at preventing other entities from benefiting from technologies and ideas developed inside the company.

However, this model of innovation has several limitations and inefficiencies that significantly restrict the ability of companies to produce innovation and reach all of its strategic benefits. In fact, many opportunities, even promising ones, are lost because they require external technologies, but not all companies have the resources and the capacity to absorb them internally. Furthermore, projects developed within the company, but not consistent with the business model adopted, are discarded without seeking an alternative use, either in another market or by selling them, thus losing the possibility to obtain additional revenues through the sale of the company's intellectual property to other companies or organizations.

These factors, along with the rapid economic and technological transformations emerged in the early 2000s, have led to the development of new approaches, in particular the open innovation model [44].

Table 9.9 summarizes the comparison between the two fundamental paradigms of innovation over seven key dimensions: (1) the placement, internal or external, of R&D resources and skills; (2) the degree of control exercised by the company

Table 9.9 Comparison between closed and open innovation

	Closed innovation	Open innovation
Location of R&D resources	Internal R&D	Internal and external R&D
The role of R&D in the creation of value	The whole innovation process is controlled directly from the company	R&D is external and is significantly involved in the creation of value
Management of intellectual property	Property and defense of internally generated intellectual property	Purchasing and selling of intellectual property
Distinctive competence	Development of internal knowledge	Integration of internal and external knowledge
Strategic objective	Being the first to market the research and defending the revenues	Building the best business model involving external actors
Degree of collaboration among companies	None, collaboration present only internally among R&D teams	An articulated network of interactions which involve vertical and horizontal alliances among different companies and industries
Relation between research and the adopted business model	The results of research are necessarily tied to the company's internal operational model	

over the innovation process aimed at creating value; (3) the policy for managing the intellectual property of the innovations generated and used by the company; (4) the strategically prioritized capability for the company; (5) the main objective which defines the coordinates of the companies' strategic action; (6) the degree of collaboration between different companies; (7) the type of relationship that exists between the results of the conducted research and the particular business model put in place by the company.

The fundamental idea of the paradigm of open innovation is that the company needs to look beyond its boundaries, integrating its own corporate resources with the external resources of a multiplicity of actors who can offer their specific expertise, thus increasing the potential for overall innovation.[4] The innovation process can be launched and activated by both internal and external sources and, at any time, can be integrated through various collaboration tools, such as, for example, technology investments, licenses, joint venture agreements and participation in research consortiums. Even the commercialization of innovation and its placing on the market may not be limited to distribution channels inside the company, but also take advantage of the paths provided by external actors.

Within the open innovation model knowledge and information flow in two directions: from the outside towards the company and from the company to the outside. The first involves the acquisition of ideas and technologies produced outside the company, reducing the costs and risks of research and significantly

---

[4] See also for these topics the discussion about digital work and collaboration in Chap. 6.

broadening the portfolio of solutions and projects which a company is able to access. The second stream involves the transferring of unused innovations developed within the company to other actors, allowing the increase of profits through the transfer of these technologies and projects, for example through processes spinning-off and the outsourcing of unused intellectual property. Such bidirectional knowledge flows, on the one hand, accelerate and improve the innovation process; on the other hand, they create and expand the markets that will use the produced innovation.

The paradigm of open innovation is based on the awareness that the knowledge generated outside the company is as important for the creation of value as the one generated inside. This results in a significant transformation in the way the research and development function has been thought of until now. In fact, this function is part of the business offer not only as a cost center anymore, but also as a profit center, because it operates within a business model capable of transforming the output of R&D in economic value, not only through the direct marketing of ideas and technologies, but also through the management of intellectual property of these ideas and technologies that are then marketed elsewhere. Furthermore, R&D is called to operate as a mechanism of connection and reinforcement of knowledge and competences present outside the company, managing an increasingly complex network of inter-organizational relationships that include new producers and co-producers of innovation, such as, e.g., universities, research centers, industrial companies, but also suppliers, manufacturers of complementary products as well as end users. The ideas and projects developed internally are only a part of the value that can be generated by the company; thus, the skills related to capturing, transforming and exploiting external expertise and, secondly, to the transferring of knowledge outside the company, become crucial. As a consequence, the creation of value and the ability to win on the market no longer depend exclusively on the development of research within a company, but it becomes more important to build a business model that can collect, integrate and enhance the best ideas, selecting and involving all stakeholders, both internal and external, in the process of innovation through the creation of strategic alliances. This exchange of ideas and technologies from the outside to the inside of the company and from the inside to the outside environment must be enabled and supported by an open business model as a fundamental source of innovation advantage, aimed at expanding the knowledge base of the company, reducing and sharing the risks and improving competitive performance, likewise.

9.6 Summary

This Chapter has provided an overview of the digital innovation impact on Business Models (BMs). Furthermore, the Chapter has presented the main concepts underlying Business Model Innovation (BMI), providing insight on the relevant literature and the tools for a solid definition and conceptualization. Understanding the effect of digital innovation on the business strategy and its potential for generating value and bringing revolutions and evolutions in BMs is a key factor for analyzing and effectively evaluating the ideas and opportunities for innovation presented in Chap. 10.

References

1. Bellman R, Clark C (1957) On the construction of a multi-stage, multi-person business game. Oper Res 5(4):469–503
2. Jones GM (1960) Educators, electrons, and business models: a problem in synthesis. Account Rev 35:619–626
3. Teece D (2010) Business models, business strategy and innovation. Long Range Plann 43:172–194. doi:10.1016/j.lrp.2009.07.003
4. Van de Ven A, Walker G (1984) The dynamics of inter-organizational coordination. Adm Sci Q 29:598–621
5. Bergvall-Kåreborn B (1999) Review: "information, system and information System" By Peter Checkland and Sue Holwell. Cybern Hum Knowing 6:91–95
6. Checkland P, Holwell S (1998) Information, systems and information systems: making sense of the field. Wiley, Chichester
7. Osterwalder A, Pigneur Y, Tucci C (2005) Clarifying business models: origins, present, and future of the concept. Commun. AIS 16(1):1–25
8. Alt R, Zimmermann H-D (2001) Preface: introduction to special section—business models. Electron Mark 11:3–9
9. Zott C, Amit R, Massa L (2011) The business model: recent developments and future research. J Manage 37:1019–1042. doi:10.1177/0149206311406265
10. Birkinshaw J, Bouquet C, Barsoux JL (2012) The 5 myths of innovation. MIT Sloan Manag Rev 52:43–50
11. Chesbrough H, Rosenbloom R (2002) The role of the business model in capturing value from innovation: evidence from Xerox Corporation's technology spin-off companies. Ind Corp Chang 11:529–555
12. IBM (2009) IBM Institute for Business Value's Biannual Global CEO Study 2009
13. Casadesus-Masanell R, Ricart JE (2007) Competing through business models—WP no 713. Work Pap IESE Bus Sch 3:1–28
14. Hammer M (2004) Deep change: How operational innovation can transform your company. Harv Bus Rev 82(4):84–93
15. Shafer S, Smith H, Linder J (2005) The power of business models. Bus Horiz 48:199–207. doi:10.1016/j.bushor.2004.10.014
16. Casadesus-Masanell R, Ricart J (2010) From strategy to business models and onto tactics. Long Range Plann 43:1–25
17. Tapscott D, Lowy A, Ticoll D (2000) Digital capital: harnessing the power of business webs. Harvard Business School Press, Cambridge
18. Amit R, Zott C (2001) Value creation in E-business. Strateg Manag J 22:493–520
19. Hedman J, Kalling T (2003) The business model concept: theoretical underpinnings and empirical illustrations. Eur J Inf Syst 12:49–59. doi:10.1057/palgrave.ejis.3000446
20. Mansfield GM, Fourie LCH (2004) Strategy and business models-strange bedfellows? a case for convergence and its evolution into strategic architecture. South African J Bus Manag 35:35–44
21. Magretta J (2002) Why business models matter. Harv Bus Rev 80:86–92. doi:10.1016/j.cub.2005.06.028

22. Zott C, Amit R (2010) Business model design: an activity system perspective. Long Range Plann 43:216–226. doi:10.1016/j.lrp.2009.07.004
23. Venkatraman M, Henderson J (1998) Real strategies for virtual organizing. Sloan Manage Rev 44:33–48
24. Bouwman H (2002) The sense and nonsense of business models. International workshop on business models. Lausanne, 4–5 October 2002, pp 1–6
25. Torbay MD, Osterwalder A, Pigneur Y (2002) eBusiness model design, classification and measurements. Thunderbird Int Bus Rev 44:5–23
26. Leem C, Suh H, Kim D (2004) A classification of mobile business models and its applications. Ind Manag Data Syst 104:78–87
27. Haaker T, Faber E, Bouwman H (2006) Balancing customer and network value in business models for mobile services. Int J Mob Commun 4:645–661
28. Hamel G (2000) Leading the revolution. Harvard Business School Press, Boston
29. Afuah A, Tucci C (2003) Internet business models and strategies. Harvard Business School Press, Boston
30. Johnson MW, Christensen CM, Kagermann H (2008) Reinventing your business model. Harv Bus Rev 86:50–59
31. Gopalakrishnan S, Kessler EH, Scillitoe JL (2010) Navigating the innovation landscape: past research, present practice, and future trends. Organ Manag J 7:262–277. doi:10.1057/omj. 2010.36
32. Sawhney M, Wolcott RC, Arroniz I (2006) The 12 different ways for companies to innovate. MIT Sloan Manag Rev 47(3):75–81
33. Dyer J, Gregersen H, Christensen CM (2011) The Innovator's DNA: mastering the five skills of disruptive innovators. Harvard Business Review Press, Boston
34. Porter ME (2011) The five competitive forces that shape strategy. HBR's 10 must reads strateg. Harvard Business Review Press, Boston, pp 39–76
35. Matulich E, Squires K (2008) What a dog fight! TKO: Pets.com. J Bus Case Stud 4(5):1–6
36. Ghoshal S, Bartlett CA, Moran P (1999) A new manifesto for management. Sloan manage review 40(3):9–20
37. Rayport J, Sviokla J (1995) Exploiting the virtual value chain. Harv Bus Rev November:75–85
38. Earl MJ (1999) Strategy-making in the Information Age. In: Currie WL, Galliers R (eds) Rethinking management information systems: an interdisciplinary perspective. Oxford University Press, Oxford, pp 161–174
39. Anderson D, Lee HL (2000) The Internet-enabled supply chain: from the "first click" to the "last mile." Achiev. supply Chain Excell. 1–7. http//anderson-d.ASCET.com
40. Bower J, Christensen C (1995) Disruptive technologies: catching the wave. Harv Bus Rev 73:43–53
41. Lee C (2001) An analytical framework for evaluating e-commerce business models and strategies. Internet Res 11:349–359
42. Winer RS (2006) Marketing management, 3rd edn. Pearson Prentice Hall, Upper Saddle River
43. Amit R, Zott C (2012) Creating value through business model innovation. MIT Sloan Manag. Rev. 53(3):41–49
44. Chesbrough H (2003) Open innovation: the new imperative for creating and profiting from technology. Harvard Business Review Press, Boston

Chapter 10
Innovation Practices

Abstract This Chapter focuses on examples of digital innovation in practice, providing fact-sheets of 10 of the most interesting ideas in the field of digital innovation worldwide in 2013. The genesis of the selected ideas lies in innovative research projects that have been developed successfully, becoming start-ups and spin-offs and reaching the market, where they are currently applied. For each innovation we provide an introduction to the main characteristics of the solution, information about its developer coupled with company competitiveness indicators for time-to-market, as well as some indicators of user value in terms of perception, such as the user Experience and the so called «Wow» effect, and impact on current processes.

10.1 Introduction

The shifting sands of innovation require from those who wish to stay on top to understand where to go, to plan each careful step, and to be ready for the next one, moving fast and following valuable opportunities. Translated in managerial terms, to solve the "innovator's dilemma" [1] companies need ambidexterity as a dynamic capability to explore new areas of innovation while also working on their day-to-day exploitation of current assets and incremental improvement [2]. The latter is often an effective routine in companies, while the first is far from trivial. Current processes and successes provide a very good guide for effective incremental innovation, but finding a trail and choosing a direction for the next revolution is not typically in the DNA of a company. One way to resolve the issue of discerning relevant innovations from temporary fades is to observe the projects and topics research centers are working on. When the idea is valuable the underlying research project often becomes a spin-off or a start-up, reaching to the market in short time and developing through experience and collaboration the execution capability to make it possible. The ideas selected and presented in this Chapter originate in effective research projects launched first by excellence centers all over the World, that have been developed and brought to the market, and are now applied. The continuous scouting activity conducted to prepare this part of research gives us tools to evaluate and select interesting topics and ideas to keep in the innovation radar.

10.2 Instabank

Instabank [3] is a Mobile Banking app developed by a Russian Start-up in collaboration with VTB Bank, a leading Russian Financial Institution. It is designed as a mix between the style and appearance of iOS with the convenience of Facebook. The app is permanently linked to a virtual credit card, based on the Mastercard circuit, and allows to keep easy track of movements in a visualization similar to the timeline in Facebook. Furthermore, it lets subscribers to link banking information with social networks allowing quicker transfers or direct use of Facebook wallet. Through the app it is possible to send and request money to friends through Facebook messages, even if they don't have an Instabank account, add pictures and personal notes to transactions, and keep track of movements and link them to position through geolocalization functionalities.

Transfers can easily be made between users, requested from friends or relatives and grouped from multiple sources. The app includes a simple and free money transfer system available through wireless communication between devices, and other functionalities for "bill splitting" as well as small transfers in social occasions. Subscribers can pay with Instabank on-line wherever Mastercard is accepted as well as in physical shops using Instabank to accept payments. Diffusion is, as of now, very low, but the fact that there is no need for specific assets and investments on the merchant side may contribute to a rapid growth in adoption.

10.2.1 Developer

Instabank is a Russian startup, born out of the experience of the founders with traditional mobile banking apps. One of the developers has an engineering background and experience on Google software, developed at the IBM Research Lab in Haifa, while his two partners both have extensive experience in the banking industry. Instabank is focusing all its energies to develop an easy to use and simple on-line banking application, while the core of the banking activity behind it is managed by a traditional Russian Bank (VPB). In 2012, Instabank received a $4 million investment from a fund by a coalition of large banks investing in financial services projects. Its first steps have been very promising and it's not hard to believe the claim of the funders who plan on expanding the business in the USA.

In Table 10.1 there is a synthetic representation of some of the drivers of competitiveness on a time-to-market basis. The measures are intended to capture

Table 10.1 Company
competitiveness indicators
for time-to-market

Company	Instabank
Funded	2012
N° Products	1
Clients	Invite only
Partners	VPB
Market dimension	Growing interest
Competitors	Yes
Enabling infrastructure	Ready

the readiness of the technology, of the company, of the market (both demand and offer side) and of the complementary infrastructure. In particular: the year of foundation and number of products are presented as a proxy of the stability of the company. Furthermore, the presence of clients substitutes a measure of the product readiness; while the presence of strong incumbent companies as partners in the development phase is another indicator of solidity.

The dimension of the market and the presence of competitors indicate a state of readiness of the demand, which signals a higher likeliness of a fast rate of diffusion of the product. Finally, the presence of the enabling infrastructure is a complement to the readiness of the technology itself, since whenever it is ready it can be effectively deployed only if the infrastructure is ready as well. As appears from the Table Instabank shows good promise for a rapid diffusion, after its official launch. For now it's going through the last phases of development and it is not yet available to customers.

10.2.2 Applications

The value behind such kinds of innovation lies mainly in an increased customer intimacy by means of becoming part of the daily routine operations of the user.

This application, as many other next-generation mobile banking apps, gives customers more interactivity, by greatly simplifying complex operations into one click experiences and blurring the boundaries between financial transactions and their personal and social context. Uploading a picture of what you just bought into your banking statement helps users recall where they spend their money, sending a Facebook message with a payment to a friend is an easy way to make a transfer. It's one of the many ways in which service oriented companies are trying to blend into the habits of their customers, instead of trying to induce them to act in a specific way.

Another similar experience is *Simple*, the American banking application developed with a "mobile-first" approach, launched in 2012. The features are similar, though the social and viral aspects of Instabank are more developed.

Table 10.2 shows a set of drivers used to capture the concept of *User Value*. In this case the user is the customer, therefore the relevance of a good user interface

Table 10.2 User value indicators

Fast learning	Yes
User interface	Good
User experience	Good
Process impact	Low
User feedback	Good (initial)
«Wow» effect	High

and user experience is even higher. The application is simple and does not require much learning. The impact is intended as a measure of how much this innovation changes the established processes for the user, therefore impacting on their willingness to change it. In this case it is low, as Instabank blends in a well-established routine. First feedbacks from users has been good, and the "wow" effect (i.e. the perceived novelty and interest in the idea) in first adopters and, more generally, in people who are presented with the application is quite high. The visible and customer-friendly characteristics of Instabank contribute to its high User Value perception.

10.3 Macrosense

Macrosense [4] aggregates and analyzes large amounts of real-time mobile location data, collected through mobile phones, GPS, WiFi, cell tower triangulation, RFID and other sensors. Using powerful machine learning algorithms, it provides extremely accurate profiling and segmentation of consumers based on habits and spending preferences. This tool allows to transform existing data into predictive behavioral data, leading to a better understanding of customers without requiring any change in behavior. It is also a key element for effective real-time marketing campaigns, for prediction of specific group behavior and for understanding the underlying reasons of the direction and intensity of passage in specific areas. On the consumer-side of the platform, the system is able to suggest the best bar for a user (based on their past behavior and that of individuals in the same group), the best corner to get a cab in New York, the best restaurant in a new city for a person with a registered behavior pattern, and other useful location-based advice. Macrosense currently process 170 billion location points per month, which is more than what any company, other than Google or Facebook, does.

The simple idea behind Macrosense and the other related services developed by Sense networks is that actual behavior is a very good predictor of future behavior. Models based on thorough analysis and observation of large quantities of data on geo-location of specific individuals provide a significant insight into human behavior.

Table 10.3 Company competitiveness indicators for time-to-market

Company	Sense networks
Funded	2006
N° Products	8
Clients	Large number
Partners	N.R.
Market dimension	Large
Competitors	Many
Enabling infrastructure	Ready

10.3.1 Developer

Sense Networks is a New York based company, founded in 2006 with the goal of empowering companies and investors to better understand and predict human behavior on a macro scale. The founding team includes MIT and Columbia University Professors in computer science, who were fascinated by the prospect to understand human behavior through the analysis of location data over time. Back then location data was increasing thanks to the diffusion of mobile phones, which soon became smarter and smarter and started generating even richer data (e.g. Foursquare voluntary check-in, automatic collection of location by different apps, Wi-fi recognition).

One of the founders is Alex Pentland, Toshiba Professor at MIT, serial entrepreneur and one of the most cited authors in computer science. His research at the MIT Human Dynamics Lab has been an important brick in the development of the interpretation models, while, at the same time, the large amount of location data was fundamental for testing hypotheses about human behavior.

In Table 10.3 the representation of the drivers of competitiveness on a time-to-market basis shows, in synthesis, an advanced development both of the technology behind Macrosense and of the demand and offer side of the market, with many clients and competitors.

10.3.2 Applications

Macrosense can identify group dynamics, understand the significance of particular behaviors in predicting consumer response and automatically find and present the most relevant suggestions to a particular audience. It is a great tool for market segmentation, for customized campaign management, for predictive analytics and for mobile advertising. It allows its adopters to understand and predict a common shopping journey, to understand activities of groups of people with similar preferences, find correlations and significant similarities among users' preferences, tastes and behaviors, improve the planning of public or private transport supply according to data about stream of people, weather forecast, specific news, traffic

Table 10.4 User value indicators	Fast learning	Yes
	User interface	Good
	User experience	Good
	Process Impact	Low
	User feedback	Very good
	«Wow» effect	High

information, etc. As the other advanced analytics systems, it allows a deeper understanding of the customer's dynamics, of the different habits of customers and non-customers, and of the logistics of a specific activity.

In Table 10.4 the set of drivers show a very high level of *User Value*. The design of the application is simple and easy to grasp. The impact on established processes is not too high, as the improved decision making fits in almost any process structure. Feedback from users has been very positive, and it is fueling the development and adoption of many other solutions based on the same core algorithms.

10.4 BillGuard

BillGuard [5] is a personal finance security system scanning credit card activity daily for hidden charges, billing errors, forgotten subscriptions, scams and fraud. The main purpose is to protect customers from the so-called Grey Charges, deceptive and unwanted credit/debit card charges resulting from misleading advertisement and ill-defined billing systems. The most common type of grey charge is the "free trial" converted in paid subscription without proper notice. It is not illegal per se, but it results in a loss of money by an unwilling customer who frequently does not even realize it. The annual impact of grey charges on USA card holders has been estimated around $14.3 billion per year. It alerts the subscriber via e-mail or mobile app notification when attention is required. Each new transaction is analyzed by over 100 automated tests to prove its authenticity. In addition to the fraud data possessed by the system, BillGuard automatically scouts the web, using crowdsourced data to harness the collective knowledge of millions of consumers reporting every day about billing complaints and suspicious merchant lists to their banks and to on-line communities.

The underlying concept is that single users seldom take the time to check their balance sheets at the end of the month, and even when they do, they rarely notice the small charges applied by unwanted subscriptions. The BillGuard monthly report expands the information about each transaction and highlights automatically the suspicious transactions. Whenever a transaction is labeled as a fraud, BillGuard activates a support service to help the customers get their money back. The experience and knowledge of BillGuard build on each single case, developing skills and tools for streamlining the process for the consumer.

Table 10.5 Company competitiveness indicators for time-to-market

Company	BillGuard
Funded	2010
N° Products	3
Clients	Large number
Partners	N.A.
Market dimension	Large
Competitors	Few
Enabling infrastructure	Ready

10.4.1 Developer

BillGuard was founded in Tel Aviv in 2010 by Yaron Samid. Besides being in the board of several other initiatives, Samid is also founder and organizer of TechAviv, an Israeli club for startup founders with branches in Silicon Valley, New York, Boston and Tel Aviv, as well as a member of the White House Business Council under the Obama Administration. BillGuard has a New York based office and provides its services mainly in the USA market. The management team is composed of data scientists, mathematicians, security experts and industry specialist, supported by the investments of some of the founders and CEOs of Google, PayPal, Verisign and Sun Microsystems.

In Table 10.5 the time-to-market drivers of competitiveness display an advanced development of the company and the market, with a ready technology and no issues of integration with established processes and enabling infrastructures, while there is still a lack of competitors.

Notably many important American Banks are trying to integrate the service in their own on-line banking platforms, in order to regain trust and intimacy with their customers.

10.4.2 Applications

The declared purpose of this free-of-charge application is to help users in not losing money to frauds, scams and grey charge policies, leveraging the collective knowledge of society. Additional services are provided to merchants, in form of tools for resolving billing issues before they become disputes, increasing customer satisfaction and reducing litigation costs. The only side that appears to be charged in this multi-sided-platform business model is the Financial Institution willing to get the integrated bill monitoring and direct-to-merchant resolution management services. The underlying idea is that the global value of BillGuard increases with the number of customers and merchants using it, while the involved financial institutions value their exclusivity and are willing to spend in order to integrate this kind of services, enabling them to increase customer satisfaction and decrease the cost of dispute management.

Table 10.6 User value indicators

Fast learning	Yes
User interface	Good
User experience	Very good
Process impact	Low
User feedback	Very good
«Wow» effect	High

Table 10.6 shows an extremely high level of *User Value*. The application design is simple and well-conceived, and the functionalities are straightforward and easy to use.

The impact on established processes is very low, in fact it is a simplification of an existing process and it blends seamlessly with the incumbent systems. Feedback from users has been very positive, and the reception of BillGuard has been enthusiastic at all the conventions and competitions it has taken part, winning the company a widespread support and a number of awards.

10.5 Mezzanine

Developed on the concept used in the Sci-fi movie *Minority Report*, Mezzanine [6] is a collaborative conference room, enabling multi-user, multi-screen, multi-device interaction both in a physical and virtual meeting space. The room has built-in technology enabling enhanced telepresence functionalities for remote collaboration and easy connection with all the devices in the room. The participants of a meeting can contribute with multiple streams of information, connecting to the screens and the distant communication systems seamlessly. Mezzanine wishes to transform the *telepresence* in *infopresence*, incorporating multiple users and devices, all sharing and manipulating information at the same time, increasing collaboration and effectiveness of meetings. The system allows easy aggregation of all the video signals in the room across a series of displays, which function as a single interactive workspace. Additional input sources can come from remote participants, video cameras, whiteboards, web-based or networked media, or applications running elsewhere. Digitization of physical content is also possible by scanning paper documents with a smartphone camera. Content of the session can be shared and stored easily in the virtual meeting space.

10.5.1 Developer

Oblong was founded in 2006 as a spin-off of the MIT Media Lab project by John Underkoffler, with the goal of creating the next generation of computing interfaces. It is a company of designers, programmers, and hardware engineers, committed to

Table 10.7 Company competitiveness indicators for time-to-market

Company	Oblong
Funded	2006
N° Products	2
Clients	Large number
Partners	Many
Market dimension	Large
Competitors	Some
Enabling infrastructure	Ready

technology development and innovation. The core purpose of Oblong is to find ways to make computers more flexible, capable, interactive, and empowering. The system designed for *Minority Report* was considered futuristic at the time, but it has largely been transformed into reality in the last years. Oblong's systems allow a fine grained gestural recognition through space-aware, networked, multi-user, multi-screen, multi-device computing environments. The core technology platform, called g-speak, enables applications to run across multiple screens and multiple devices.

In Table 10.7 competitiveness appears to be high on time-to-market drivers. The company is solid and growing and the technology is developing and integrating with more and more partner technologies. The market is interested, especially in design-intensive companies and for advanced decision making activity. Competitors are present with more traditional solutions, but none appear to have the same level of integration and collaboration. The infrastructure is provided by Mezzanine as a complete solution, besides a good internet connection there is no major requirement for installation.

10.5.2 Applications

The interactive setting makes meetings and working sessions more effective by helping multiple team members share and compare data, increasing engagement and allowing parallel working and synchronous data visualization. The new technology challenges the traditional linear view of meetings and creates a disruptive need for a different governance of meetings. Anyone in the room and from remote can contribute, collaborate, present, interact at the same time, but it requires new practices and routines to get managers to use the tool effectively.

The main pitfalls are underusing the system's capabilities, by carrying on with the linear meeting habit, thus, using it without fostering and developing a behavioral change in the way meetings are conducted. If, however, the technology is absorbed by the team using it, it provides a high level collaboration which can create great advantages of collaborative decision making, collaborative design, unified virtual collaboration and increased engagement in meetings.

Table 10.8 User value indicators

Fast learning	No
User interface	Good
User experience	Very good
Process impact	Medium
User feedback	Very good
«Wow» effect	High

Table 10.8 suggests a high level of perception for the *User Value*, but with the caveat of integration with existing processes. The gestural recognition takes some time getting used to, but it's very effective and convenient once mastered. Feedback from users has been very positive and the "wow" effect is very high: people involved in demos of Mezzanine sessions generally report a very strong positive impression.

10.6 Tykoon

Developed with the goal of increasing spending awareness and personal finances management capabilities in the new generations, Tykoon [7] is a financial education tool for kids and their parents, empowering the children to develop stronger financial values under the watchful eye of their parents. Early financial education in children is considered very important for developing values like work ethics, spending awareness, long term planning ability as well as for understanding the value of earning money. Tykoon enables kids to plan and manage their personal finances, using chores and other goals set by their parents to earn money, managing their wish-lists and savings, setting savings goals, donating for charity and eventually shopping in a parent-controlled environment. Parents can completely customize their kids' platform experience according to their personal financial values. The virtual environment is safe, secure and private and there can be no interference from external sources. Experiences of parents using the application are very good, and the customization potential is very much appreciated.

10.6.1 Developer

Tykoon is a New York based startup, founded in 2011. The management team is made up of financial experts, kids entertainment professionals, software developers, startup experts and creative. The idea of a financial education tool for children has been developed also by other companies, but with a somewhat lower level of user experience. The platform is simple and easy to use on the parents' side, game-like and fun on the children's side. The purpose is to develop a sense of commitment and fulfillment in kids earning and managing their own money.

Table 10.9 Company competitiveness indicators for time-to-market

Company	Tykoon
Funded	2011
N° Products	1
Clients	Many
Partners	N.A.
Market dimension	Small
Competitors	Some
Enabling infrastructure	Ready

In Table 10.9 time-to-market drivers show a ready and on the market company facing a somewhat small demand yet to develop. The company is growing and the development of the platform is continuing. Competitors are few and exhibit a more traditional approach. The infrastructure is ready as there is no need for anything other than a pc and an internet connection.

10.6.2 Applications

The interactive and game-like experience of Tykoon make it a very appreciated application by those who are using it. Parents in developed countries often struggle to teach their children the value of money, especially in high income families. It is of great support to these families to have an instrument to help them transfer their values to their children, through an interactive game to play. Some banks have been showing interest in including Tykoon in their "family account" packages or as an additional service to parents.

Table 10.10 shows a good level of perceived *User Value*, based on a great user interface and user experience, a very high level of personalization and a gamified structure of the application. Feedback from users has been very positive even if the novelty and "wow" effect are not that high: the impact on the personal life is not huge, but it has to do with the education of the children, so it happens to be a very sensitive topic.

10.7 Noldus Face Reader

Noldus Face Reader [8] is an affective computing tool designed to capture and interpret emotions in individual subjects, through the recognition of uncontrollable micro-expressions. Unlike many similar solutions, Face Reader is not only able to recognize stress and other alterations of normal state: it is actually developed for capturing expressions corresponding to happy, sad, angry, surprised, scared, disgusted, and neutral feelings. The system uses live video or recorded footage indiscriminately as input for the expressions analysis. The external stimuli

Table 10.10 User value indicators	Fast learning	Yes
	User interface	Very good
	User experience	Very good
	Process impact	Low
	User feedback	Good
	«Wow» effect	Middle

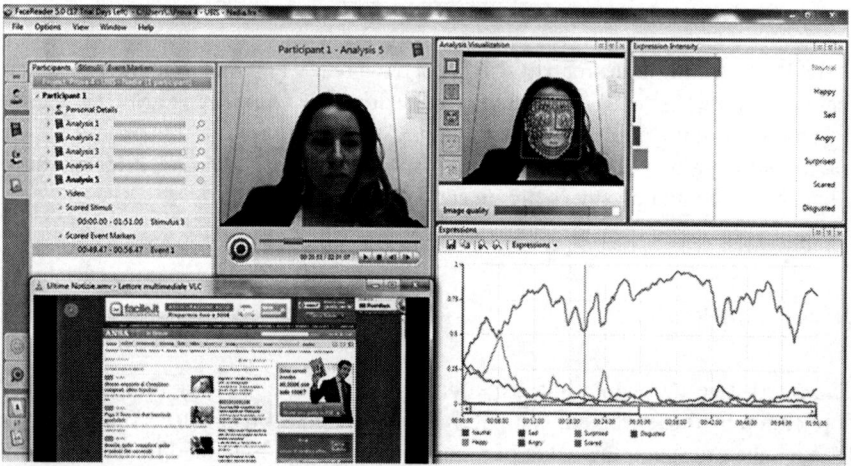

Fig. 10.1 Noldus face reader features

producing the emotional reaction can be incorporated in the analysis, in order to couple the moment of reaction with the specific cue, increasing the explanatory power of the affective data (Fig. 10.1). The system has been extensively tested with scientific research accuracy and the underlying science of emotions is the result of years of studies.

The advantages, compared with traditional expert recognition of emotions, lay in a higher objectivity, the ability to capture all the micro-expressions, even when they are not perceivable by a human eye, and lower costs thanks to automation of the process. The reports' data can be easily exported and the software itself is developed for easy integration with other systems.

10.7.1 Developer

Noldus Information Technology was established in 1989, currently having headquarters in the Netherlands as well as in the United States. The president of the company, Lucas Noldus, holds a Ph.D. in animal behavior and, during his research on parasitoid wasps, he developed the first version of *The Observer*, a software

Table 10.11 Company
competitiveness indicators
for time-to-market

Company	Noldus information technology
Funded	1989
N° Products	Many
Clients	Many
Partners	Many
Market dimension	Average
Competitors	Some
Enabling infrastructure	Ready

package for behavioral recording and analysis, independent of the organism being studied.

This tool attracted attention from researchers within many other fields of study and led to starting a company for the development of software dedicated to behavioral research. Later, in 2011, was founded Noldus InnovationWorks, a research and innovation lab serving as an incubator for high-risk projects at the edge of technology advances.

In Table 10.11 the representation shows a short time-to-market, if we consider the presence of competitors, the enabling infrastructure, and the solidity of the company. There is some more doubt about the market dimensions, as the implementation of automatic emotion recognition is only useful when the company intends to make use of the tool to conduct experiments involving the evaluation of human affective response.

10.7.2 Applications

Face Reader can be used to raise understanding of the relationship between emotions and business results, by means of many different experimental activities to conduct with employees and customers.

As an example, it can be used to test whether a given set of information affects emotions or not - whether in customers or in employees - while executing a process or interacting with a tool; to test whether different affective states in the customer service operator, while talking with a customer, result in different and correlated perception of quality and/or competence, or not; to test whether a product's characteristics are perceived favorably or not, and whether an operation consumers have to complete is generating negative emotions.

In Table 10.12 it appears the *User Value* is quite high, with good user experience and positive feedback from users. The impact on existing processes is due to the need to modify interaction processes and transform them in more dynamic and adaptable ones.

Table 10.12 User value indicators

Fast learning	Yes
User interface	Good
User experience	Good
Process Impact	Average
User feedback	Very good
«Wow» effect	Middle

10.8 Cogito

Cogito [9] is a real time analytics solution developed to capture distress, anxiety, engagement and excitement in the interaction between people. It works on the analysis of speech pattern, tone of voice, semantic analysis, body language, facial recognition. Cogito's systems continuously collect and interpret social signals underlying telephone conversations, video chats, and live behavior, based on clinical studies on post-traumatic stress disorder (PTSD) patients. The system automatically tracks and analyzes facial expressions, body posture, acoustic features, linguistic patterns and higher-level behavior descriptors (e.g. attention and fidgeting), in real-time.

Cogito helps companies gain valuable data about their clients' behavior and increase the quality of interaction. Agents see in real time a display showing customer engagement and distress level, providing also feedback on the quality of their own behavior. All data are combined with traditional performance indicators, in order to create detailed predictive models.

10.8.1 Developer

Founded in 2006, Cogito is a Boston-based technology company developing fundamentally new ways of analyzing and understanding human communication and perception. They combine a decade of MIT Human Dynamics Lab research, represented by the Co-founder Professor Alex Pentland in the Management Team, with advanced signal processing and computational engineering capabilities, in order to track and model social signals exchanged in conversation and monitored through Smartphone-enabled mobile sensing systems.

In Table 10.13 the time-to-market competitiveness appears to be high, with a solid company, facing some competition but with a large market to tap, showing no need for additional enabling infrastructure.

Table 10.13 Company competitiveness indicators for time-to-market

Company	Cogito
Funded	2006
N° Products	3
Clients	Many
Partners	Some
Market dimension	Large
Competitors	Many
Enabling infrastructure	Ready

10.8.2 Applications

Companies use Cogito to gain insight into buying behavior, satisfaction, follow-through, and intervention needs of their customers. This improves decision-making, workflows, and consistency of service, and successful interactions. Feedback from clients report benefits as increase in productivity, improved sales performance, better data collection, and higher customer retention.

As shown in Table 10.14, the *User Value* is quite high, with positive feedback from users. The impact on existing processes, though quite high, is bounded from the fact that the solution requires to set specific actions and procedures to make use of it, unless it is integrated in an existing activity as an improvement of sentiment recognition.

10.9 True Link

True Link [10] is a prepaid Visa card developed specifically for the elderly and their close relatives seeking ways to protect them from scam and fraud, without taking away their financial independence. It works like a regular Visa Card, both on-line and off-line, but it's linked to a control system that allows to prevent purchases from specific stores and types of merchants, to control if any unexpected or suspicious activity has been made, and to recognize automatically the most common scams. The close relative in charge of the control receives a notification for every suspicious transaction and can choose to confirm or reject it, and even to contact the elderly relative to discuss it before deciding. The rules for blocking payments are highly personalized and can include specific limits for type of activity (e.g. maximum 10 % to charity, or donations only to approved list of charities) or for means of purchase (e.g. only physical payments allowed). In case a fraud, or scam is not detected and there is the need to resolve already concluded transactions, True Link offers the support of a toll-free customer service dedicated to recovering lost charges.

Table 10.14 User value indicators

Fast learning	Yes
User interface	Good
User experience	Good
Process impact	Average
User feedback	Good
«Wow» effect	Middle

10.9.1 Developer

Founded in 2013 in San Francisco, True Link Financial is managed by a group of young and promising entrepreneurs with experience in payments, startups and services. The card itself and the underlying financial services are provided by Sunrise Banks, while True Link Financial is focused on developing the interface on the user side. The business development plan is to secure partnerships with large retirement homes and organizations for caregiving, retirement home placement services, and health care organizations.

In Table 10.15 the time-to-market drivers show a very young and promising company (launched in August 2013), going through the first adoption but already having a hard time to service the many requests. Enabling infrastructure is ready, there are not many relevant competitors and the demand is potentially very large.

10.9.2 Applications

With a growing number of senior citizens and an increasing impact of different kinds of fraud, scam, aggressive marketing and commercial pressure, it's ever more important for people facing the hard issue of helping elderly relatives stay on top of their financial situation. Traditional methods require, in most cases, to take away the financial independence as a whole, keeping allowances and other methods which people perceive as painful and heartbreaking. This simple system is designed to enable a lightweight control and decision support, which has so far been really appreciated. Financial Institutions dealing with an aging population of clients and prospects, should devise similar services to avoid being cut out of the game.

Table 10.16 shows a good *User Value*, with very positive feedback from the first adopters. The impact on existing processes is very low and, even if there is no "wow" effect, the value in simplification and reduction of unwanted expenses is very much heartfelt.

Table 10.15 Company competitiveness indicators for time-to-market

Company	True link financial
Funded	2013
N° Products	1
Clients	First adopters
Partners	One
Market dimension	Large
Competitors	Some
Enabling infrastructure	Ready

Table 10.16 User value indicators

Fast learning	Yes
User interface	Good
User experience	Very good
Process impact	Low
User feedback	Very good
«Wow» effect	Low

10.10   AcceptEmail

AcceptEmail [11] is a very simple innovation which enables customers to pay bills, in form of e-mails, safely and conveniently through online banking, PayPal, debit card or credit card. The customer receives in his mailbox an e-mail with prefilled information about the payment (i.e. sum, identity of requesting side, quantity and type of purchase, due date, etc.) and, directly from his notebook, table or smartphone, he can complete the payment online with very few steps. It enables a quick and timely payment initiation, perfectly aligned with the receiver's administrative records, error free since all necessary payment details are already prefilled. It is also a very convenient way of sending reminders about due payments, as it allows to complete the transaction right away. Once the bill has been paid, the banner in the e-mail turns green and the payment request now changes into a payment receipt, to store and use as convenient. Many companies use AcceptEmail for sending its friendly reminders of a due date, of a special offer, of a charity donation option, or as a reminder when a direct debit has bounced.

10.10.1 Developer

Set up in 2007, AcceptEmail is located in Amsterdam. The management team used to be closely involved in numerous online payment initiatives throughout Europe and, since its advent, in e-mail marketing as communication medium. AcceptEmail is independent from payment methods, banks, PSPs and BSPs, as it does not collect money on behalf of its customers, it only enables the payment initiation.

Table 10.17 Company
competitiveness indicators
for time-to-market

Company	AcceptEmail
Funded	2007
N° Products	1
Clients	Many
Partners	Many
Market dimension	Large
Competitors	Many
Enabling infrastructure	Ready

In Table 10.17 the drivers for time-to-market describe a solid company facing a large and mature market, with a strong link to partners in the same technological ecosystem. Enabling infrastructure is ready and the demand is very large.

10.10.2 Applications

Managing timely payments is a big issue for many industries, and especially for utilities and telecommunications. Indeed, automatic payments are often denied from the bank, reminders reach the customers much later and require additional procedures to recover payments. On the customer side, reminders and requests for payment are unpleasant hassles and are seldom followed through immediately. The result is a lengthy process of recovery in which companies lose liquidity and customers feel stressed. Bringing the payment platform to a simple e-mail helps in mitigating this issue, with a "3 clicks" approach to the completion of the transaction, and a secure underlying instrument.

In Table 10.18 the *User Value* is high, with very good feedback on user interface and experience, and a minimal process impact (it's actually an improvement and streamlining of existing procedures). The "wow" effect is low, as in most innovations focused on cost reduction and simplification.

10.11 Starbucks Digital Ventures

It appears, looking at the case of Starbucks [12], that coffee shop differentiation in modern times is happening in the digital environment. After the first success with the mobile payments enabled Loyalty Card, launched in 2011, the company has developed a comprehensive digital strategy. The main areas of intervention are: in-store experience, Mobile Payments, and crowdsourcing. Adding digital features to the point of sale enables a better multichannel experience for customers. Moreover, thanks to the Starbucks Digital Network, customers are offered extra content and entertainment when connected to the facility's Wi-Fi (e.g. on-line Music,

Table 10.18 User value indicators	Fast learning	Yes
	User interface	Good
	User experience	Very good
	Process impact	Low
	User feedback	Good
	«Wow» effect	Low

The New York Times, The Economist, The Wall Street Journal and other publications). On the Mobile Payments side, the iOS and Android app, on the one hand, allows customers to pay with their smartphone, with no need for cards or cash, reducing by 10 s the single transaction; on the other hand, it allows the business side gathering meaningful data about their customers. Around 10 % of all transactions are currently completed through the mobile app.

The last point of the digital strategy is the development of an on-line community for crowdsourcing called "My Starbucks Idea", where customers can submit suggestions on how to improve products, customer experience and corporate initiatives. Besides a strong positive effect on corporate innovation, the initiative is having a viral diffusion effect, contributing to a continuous growth of interest in the digital activities of Starbucks.

10.11.1 Developer

Starbucks Digital Ventures' initiation dates back to 2008, when the CIO Stephen Gillett decided to promote the development of an internal venture-capital-style incubator for digital technology initiatives. Since then, also thanks to its Chief Digital Officer Adam Brotman, appointed in 2012, the division has focused on developing digital innovation in collaboration with Starbucks' IT and Marketing functions, pioneering a set of initiatives.

The choice to not follow on the NFC mobile payments trend but to go for a simpler approach based on a 2D bar code has been positively accepted by the first adopters, enabling a fast diffusion also thanks to the low implementation costs, since bar code readers were are already installed in all physical stores. Looking back at Starbucks' history, the first declaration of a digital strategy is considered to be the moment when the top management first decided that Wi-Fi should be a feature of all Starbucks coffee shops, giving customers the clear message that the company intends to leverage IT value in its business model.

In Table 10.19 the representation shows a short time-to-market, if we consider the presence of competitors, the enabling infrastructure, and the solidity of the company. There is some more doubt about the market dimensions, as the implementation of automatic emotion recognition is only useful when the company intends to make use of the tool to conduct experiments involving the evaluation of human affective response.

Table 10.19 Company
competitiveness indicators
for time-to-market

Company	Starbucks digital ventures
Funded	2008
N° Products	A few
Clients	Many
Partners	Few
Market dimension	Very large
Competitors	Many
Enabling infrastructure	Ready

Table 10.20 User value
indicators

Fast learning	Yes
User interface	Very good
User experience	Very good
Process impact	Low
User feedback	Very good
«Wow» effect	Middle

10.11.2 Applications

Starbucks Digital Ventures' strategy aims at developing a digital media company business model dedicated to all Starbucks customers. All services and initiatives share a customer-oriented approach, dedicated to increasing customer intimacy, loyalty, engagement and viral diffusion.

The current digital presence of Starbucks (both on-line and through mobile apps) drives nearly 35 million monthly visitors, a number that is comparable to the customer base of a large media company. The fact that Starbucks Digital Ventures is independent from the IT function and Marketing function, reporting directly to the CEO, helps in developing an independent strategy, adding up to the company's value. In Table 10.20 the User Value is very high, with great User experience and interface, very positive feedback and very low impact on existing processes, coupled with a relevant "wow" effect.

10.12 Summary

This Chapter has discussed examples of digital innovation in practice, providing fact-sheets of 10 of the most interesting ones available worldwide in 2013. The selection has been focused on those innovations that have already had some diffusion among specific target users or even to a wide audience. However, we have also considered some evaluation parameters in the selection, namely: the impact on current processes and the steepness of the learning curve; the perceived value of the specific user, based on ease of use, pleasure and the so called «Wow» effect, which makes the innovation potentially inedited if not disruptive.

The time-wise competitive evaluation of the ideas comes from the observation of the technology readiness, the presence of a strong demand, the development stage of the competitors and of the target. As a consequence, the considered practices covered different implementations areas, spanning from financial services (Instabank), to ageing and education issues (TrueLink, Tykoon), through advanced behavioral analysis (Cogito), and affective computing (Noldus Face Reader). Furthermore, the selection has shown a majority of digital innovations coming from US based companies (among them a "big" player such as Starbucks), while Europe has been represented by the Netherlands in two cases as well as other countries, namely Russia and Israel (one innovation each). In addition, the examples of digital innovation considered in this Chapter cover some of the topic discussed in the previous two Parts of this volume. In particular, it is worth noting a prevalence of digital innovations focusing on the converge of *mobile services* (Instabank, TrueLink, AcceptEmail, Starbucks Digital Ventures), *social listening* (BillGuard, Starbucks Digital Ventures), and the use of sensors for *social sensing* (Macrosense, Cogito, Noldus Face Reader). However, among the discussed digital innovation practices we have found also a coverage of *digital work and collaboration* (Mezzanine) as well as *digital business identity* (Tycoon) issues.

Taking these issues into account, it is worth noting that the potential evolution trends are going to concern a further focus on convergence of mobile services and social sensing, that is an increased exploitation of advanced analytics for behavioral analysis from intensive data streams as well as from Big Data.

References

1. Christensen CM (1997) The innovator's dilemma: when new technologies cause great firms to fail. Harvard Business School Press, Boston, MA
2. O'Reilly III CA, Tushman ML (2008) Ambidexterity as a dynamic capability: resolving the innovator's dilemma. Res Organ Behav 28:185–206. doi: http://dx.doi.org/10.1016/j.riob.2008.06.002
3. Instabank (2013) https://instabank.ru/en. Accessed 18 Nov 2013
4. Macrosense (2013) https://www.sensenetworks.com/products/macrosense-technology-platform/. Accessed 18 Nov 2013
5. BillGuard (2013) https://www.billguard.com/. Accessed 18 Nov 2013
6. Mezzanine (2013) http://www.oblong.com/mezzanine/. Accessed 18 Nov 2013
7. Tykoon (2013) http://www.tykoon.com/moneysmart/. Accessed 18 Nov 2013
8. Noldus Face Reader (2013) http://www.noldus.com/human-behavior-research/products/facereader. Accessed 18 Nov 2013
9. Cogito (2013) http://www.cogitocorp.com/research-showcase/. Accessed 18 Nov 2013
10. True Link (2013) https://www.truelinkcard.com/. Accessed 18 Nov 2013
11. AcceptEmail (2013) http://www.acceptemail.com/en/. Accessed 18 Nov 2013
12. Starbucks Digital Ventures (2013) http://www.starbucks.com/coffeehouse/mobile-apps/mystarbucks. Accessed 18 Nov 2013

Chapter 11
Conclusion

Abstract The book has discussed and presented the main trends and challenges in Digital Business Innovation to a composite audience of practitioners and scholars. In this Chapter conclusive remarks are provided as well as key advices for strategic actions as a result of the discussion of the digital trends and practices analyzed in this volume.

11.1 Making Digital Business Innovation Real

In this book we have discussed the main challenges and trends of digital business innovation to a composite audience of practitioners and scholars. As for the digital trends we have considered the business challenges of Big Data as a core component of the information infrastructure upon which our society is building its own open environment. Taking this issue into account, we have investigated the strategic drivers and drawbacks of Cloud computing, considered an innovative IT model for providing on-demand network access to a shared pool of configurable resources such as networks, servers, and software applications. Furthermore, we have analyzed the challenges to digital business innovation by the diffusion and convergence of mobile services, sensors technologies, and social networks. Accordingly, we have outlined the main implications of new marketing perspectives and analytics methods for extracting business value from them as well as an improved knowledge of customers' needs and lifestyle for a consequent better user experience.

Lastly, in Chap. 5 we have discussed what can be considered as the core trend of the year, perhaps resulting from or else enforcing the previous ones: IT Consumerization. The latter can be seen as the trend for new technology innovations to begin first in the consumer market then to enter business environments. Likewise, this phenomenon has important consequences also for workplace habits and routines, due to the increasing relevance of another connected phenomenon,

Fig. 11.1 Key areas for
digital business innovative
organization

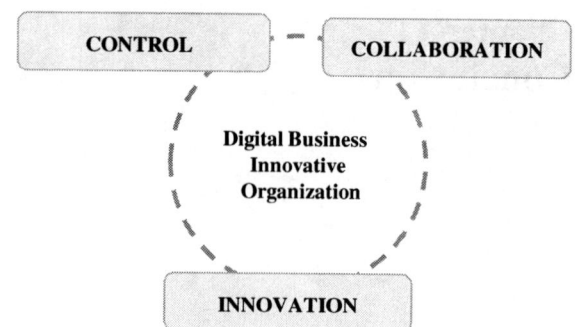

'Bring Your Own Device' (BYOD): individual employees can choose their own type of device to do their work, and this can be their own private personal one, with consequences on IT policies as for security, disclosure of data, and privacy.

Taking the digital trends challenges into account, Fig. 11.1 summarizes the areas for digital management intervention by IT executives and the other CxOs[1] interested in initiatives for digital business innovation. Notwithstanding collaboration evolution enabled by different digital technologies has been introduced in Chap. 6, here it is worth to be emphasized the contribution it has received from the advancement of mobile technology, digital services, social networks, sensors, and IT Consumerization, likewise. Besides the benefits, collaboration contributed to "open" work practices, blurring the boundary between the inner and the outer context of a company. This openness asks for a consequent need for control (see left hand side of Fig. 11.1) of the digital business identity, on the one hand, preserving it through, e.g., policies for privacy and security of data and information flows; on the other hand, promoting it in terms of brand in an ever-changing and dynamic digital market (see Chap. 7). Thus, these challenges require also control as improved and inedited digital governance, relying on and evolving from traditional IT governance, likewise (as outlined in Chap. 8).

As a consequence, digital business innovation necessitates that IT leaders have to be able to combine an appropriate knowledge of business benefits and drawbacks of the current digital systems trends, to the ability to implement digital management solutions considering the above key areas. As for these issues, this book has tried to provide insights as well as inspiring "templates" for putting in practice digital business innovation. Accordingly, a set of characteristics have been identified for telling what could be called "10 short stories" about those which have been selected as the most interesting "global" experiences of the 2013. As for this selection, it is worth mentioning that also in this case the choice concerns innovations that are actually applied and "in use"; thus, a pragmatic approach have been adopted, balancing between the so called «Wow» effect (i.e. the

---

[1] C-level managers, such as, e.g., Chief Executive Officer (CEO), Chief Financial Officer (CFO), Chief Information Officer (CIO), etc.

perceived novelty and interest in the idea), feasibility, and actual user adoption. Consequently, not only digital innovations potentially inedited if not disruptive, but also "ready-to-use" ones, have been selected and analyzed.

As a conclusion, three key advices (rather than guidelines) for actions are provided as a result of the discussion of the digital trends and practices in this volume:

1. *Generate digital business value* from new systems and technologies not only enabling it; thus, transforming digital infrastructures into digital business platforms.
2. *Manage talents*, not merely resources; thus, effectively exploiting digital work and collaboration.
3. *Promote business agility*, not only efficiency; thus, constructing dynamically your digital business identity through innovative business models and an effective digital governance.

The above directions require that IT must be able to generate value from current digital information infrastructure, leading to a change of perspective on its strategic role as the "guardian" of a company digital business assets and "heritage". In a sense, the new strategic role of IT should transform it in the interpreter of the "desires" of digital business innovation of organizations as well as of their internal and external users.

Index

Lightning Source UK Ltd.
Milton Keynes UK
UKOW05n0728190214

226736UK00001B/50/P